CW00747022

123 Places in Turkey

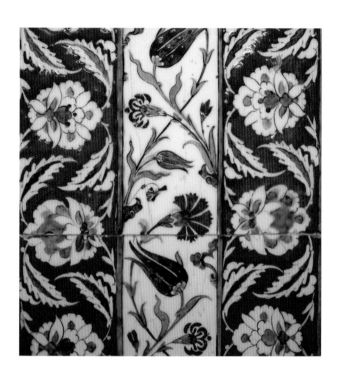

123 Places in Turkey
A Private Grand Tour

FRANCIS RUSSELL

WILMINGTON SQUARE BOOKS
an imprint of Bitter Lemon Press

WILMINGTON SQUARE BOOKS
An imprint of Bitter Lemon Press

First published in 2017 by
Wilmington Square Books
47 Wilmington Square
London WC1X 0ET

www.bitterlemonpress.com

Copyright © 2017 Francis Russell

All rights reserved. No part of this publication may be
reproduced in any form or by any means without
written permission of the publisher

The moral rights of the author have been asserted in accordance
with the Copyright, Designs and Patents Act 1988

Some portions of this book were previously published in
Places in Turkey (Frances Lincoln Limited, 2010)

A CIP record for this book is available from the British Library

ISBN 978-1-908524-874

2 4 6 8 9 7 5 3 1

Designed and typeset by Jane Havell Associates
Index by Marianne Ryan
Printed in China

In memory of my mother,
Anne Russell (1923–2015),
who came to share my love of Turkey

CONTENTS

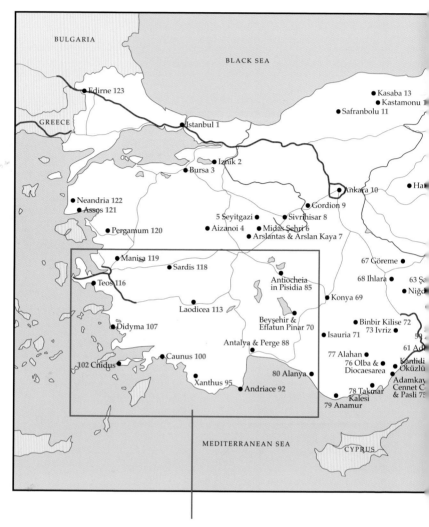

For detailed map of this area, see pages 10–11

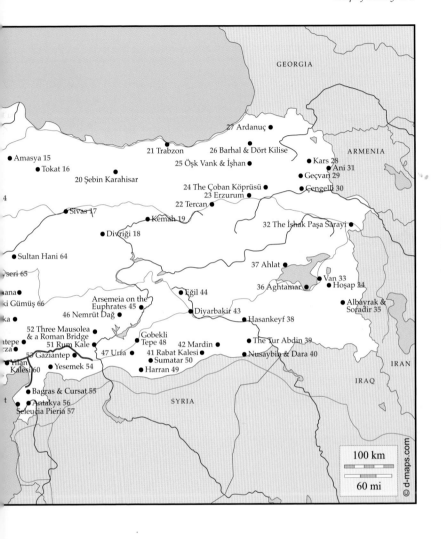

GEORGIA

27 Ardanuç ●

21 Trabzon ●   26 Barhal & Dört Kilise ●

ARMENIA

● Amasya 15   25 Öşk Vank & İşhan ●   ● Kars 28
    ● Tokat 16   ● Ani 31
        20 Şebin Karahisar   ● Geçvan 29
                              24 The Çoban Köprüsü ●   ● Çengelli 30
                              23 Erzurum ●
                              22 Tercan ●
    ● Sivas 17   32 The İshak Paşa Sarayi ●
        ● Kemah 19
        ● Divriği 18

● Sultan Hani 64   37 Ahlat ●
                                          ● Van 33
seri 65   36 Aghtamar ●   ● Hoşap 34
                    Eğil 44 ●
ana ●   ● Albayrak &
ki Gümüş 66   Arsemeia on the   Sofadir 35
ka ●   46 Nemrüt Dağ ●   ● Diyarbakir 43
                              ● Hasankeyf 38
    52 Three Mausolea   Gobekli
    & a Roman Bridge ●   Tepe 48 ●   42 Mardin ●   ● The Tur Abdin 39
atepe ●   51 Rum Kale ●   41 Rabat Kalesi ●
rza ●   53 Gaziantep ●   47 Urfa ●   ● Sumatar 50   ● Nusaybin & Dara 40
Yilan
Kalesi 60   ● Yesemek 54   ● Harran 49   IRAN

    ● Bagras & Cursat 55   IRAQ
t ● ● Antakya 56   SYRIA
Seleucia Pieria 57 ●

100 km

60 mi

© d-maps.com

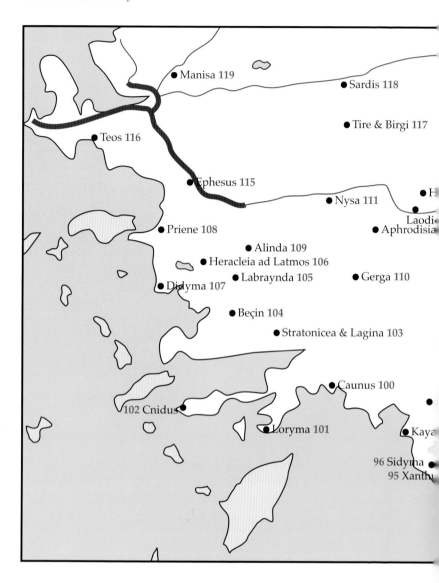

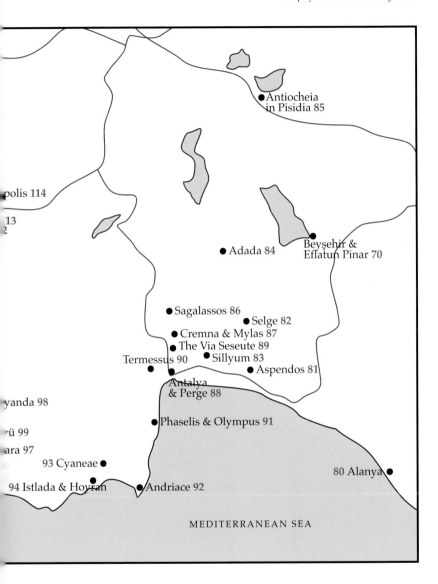

polis 114

13
2

● Antiocheia in Pisidia 85

● Adada 84

Beyşehir & Eflatun Pinar 70

● Sagalassos 86

● Selge 82

● Cremna & Mylas 87

● The Via Seseute 89

Termessus 90

● Sillyum 83

● Aspendos 81

Antalya & Perge 88

yanda 98

ü 99

ara 97

● Phaselis & Olympus 91

93 Cyaneae ●

80 Alanya ●

94 Istlada & Hoyran

● Andriace 92

MEDITERRANEAN SEA

INTRODUCTION

TURKEY is a daunting, yet infinitely rewarding, proposition for the tourist. Like most Englishmen, I first met the word when confronted with the over-rated meat of an ungainly domestic fowl; our ancestors might have associated this rather with a type of carpet, imported no doubt through the agency of a Turkey merchant. And we, at school, learnt how close the Ottomans came to penetrating the heart of Europe at the siege of Vienna and of British endeavours to support Turkey, as the 'Sick Man of Europe', in the Victorian era. Yet this is a misleading association. For, although it does succeed to former territories of the Macedonian and Roman Empires, Turkey, despite the aspirations of some of her rulers, has never been European. Her political complexion is owed to the Asiatic credentials of her peoples, her strategic power to control of Anatolia.

My own interest in Turkey was aroused by the later books of Freya Stark. But other priorities and a sense, not incorrect, that Turkey needed time, meant that for many years I made no effort to go there. Late in 1986, however, an act of injustice to a colleague on the part of an already undependable chief executive made me decide to escape from Christie's. Playing with books over Christmas settled my destination. My anger cooled when I found how widely it was shared, but my plans had by then developed their own momentum. The following August I set out in a much-loved white BMW, conscious only that Christie's insurance wouldn't carry me beyond the Bosphorus. On the journey I paused for a quiet day by the swimming pool at Langenburg and then stopped at Passau, before driving on through Yugo-slavia. Failing to find a hotel, I slept – with the aid of a pill – in my motor in the central square at Zagreb. The road south was narrow. Lorries outnumbered motors and overtaking with a car made for the English market was almost impossible. After twenty painfully slow miles, a larger white BMW overtook me. The driver, a Turk, settled as his number plate implied in Germany, sensed my predicament: he waved – and for over three hundred miles signalled when I could safely overtake behind him.

Tito's Zagreb at least seemed like many other central European cities. Further south, I was astonished that the Turks could have controlled so vast a territory without leaving more crumbling fortifications in their wake. Beyond the Bulgarian border things changed. The Iron Curtain had not rusted. At major intersections there were control towers, manned by sinister-looking observers. Occasionally I passed a concrete monument in the mock-heroic idiom preferred by dictatorships. There were fewer lorries on the road as the afternoon drew on. The shadows lengthened, and the towering white blocks of flats that circled the few towns looked unexpectedly impressive. It was dark when I got to the border. No other car was in sight. The young guard, impeccably dressed in white, tried to dissuade me from changing my Bulgarian currency. He asked then why I was going to Turkey. My answer, 'to see archaeological sites', surprised him. He lent forward and half-whispered:

'What is top of the pops in London?'

'I am afraid I am not your man – I don't know.'

Then, after a pause:

'What do you think of Bulgaria?'

'The country is beautiful and your modern housing seems to be well designed.'

'But it is *all* the same.'

He waved me on my way. A minute later, across the frontier, a Turkish guard greeted me: 'Merhaba.' Still thinking of his Bulgarian counterpart, I hardly registered the greeting; so he repeated it and then told me in English that I was welcome. Starving, I stopped at a restaurant that was doing a roaring trade and then went on to Edirne, somehow finding a large and characterless hotel near the centre of the town. Only when woken by the muezzin early the next morning did I really know that I was in Turkey. I have since arrived in Turkey many times – by air. But that first morning at Edirne, the ancient Adrianople, marked, as it were, a new stage in my sightseeing, in a land of which no one can say that it is 'all the same'.

Sinan's mosque at Edirne represents the culmination of the heroic period of Ottoman architecture, and should ideally be visited after one has seen the extraordinary sequence of imperial mosques in Istanbul. So it is there that my theoretical itinerary begins. To arrive at Istanbul by car is a mixed blessing. As the press of the traffic grew more intense in the brightness of that early August afternoon, I saw, with gratitude, the sign

'Otopark'. Too much time in the ensuing days was taken up with trying to secure the insurance I needed. At length I went to Barry's great palazzo, the former embassy, high in Pera. There an official gave me a telephone number. Less than confident, I rang from my hotel, to be answered by a man who spoke the English of an earlier generation. He immediately said he could help. Then there was a sound in the background:

'I am awfully sorry. I must answer another call: please hang on!'

I did.

'So sorry to keep you. A ship I insure has just sunk in the Bosphorus.'

His office, modest enough, was by the harbour. His tweed could only have come from Scotland. Within minutes I had the necessary paperwork. He too had a request. In the event of an accident I was not to admit to having more than the minimum insurance, lest he in turn be pestered with claims.

Turkey is an inexorable land, cold in the winter with heavy snowfalls in the east, hot by English standards in the summer, not least in the heartlands of Anatolia. The beauties of the spring in coastal Turkey are almost impossible to describe – and the weather then is perfect for the long walks that sightseeing implies. By August, the great valleys are aglow with their golden crops – and the straw the harvesters leave. Later, in September or October, the light has that 'tonic' quality which Berenson found in Perugino's landscape. The cyclamen and anemones of March have been succeeded by colchicums; and the hungered visitor to a remote classical site may find fennel or figs or bursting pomegranates.

Visitors are drawn to Turkey for differing reasons. That so many go to the southern coast has encouraged me to give what many may think undue weight in this book to the places within reach of this. But the selection reflects my own tastes. I am more interested in extant buildings than foundations. I prefer unexcavated sites to those where the hand of the archaeologist is officiously evident. And I love most those whose settings are unimpaired. By the same token, the green silhouette of a tel rising above the valley floor moves me more than any systematic excavation, even one so remarkable as that at Catalhüyük. Irrationally, I do not really warm to the strange Hittites. Eflatun Pinar has a magic and Hattuşaş is extraordinary; but the search for eroded reliefs and texts which can only be seen clearly at certain times of day is, for me, too uncertain a pursuit. The Hellenistic and Roman and Byzantine sites of Turkey represent an evolving world that touched on and indeed affected the civilization we think of as our own; and it is to these that I am most powerfully drawn. The Armenian and Georgian churches are beautiful offshoots of the same growth. Equally remarkable are the great monuments of the Seljuk and Ottoman civilizations, the hans and, of course, the very remarkable religious monuments. With the exception of the hans, most of the great buildings of Islamic Turkey are concentrated in her former capitals. There are, of course, marvellous mosques and medreses elsewhere; but often these have been too energetically restored for my personal taste and almost invariably their urban context has suffered as a result of recent development.

Building proceeds apace. It is easy to regret this. Yet without the prosperity such development represents, travelling in Turkey would be far less easy than it is. Places that were until quite recently almost impossible to reach are now readily accessible by road. And driving is an excellent way to understand the daunting size of the modern republic, itself only a small part of the former Ottoman Empire. While in Lycia, for example, ancient settlements are often within easy walking distance of each other, things are very different on the vast plains of Anatolia. The sightseer in Turkey learns to measure, and respect, distance. The high roads of medieval Anatolia are punctuated by the great Seljuk hans, their successors by petrol stations and the restaurants that cater for those who take the buses that are the descendants of the traditional caravans. On the road, buses assume precedence as if of hereditary right, their destination clearly proclaimed. More varied are the lorries, although the elaborate traditional decoration of these, in patterns of blues and pinks, has now fallen from fashion. Peasants go to market in open-sided pickups and donkeys are still put to service.

Even without a knowledge of Turkish or Kurdish one learns much from offering lifts. I first did so on the way to Gordion. It was a hot afternoon and four labourers filled my motor with mud and dust. Memories of many such encounters remain: women heavily laden on the way to market their wares; an elderly patriarch who with much ceremony gestured to two large veiled ladies wilting in the Cappadocian sun. As Richard Chandler in the eighteenth century noted, Turks are curious and interested in words. The women are silent, but men will ask where one is going and whence. Next may come the enquiry:

'Alleman?'

'English.'

'Ingilterra, Ingilterra!'

To which the young may add 'Munch-

ester Eunited', 'Shell-say' or 'Leeverpul';
or, like a wiry veteran near Kayseri,
'Magret Tatcher, Magret Tatcher'.

Particularly in the east, Kurdish
youths, natural linguists, fall upon the
ostensibly solvent tourist, intent on coax-
ing him or her to visit whichever carpet
dealer pays the best retainer.

It is not only the decoration of lorries
that has changed over the last twenty
years. The chrome-adorned cast-off
American motors that used to be so
picturesque an element of the scene, not
least in Istanbul, have almost gone. Western clothes are more in evidence for men,
while in some areas for women the black
veil now prevails where brightly patterned prints used to predominate.
Towns have grown; and, alas, some
monuments have been damaged. While
many restoration programmes have been
exemplary, others can only be regretted.

Like any sightseer or tourist, I have
owed everything to the books that have
determined my itineraries: Ekrem
Agurkal's *Ancient Civilizations and Ruins
of Turkey* (1969), which my brother,
Andrew, gave me after a school expedition to Mount Ararat; Freya Stark's
marvellously observed and now under-
estimated books about Turkey – *Ionia, a
Quest* (1954), *The Lycian Shore* (1956),
Alexander's Path (1958) and *Rome on the
Euphrates* (1966); Professor Bean's four
lucid volumes covering the classical
monuments of south-western Turkey;
numerous articles in both *Anatolian Studies*, the journal of the British School of
Archaeology at Ankara, and *Cornucopia*;
the fine illustrations in Derek Hill's
Islamic Architecture and its Decoration
(1964); and, not least, for the east, the
four indispensable volumes of T. A. Sinclair's *Eastern Turkey: An Architectural and
Archaeological Survey* (Pindar, 1987–90):

these have directed me to many places of
which I would otherwise have been
unaware: it was not surprising to be told
by a French scholar in the Tur Abdin that
the book is his bible. Of general guidebooks, I have usually found the *Blue
Guide* and the *Rough Guide* to be the most
helpful in practical matters.

The selection of illustrations here is
intended to give some sense of the range
of what there is to see in Turkey. My
snapshots imply an obsessive wish to
avoid visual distortion. Some of the
details may surprise. But it is only by the
close examination of buildings that one
begins to understand these. And as some
of the views of Istanbul and Kayseri
imply, the great monuments of the past
are not insulated from the living world.

I am indebted to Omer Koç, to Rupert
Scott for hospitality at Kargi, and to Hen-
rietta Nevill and Joe Bunting, who in
1987 found my car less uncomfortable
than a bus and taught me that it is perfectly possible, indeed enjoyable, to stay
in the simplest of Turkish pansiyons. I
alone am aware how much I owe to
ideas raised in conversation with others
who love Turkey: Patricia and Timothy
Daunt, Lavinia Davies, the late Alican
Ertüg, Philip Mansel, Barnaby Rogerson,
John Scott and Norman Stone; while
Sébastien de Courtois was able to reas-
sure me about the fate of the murals at
Kaymakli about which I, and no doubt
others, had made determined representations to the authorities. The original
edition of this book owed much to the
sympathetic attention it received from
John Nicoll and everyone concerned at
Frances Lincoln and I am doubly grateful to John who asked me to prepare this
expanded edition and thus to cover so
many places that were reluctantly omit-
ted in 2010.

1

ISTANBUL
✿

NO CITY has a more imperial past than Istanbul, which for more than fifteen centuries was the capital of successive empires. The site, on the western side of the Bosphorus, which divides Europe from Asia Minor, has been settled for three millennia; and the city owes its early name, Byzantium, to Byzos of Megara, who founded it in 667 BC. His city was built near the extremity of a triangular peninsula between the Sea of Marmara and a deep inlet, the Golden Horn. Taken by the Persians in 512 BC, but recovered by Pausanias in 478 BC, Byzantium was subsequently subject to Athens, to Sparta, to Alexander and eventually to Rome. Her strategic importance was obvious and the expanding commitments of the Roman Empire in the east led the Emperor Constantine to nominate Byzantium as his capital in AD 330.

The New Rome, or Constantinople as it was generally to be known, grew rapidly and the process continued under Constantine's successors, notably Theodosius II (408–50), who built the prodigious Land Walls, thus significantly extending the city westwards, and Justinian (527–65), who constructed the great cathedral of Haghia Sophia. Constantine's empire, interrupted by the disastrous episode of the Fourth Crusade in 1204 and its Latin aftermath, was to endure until 1453. Its 'decline' was a long-drawn-out and by no means inevitable process, punctuated by periods of military revival and by successive phases of artistic renewal. The great monuments of Constantinople, and above all Haghia Sophia, testify to the enduring authority of an empire in which the Emperor was also Christ's regent. And, despite the evident and increasing impotence of the successors of Michael VIII, who recovered Constantinople in 1261, the city's fall to Sultan Mehmet II in 1453 was rightly seen throughout Western Europe as a cataclysmic event.

Mehmet II was well aware of the importance of his prize. Haghia Sophia, cleared with ruthless efficiency of those who had taken refuge there, was immediately turned into a mosque. The Sultan's own mosque, the Fatih Camii, became the first of the prodigious sequence of imperial mosques that now dominate the skyline of the city. Mehmet built two palaces that vied in scale with their Byzantine predecessors. In the second and larger of these, the Topkapi Sarayi, the visitor can still experience something of Ottoman court life and the ceremonial of the Sublime Porte. The Ottomans devised a sophisticated system of government depending on trusted officials – two of whom, Rüstem Paşa and Sokollu Mehmet Paşa, built the most appealing mosques of sixteenth-century Istanbul. Not the least effective of Ottoman ways of controlling subject peoples was to appropriate the most promising boys born to them: many were recruited to the feared corps of the Janissaries. One such was Sinan, who served as a military engineer in four of Süleyman the Magnificent's campaigns and was, in 1538, appointed Chief of the Imperial Architects. As Süleyman's conquests marked the high noon of Ottoman power, so Sinan's buildings represent the zenith of Ottoman architecture.

The long period of expansion came to an end with the failure to capture Vienna in 1683, but the Ottoman Empire none the less remained a major power. European attitudes changed. Thus the letters of Lady Mary Wortley Montagu demonstrate that Turkey came to fascinate rather than terrify commentators from the West. And as the eighteenth century wore on, there was a greater interest in the advances of European civilization in Turkey. This was reflected in political developments and is also echoed in the detail of buildings of the period.

Nineteenth-century architecture in Istanbul is equally eloquent. The imperial palaces of Dolmabahçe and Yildiz, completed by Abdül Hamid II, are grandiloquent yet vapid statements, impressive in size no doubt, yet oppressive in detail. Abdül Mecid's Küçüksu is perhaps redeemed by its smaller scale. Abdül Hamid II's long, reactionary reign (1876–1909) saw the loss of most of Turkey's European empire. He was deposed in 1909 by the Young Turks. Their leader, Enver Paşa, took the German side in 1914 and as a result of the Allied victory in the First World War, the Ottoman Empire dissolved. A rash, but initially successful, Greek advance in 1919, irresponsibly encouraged by the Western powers, might have left Constantinople as the capital of a much-reduced rump of Anatolian territory. But Turkish Nationalists under Mustafa Kemal, later Atatürk, drove the Greek forces back, at terrible cost. Turkey officially became a republic on 29 October 1923 and the capital was definitively transferred to Ankara.

Istanbul may no longer be the political centre of the state, but with a population of over 14 million, it is unquestionably the fulcrum of Turkey's economic prosperity. Exponential growth has choked much of the ancient city, and the great walls now defend this not from the rolling wastes of Thrace but from a vast conurbation that stretches relentlessly westward. The major monuments of Istanbul survive. Most of the traditional wooden houses do not, and much that replaces these is tawdry. But despite everything the city still works, and its transport systems are comprehensible even to the outsider.

Early visitors had the unforgettable experience of arriving by sea in the Golden Horn and seeing both Constantinople proper, the rising line of its ridge bristling with imperial mosques and minarets, and the commercial quarter of Galata and Pera on the opposite, eastern, shore. While those who travelled by land from Adrianople, now Edirne, following the line of the Roman Via Egnatica, would have been awed by the immense scale of Theodosius II's walls, today's traveller, arriving from the airport, will also have a glimpse of these as he or she is driven to the city. Istanbul instantly asserts its magic. But it is not a city that can be taken by storm. It yields its secrets slowly; and those who have the patience to unravel the impacted strata of these will find the process deeply satisfying.

A sensible itinerary demands time – at least a week – and calls for a good deal of walking. The challenge is to balance the claims of the Byzantine and Ottoman buildings with those of the major museums. But there is no doubt as to where to start. Haghia Sophia is the quintessential building of Byzantium, prodigious in both scale and ambition, placed on commanding ground to the south of the Roman *cardo*, which remains the principal street of the modern city. The third church on the site, Haghia Sophia was begun in 532 and dedicated in 537. The

Emperor Justinian employed two leading architects, Anthemius of Tralles and Isidorus of Miletus. Partly because of earthquake damage, the church had to be reconstructed under the supervision of Isidorus's eponymous nephew in 558–63: he was responsible for the earliest of the additional buttresses and raised the shell of the dome to diminish internal thrust. Given the impressive size of the dome, it is not surprising that it collapsed in 989 and again in 1346. Mehmet's decision to turn the cathedral into a mosque necessitated another structural campaign; and a further major restoration was undertaken in 1847–9. None the less the rectangular structure of Justinian's great building can still be experienced. The building is orientated on sunrise during the winter solstice. The visitor now enters on the west side, through the narrow outer narthex of nine bays, to the deeper narthex behind. The vaults here are decorated with mosaic in gold. Doors open to the basilica, that at the centre originally being the Imperial Gate, surmounted by a mosaic of Christ adored by a prostate emperor, probably Leo VI the Wise (886–912).

However often one enters it, Haghia Sophia overwhelms, both for its sense of captive space and for the way the light plays on the surfaces, for the glow of the gold ground of the mosaic, the drama of the seraphs of the dome, the nobility of the Virgin of the apse, the colours of the marble columns and facings – many of course ruthlessly recycled from Roman buildings – and the crisp detail of the capitals. One is at first unaware of the engineering feat of supporting the dome on the four great lateral piers. The visitor moves through what was clearly conceived as a processional space. But the majesty of this central axis does not detract from the beauty of the aisles. In these it is easier to see how the Ottomans sought to disguise the Byzantine crosses of the mosaic vaults by overpainting them with decorative designs.

At the north-west corner of the narthex, a ramp mounts in easy stages to the galleries. A circle of green marble in the west gallery marks the place of the empress's throne. In the westernmost bay of the south side, among other early graffiti, is the runic scratching of an understandably astonished Viking. A *trompe l'oeil* marble screen leads to the next section in which is what some claim to be the finest mosaic in the cathedral, the late thirteenth-century *deësis* with Christ between the Virgin and St John the Baptist. Opposite is the lid of the sarcophagus of Enrico Dandolo, the octogenarian Doge of Venice who had a decisive role in the seizure of the city in 1204. On the eastern wall of the third section of the south gallery are two further royal mosaics, one with Christ between the Empress Zoë and her third husband, Constantine IX (1042–55), and beside this that of the Virgin with John II Comnenus, his consort Eirene and their eldest son, Alexius (1122). There are other mosaics in the north galleries. But more memorable than any individual works of art are the views over the nave and to the dome.

The tourist now leaves Haghia Sophia through the vestibule at the south end of the narthex, the Vestibule of the Warriors, which was originally reserved for imperial use. The vault is covered with gold mosaic, like that throughout the body of the church, of Justinian's time. Above the inner door is a mosaic of the Emperor himself before the Virgin and Child, executed in the late tenth century. The fastidiously decorated bronze doors are apparently also of Justinian date.

Other Byzantine monuments are in easy reach of Haghia Sophia. Haghia Eirene, the second in importance of Istanbul's early churches, is to the east, in the outer court of the Topkapi Sarayi. This too was built to the order of Justinian. It is a masterpiece of Byzantine brickwork, with an impressively austere interior, the intended richness of which can be judged from the quality of the marble capitals. West of Haghia Sophia, flanked by the Sultan Ahmet Mosque, to which we will return, is the hippodrome, the focal point in the secular life of Byzantium. The terraces have gone. But the central spina is still punctuated by three remarkable monuments: the fragmentary obelisk of Thutmosis III (1549–1503 BC), brought from near Luxor and placed by Theodosius I in AD 390 on a base with reliefs of himself and his family presiding over events at the stadium; the bronze serpentine column originally set up at Delphi to celebrate the Greek victory at Platea in 479 BC; and a tapering pillar restored in the tenth century AD which was formerly coated in bronze.

The hippodrome could sit 100,000. And the Byzantines were well aware that cities of such a population needed dependable water supplies. A substantial Byzantine cistern, the Binbirdirek, is to the north-west of the hippodrome. Monumental as this is, it pales into insignificance by comparison with the Yerebatan Saray, north-west of Haghia Sophia. Supported on 336 massive columns, this is an eerie place, with wooden walkways that lead the visitor out over the water. At the furthest end, two columns are set on bases of Medusa heads, one on its side, the other upturned: for Christian Byzantium had no tolerance for the religions it supplanted.

Several early churches in Istanbul now do service as mosques. South-west of the hippodrome, just within the Sea Wall, is the recently restored church of St Sergius and St Bacchus, where happily the galleries are accessible. Other former churches are only open at prayer times, so that it is difficult to plan a circuit on foot: the Kalenderhane Camii, which retains its original marble facings; the nearby Kilise Cami, with a fine arcaded exterior; and the monumental Pantocrater further west, in fact two churches side by side, both in urgent need of sympathetic attention. To see these patience and persistence are called for.

The one church that no visitor should miss is the Kariye Camii, St Saviour in Chora, rebuilt in 1315–21 for Theodorus Metochites, minister and Grand Logothete to the Emperor Andronicus II Paleologus. The extensive mosaic decoration that is complemented by the murals of the parecclesion to the right of the church represents a high point of Byzantine art. The cycle begins with the Christ Pantocrator above the door from the outer narthex to the narthex proper. There are other dedicatory panels, the most hauntingly beautiful of which is surely the *deësis* below the right-hand dome of the narthex. These are complemented by cycles of scenes: that in the outer narthex is of the Infancy of Christ and his Ministry, which is continued in the narthex proper, where the Ancestors of Christ in the domes are followed by the Life of the Virgin. In the nave are representations of Christ paired with the Virgin Hodegetria, and a noble scene of her Dormition. The production of mosaic has been wrought to the most refined pitch, yet inevitably restricted the range of expression of the anonymous artist whom

Metochites enlisted. His visual imagination and sense of scale is thus more perfectly expressed in the parecclesion murals and not least in the prodigious and radiant Resurrection in the apse.

The Kariye Camii is near Theodosius's Land Walls and makes a memorable complement to a survey of these. This would best begin at the southern end with the Marble Tower, built with the spoil of earlier monuments, which marks the end of the reasonably well preserved line of the Sea Walls along the Sea of Marmara. Theodosius and his engineers faced a considerable challenge, for as the ground offered few natural advantages, it was necessary to provide in-depth defences. The inner wall was originally some 12 metres/39 feet high, with towers; it was preceded by the lower protichisma, some 8.5 metres/28 feet high, set back on a terrace in turn protected by a moat which could, when necessary, be flooded. After crossing the railway line, one comes to the Golden Gate, where an earlier triumphal arch was encased by Theodosius, and many of his successors staged their triumphal entries: this now leads to the Yediküle, a fortress built for Mehmet II, later used as a prison. The great walls sweep inexorably onwards, fringed in places by vegetable gardens, punctuated in others by traffic, with a procession of towers whose original near-uniformity has been eroded and shaken by man and earthquake. To reach the Kariye Camii, enter by the Edirne Gate. But later return to see the walls of Manuel Comnenus, as these curve round to take advantage of the ground as it falls away to the north, and search out the not insubstantial carcass of the Palace of Blachernae. A road turns down through one of the more atmospheric quarters of Istanbul, to reach the three handsome

hexagonal towers built by Heraclius in 627 and defended by an outer enceinte added in 813 by Leo V.

The Ottomans sought very sensibly to build on what they found. Haghia Sophia was appropriated as a mosque; and its great dome haunted the imagination of every ambitious builder. The grandest monuments of Ottoman Istanbul are the imperial mosques, built in sequential emulation. Few visitors have the time to see these in chronological order and the earliest, the Fatih Camii built by Mehmet in 1463–70, was largely destroyed in an earthquake of 1766.

The Fatih Camii.

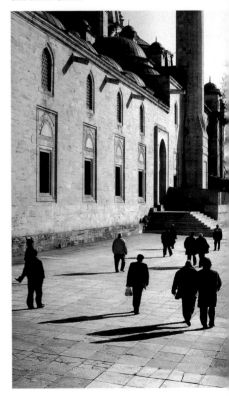

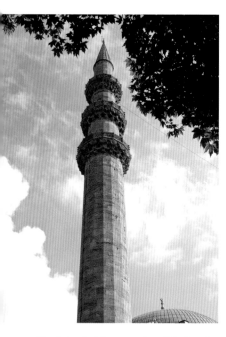

The Şehzade Mosque, minaret designed by Sinan.

While the lesser components of the complex were rebuilt to their original plan, the mosque was not, but this was indubitably the model that the Sultan's successors sought to challenge.

Mehmet's heir was Beyazit II Yildirim ('Thunderbolt') (1481–1512). While his father had chosen for his mosque a position on the ridge that gives Istanbul her unforgettable silhouette, Beyazit chose ground to the north of the Roman *cardo*. The beautiful arcaded courtyard of the Beyazidiye Camii exploits classical columns of varying colour and has a central fountain; a tremendous door opens to the prayer hall, which is an intelligent, if much smaller, variant of that of the Haghia Sophia, adapted to ensure maximum visibility for the imam. The

inverted T plan of the earlier imperial mosques of Bursa survives to echo that of a Byzantine church preceded by a narthex. Beyazit's loge – on the right – is enriched with polychrome marble, but the building as a whole is of an extreme austerity.

Beyazit's grandson, Süleyman the Magnificent (1494–1566), was fortunate in his choice of architect, Sinan. After the death of his son Mehmet in 1543, Süleyman instructed Sinan to build an appropriate memorial, the Şehzade complex, some ten minutes' walk north-west of the Beyazidiye. With its subsidiary buildings and shaded garden, the place has an immediate charm. The exterior is particularly impressive and the minarets are almost exuberant in detail. The measured rhythm of the courtyard is most satisfying, but the mosque itself perhaps less successful because of the very scale of the piers necessary to support the dome in a rigorously centrally planned structure. Sadly, the nearby türbe of Mehmet is not readily accessible.

Both sultan and architect learnt from the Şehzade Camii. For the Süleymaniye, begun in 1550 and finished seven years later, high on the ridge some ten minutes to the east, is unquestionably the most remarkable Ottoman monument of Istanbul. The scale is worthy of both men. The great rectangular enclosure of the mosque is flanked by medreses, a caravanserai and a hamam. The mosque is entered through a spectacular arcaded courtyard, with minarets at the four corners. The prayer hall itself is almost square, an impressive unitary space crowned by a vast dome, which rests on buttresses that are cleverly disguised by the flanking walls. The austerity of the architecture is relieved by panels of Iznik tiles and by a yet rarer survival, stained-glass windows by Ibrahim the Drunk-ard, who must have been aware of the Byzantines' use of the technique. Behind the mosque are two exceptional türbes. That of Süleyman is lavishly tiled and retains the original painted decoration of its dome. The smaller türbe of his wife, Haseki Hürrem, or Roxelana, is enriched with yet finer Iznik tiles. The north ter-race, with scattered trees, is a place of particular charm; and the view down across the Golden Horn is incomparable.

The Süleymaniye is, with Sinan's later mosque at Edirne, one of the consum-mate achievements of Ottoman architec-ture. But for many visitors it has a close competitor in the Sultan Ahmet I Camii, which answers Haghia Sophia across the Ayasofia Gardens. This – the 'Blue Mosque' – was built in 1609–16 under the direction of Mehmet Ağa. The plan follows that of earlier mosques. From the impressive courtyard, the central door (tourists are directed to a side entrance) leads to the enormous prayer hall, the lower walls of which are clothed in tiles, predominantly blue, many of floral motifs. The effect of these is indeed mes-merizing. The echo of Sinan is experi-enced here, in the slightly earlier Yeni Cami which overlooks the Galata Bridge and in numerous later imperial founda-tions.

But for those who love Iznik tiles, two smaller non-royal foundations, both designed by Sinan, are ultimately more appealing. The earlier, not far from the Galata Bridge, in an area of the souk that has not lost its natural vitality, is the Rüstem Paşa Camii, built in 1561 by Süleyman's grand vizier of that name. This is set on a terrace, and the arcaded porch is preceded by a porticoed projec-tion. Both façade and prayer hall are dec-orated with Iznik tiles, ablaze with

luminous blues and turquoise and ox-blood red. South-west of the Sultan Ahmet I Camii, but lower down, is the Sokollu Mehmet Paşa Camii of 1571–2, built for another grand vizier. Because of the steeply shelving ground the main approach to the courtyard is up a flight of steps. The tiles are of the highest qual-ity, which is matched by that of the marble decoration that enriches the pale stone.

By comparison with their mosques, the sultans' palace of Topkapi may seem oddly unassertive. Few, of course, were privileged to penetrate this in Ottoman times. Despite the number of visitors today, one can still sense something of the claustrophobic intimacy of the harem and respond to the charm of the finest rooms there, and to that of the Baghdad Kiosk in the fourth and lowest court, which was built in 1638 for Murat IV. Later sultans deserted Topkapi for palaces more congenial to nineteenth-century taste. But the place remained a repository for the extraordinary imperial assemblage of works of art. The collec-tions of oriental porcelain and of Otto-man kaftans and other fabrics are unrivalled. And if many Turkish visitors are most excited by the relics in the Pavil-ion of the Holy Mantle, which include Abraham's cooking pot and hairs from Mohamet's beard, other tourists will be astonished by such items as the Topkapi dagger and the booty Selim I seized in Iran in 1514.

Topkapi is an isolated survival, for time has not treated the lesser secular buildings of Istanbul kindly. Timber-framed houses burn, as Orhan Pamuk has recorded so hauntingly in *Istanbul: Memories of a City* (2001). And develop-ment has taken an inexorable toll. With other classes of buildings we are more fortunate. Istanbul is rich in baths, and one can follow a progression from those by Sinan associated with the Süleymaniye to the Cağoloğlu Hamami built for Mahmut I in 1741. Fountains abound; and in the market area there are numerous hans, which are far more atmospheric than the celebrated Kapali Çarşi to which most tourists are drawn.

It was only in the mid-nineteenth century that the Ottoman government determined to assemble antiquities from the territories it controlled. Osman Hamdi Bey was appointed director of the Archaeological Museum in 1881. The collection was originally stored in the beautiful Çinili Pavilion, built under Mehmet II in 1472, to the north of the Topkapi Sarayi, and the Archaeological Museum was constructed round this in three phases between 1896 and 1908. The style is unapologetically classical, as was indeed appropriate for a collection notably strong in Hellenistic and Roman sculpture. Most memorable are the sarcophagi from the royal necropolis at Sidon, in what is now the Lebanon, found in 1887. The Sarcophagus of the Maidens of c. 350 BC, with mourning figures in relief, would seem one of the finest works of the kind if it were not overshadowed by the technically yet more ambitious Alexander Sarcophagus nearby. Both are in remarkable condition, the latter with visible traces of original colour. The most recent contribution to the museum is an excellent suite of galleries dedicated to the history of the city. Nearby is the Museum of the Ancient Orient, with Mesopotamian, Assyrian and Hittite antiquities. The two museums are complemented by the notable holdings of the Museum of Turkish and Islamic Art, appropriately housed in the much-restored Palace of Ibrahim Paşa on the north side of the hippodrome. Particularly remarkable are the carpets. Others, lent from religious institutions throughout Turkey, are exhibited in an outbuilding of the Ahmet Paşa Mosque nearby.

Across the Golden Horn is Beyoğlu, formerly known as Pera and Galata. The Genoese built a fortress here in about 1300 and this was subsequently expanded. The Galata Tower, above the maze of streets that lead up from the harbour, marked the highest point of the enceinte. Beyond is the Istiklal Caddesi, formerly the Grand Rue de Pera, with handsome nineteenth-century embassies squeezed between more recent blocks. Barry's British Embassy, now the Consulate, is to the left just before Taksim Square. Ironically, G. E. Street's Crimean Memorial Church of 1858–69 is nearer to the former Russian Embassy, at the west end of the street, and easily reached from the Galata Tower.

Across the Bosphorus from Beyoğlu on the Adriatic shore is Üsküdar, from where pilgrims set out on the annual pilgrimage to Mecca. The landing stage, still served by ferries, is dominated by the the fine İskele Mosque, built for Mihrimar Sultan, daughter of Süleyman the Magnificent and wife of Rüstem Paşa, who inevitably employed Sinan for her complex with its outsize double portico. A few hundred yards to the south on the shore is Sinan's more intimate Paşa Camii of 1580. Back from the Iskele Camii is the ambitious if conservative Veni Valide Camii, built in 1707–10 to honour his mother by Ahmet III, with its unusual open-domed türbe. Fine as all three mosques are, these cannot compete with the Atik Valide Camii on a platform higher up. This was built by Sinan in 1583 for Nur Banu, wife of Selim II and

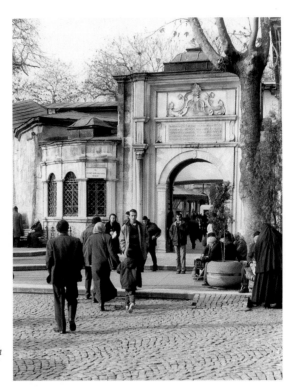

Eyüp, the gateway with pilgrims to the tomb of Eyüp Ensari.

mother of Murat III, and stands comparison with any of his more familiar masterpieces: the airy arcaded court with ancient plane trees prepares one for the harmony of the prayer hall or the radiance of the Iznik tiles that flank the mihrab.

Those with time should not miss two great monuments on the outskirts of Istanbul. Eyüp, some 4.5 kilometres/2.8 miles up the Golden Horn, retains its magic and is still a place of pilgrimage. Eyüp Ensari, the Prophet's standard-bearer, was killed during the Arab siege of Constantinople in 674–8. His tomb was venerated long before the Ottoman conquest, and it is not surprising that the complex at Eyüp was one of Mehmet II's earlier undertakings, begun in 1453. The mosque is not of particular distinction, but the türbe boasts panels of Iznik tiles of exceptional quality. There are many associated buildings of great charm, notably the Külliye of Mihnşah Valide Sultan, the mother of Selim III, of 1791, which perfectly exemplifies the so-called Turkish baroque in which decorative elements inspired by the late baroque of Western Europe are given, as it were, an Ottoman dressing.

Many secular buildings in this tradition survive on the shores of the Bosphorus, but few of these are readily accessible. The monument overlooking the Straits that deserves to be examined is very different in character. When Mehmet II determined to take Constantinople soon after his definitive accession to the sultanate in 1451, he demanded that the Emperor Constantine XI Dragases cede the ground on which to build a fortress, on the western shore of the Bosphorus. Work began on the Rumeli Hisari in April 1452 and, despite the huge scale of the project, was finished within four months. By establishing Ottoman control of the Straits, Mehmet effectively sealed the fate of Constantinople. The formidable walls, now themselves dominated by the new Bosphorus Bridge, link three large circular towers, two crowning low hills that rise abruptly from the shore and the third defending the watergate. Nothing could contrast more with the ruthless efficiency of the conqueror's fortress than the repetitive detail of his descendant's palace of Dolmabahçe, which must be passed to get to it; and indeed the two buildings may stand for the rise and fall of Ottoman Istanbul.

2
IZNIK
❖

THE TOWN of Iznik at the eastern end of the eponymous lake has had an unusually distinguished history, phases of which are represented by extant monuments. An existing settlement was enlarged in 311 BC as Antigoneia by one former general of Alexander, Antigonos, and promptly seized by another, Lysimachos, who renamed it Nicaea in honour of his wife. The modern town retains their Hippodamian plan. Briefly the seat on the kingdom of Bithynia, Nicaea fell to Rome in 74 BC, becoming the capital of the province of Bithynia. The Hellenistic town was expanded: the younger Pliny and the Emperor Hadrian were in turn responsible for public buildings. Constantine had a palace at Nicaea, and in 325 convened the first Council of Nicaea, which outlawed the Aryan heresy. Although damaged by earthquakes in the 360s and in 740, Nicaea remained a place of considerable importance. The second Council of Nicaea, which condemned Iconoclasm with momentous artistic consequences, met in 787. After a Seljuk occupation from 1081, Nicaea was recovered only seven years before Byzantium was seized during the Fourth Crusade in 1204. Nicaea then became the capital of the, much diminished, Byzantine Empire and the seat of the Patriarchate until the collapse of the Latin Empire in 1281. Its fall to Orhan in 1331 was a severe blow to the Byzantine cause. Renamed Iznik, the town became the major Ottoman centre for the manufacture of ceramics from the early sixteenth century. It is rich in Ottoman monuments, but the tiles with which the town's name is synonymous are best seen in Istanbul and Bursa.

The most conspicuous monument of Iznik is the unusually complete girdle of its walls. The inner circuit was largely built in the third century AD, but inevitably had to be repaired after earthquakes and incursions; the lower, outer enceinte, originally some 4 metres/13 feet high and incorporating much spoil from earlier buildings, was built under Theodosius at the same time as the original wall was heightened. The four gates are all of interest. The northern Istanbul Gate is particularly impressive, with a triumphal arch dedicated to Vespasian and Titus, the lower half of which is now below ground level, defended by a medieval outer gate and an inner gate, now surmounted by two masks that were presumably robbed from the Theatre. That the gate is still used by local

traffic and cyclists adds to its charm. The east, or Lefke, Gate, was, as an inscription establishes, restored by Hadrian. The aqueduct built by Justinian and in use until recently entered the city beside this. A particularly impressive stretch of wall with some well-preserved towers continues southwards, before turning towards the elegant Yenişehir Gate of 268–70.

At the centre of Iznik the Atatürk Caddesi and Mazharbey Caddesi, successors of the main Hellenistic and Roman streets, intersect. To the south-east of the crossing, sunk below the level of the modern town, is the brick carcass of Haghia Sophia. The original basilica was built by Justinian. Its successor, largely reconstructed after 1065 and converted to serve as a mosque in 1331, has been restored after a series of vicissitudes; and is now, after an interval in which it served as a museum, again in use as a

The Istanbul Gate, incorporating the Arch of Vespasian and Titus.

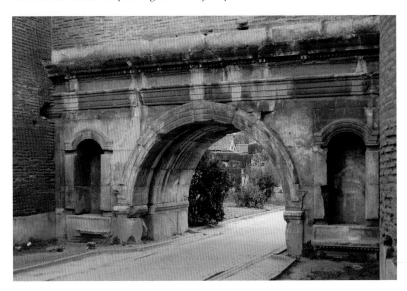

mosque. The scale of the bare structure impresses and there are hints of its former riches in a section of marble pavement near the west door and in the elegance of the white marble benches of the synthronon in the apse.

Of the numerous mosques in Iznik, the earliest is the small Haci Özbek Camii, four blocks to the east on the opposite side of Mazharbey Caddesi. More celebrated is the Yeşil Mosque of 1378–91, further east and a block to the north. The name of the architect, Haci bin Musa, is recorded. Its setting has a particular charm. To the west, across an open space, is the Nilüfer Hatun Imareti (soup kitchen), founded in 1388 by Murat I who named it after his mother, a Byzantine noblewoman. The main domed chamber and the flanking rooms of this charitable foundation are reached through an elegant arcaded portico. The building houses the town's museum, and numerous antiquities are laid out in the forecourt, among them a very handsome Roman sarcophagus. Excavations are under way behind the imareti.

South of Haghia Sophia on Atatürk Caddesi is the domed Murat Hamani, which is still in use, opposite the characteristic Ottoman Mahmut Çelebi Camii completed in 1443. Immediately to the east of the baths a number of kilns have been excavated. At the next crossroads turn right for the Roman Theatre. Turkey can boast many scores of such buildings, but no other can claim to be documented by letters of the younger Pliny, who as Governor was concerned with its construction in 111–13. Continuing excavation has demonstrated that although the theatre was systematically robbed for building material, a considerable portion of the lower section of the cavea and much of the substructure have survived.

3
BURSA

BURSA, the ancient Brusia, is named after its founder, Prusias I (228–185 BC), King of Bithynia. The last of his line bequeathed the kingdom to Rome in 74 BC. The city prospered under the Empire and Byzantium, but with the seventh century a long period of instability began. In 1326 Orhan Gazi conquered Bursa, which became the capital of his Ottoman Empire. Although supplanted as capital successively by Edirne and Istanbul, Bursa retained her commercial importance and it was there that the dynasty founded by Orhan's son, Osman, chose for two centuries to be buried.

The city lies on the northern flank of Uludağ, the Mysian Mount Olympus. The substantial acropolis of the early town, the Hisar, is on an oval hill that stands forward from the massif. Much of the circuit of the early walls survives. A long stretch on the south side is readily accessible: most of the facing blocks have been removed and the occasional re-used column drum implies post-Roman reconstruction. The small Alaeddin Mosque above the western gate of the Hisar is the earliest in the town, built inevitably with the spoil of a Christian church. Both Orhan and Osman were buried in the north-eastern section of the Hisar: their türbes, although late reconstructions, are still treated with due reverence.

The area to the east of the Hisar became the commercial centre of the Ottoman city. The Ulu Cami, built in 1394–9, was with its twenty domes the largest mosque the Ottomans had as yet constructed. Much restored, this is notable for the early carved mimbar. Behind the mosque spread the souks and numerous hans. Of these, the Koza Hani of 1451 – the han of the silk workers – has a particular charm, not least when approached from the square east of the mosque. Here one enters at the upper level and looks through plane trees to the central mescit, raised like a pavilion. Further east is the earliest of Bursa's royal mosques, the Orhan Gazi Camii, begun in 1338. The plan, an inverted T, set the pattern for later royal mosques at Bursa, but the fabric is much restored. Rather unexpectedly the mosque contains a long case clock signed by 'Chas. Hill' of Leicester.

From the Orhan Gazi Camii, make eastwards. A few old houses lurk among modern detritus, already in decay. Try to cross the not very appetizing river Gök Dere by the Irgandi Köprüsü, a restored bridge flanked by shops. Continue, passing a handsome medrese which houses the Museum of Turkish and Islamic Art and braving antiquity vendors, to the Yeşil Camii, built for Mehmet I from 1413 onwards and left unfinished in 1424. This owes its name, the 'Green Mosque', to the external tiles of the domes and minarets. The unfinished façade of pale Proconnessian marble is much restored, for two earthquakes in the nineteenth century took their toll. The interior, on the inverted T plan, is breathtaking. The four domes are beautifully handled; and the lower sections of the walls and those of the two flanking rooms are tiled: hexagons of a sustained green and a deeper blue are arranged and set off with a mathematical ingenuity. At either side of the entrance are small recessed chambers which are entirely tiled with green hexagons. The tiling of the imperial loge above the door is even more elaborate in

treatment. Artisans from Tabriz were recruited to help with the project; and Mehmet's Yeşil Türbe east of the mosque was decorated in the same way. Some way north-east of the Yeşil Camii is the mosque of 1390–5 which influenced its plan, that of Mehmet's father, Beyazit I, the Yildirim ('Thunderbolt') Beyazit Camii. The site is a commanding one, the hillside falling away abruptly to lower ground, which was not developed until recently. The portico is impressive; and the niches in the entrance are apparently the earliest recorded examples of the Bursa arch. Of several associated buildings, only the sultan's rather simple türbe and a medrese survive, the last now in appropriate use as a clinic.

The Ottomans were quick to expand on the low ground to the west of the Hisar. The Muradiye is an area of considerable charm, and much of interest survives. The Muradiye Külliyesi complex is a precious oasis of calm. Murat II chose to follow the plan of Orhan Gazi's for his own mosque (1425–6), but the use of tiles – with hexagons of turquoise, deep blue and green – was clearly inspired by the Yesil Cami. Behind, in a well-tended garden, is the Sultan's türbe, in which Byzantine capitals are put to service as column bases: the painted awning above the entrance is an enchanting conceit. Later members of Murat II's family must have responded to the charm of the place, and three of the nine other türbes built for them are of particular interest. At the western side of the garden is the türbe used for Prince Cem, who died in 1495, but which was in fact built in 1479. The tiling is of a dark and a lighter blue with gold decoration; and the upper walls and dome retain much of their original painted scheme, with patterns of blue and red and gold on a white

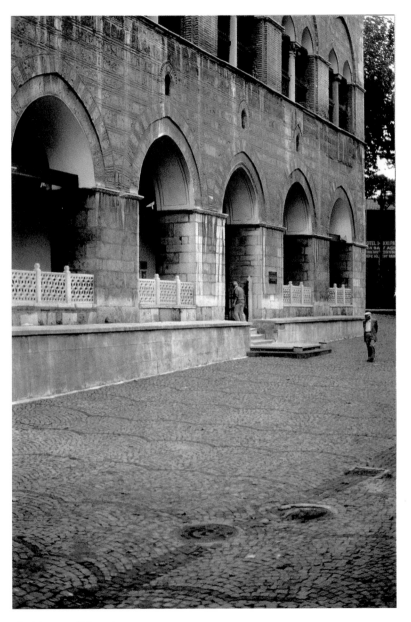

The Mosque of Murat I.

3 *Bursa* ❖ 31

ground. The türbe nearest the mosque is that of Princes Ahmed and Şehinşah, who were murdered in 1513 by their cousin, Selim I. The lower sections of the walls are tiled with blue and turquoise hexagons. Beyond Murat II's türbe is that of Prince Mustafa, built in 1573. The painted decoration of the upper walls has mostly been restored, but the marvellous Iznik tiles below are original. The continuous design of tulips and other flowers in blue, an ox-blood red, green, turquoise and white is so compelling that it takes a moment to realize that this is achieved with tiles of only two types, arranged vertically; work may have begun immediately to the left of the entrance where the pattern does not join properly.

Four kilometres/2.5 miles west of the centre of Bursa, long since subsumed by the metropolis, is Çekirge, where the hot springs were exploited by the Romans and their Byzantine successors. The Moroccan traveller Ibn Battuta saw the baths on his visit in 1333. Murat I (1359–89) reconstructed these, and his scheme largely survives, not least in the splendid chamber with Byzantine marble columns and leaf capitals in the section of the Eski Kaplica still used for men. That the sultan had a particular fondness for the place is proved by his decision to build his mosque there, high above the baths and in a position as dominant as that of any of the memorial mosques of his line. The façade reads like that of a contempo-

rary Tuscan town hall, the five arches echoed by the blind arcades above, within which paired windows are set. The explanation may be functional, for the upper floor was intended as a medrese. But none the less some degree of Western influence may be inferred, even if the belief that the building was designed by a captive Italian cannot be sustained. Inside, the familiar reversed T plan is adhered to, and there is a single dome. Understandably Murat I's mosque was the model that in their turn Beyazit I and Mehmet I would seek to challenge.

The last of the great buildings of Ottoman Bursa, at the foot of the hill on which Çekirge lies, was not a royal foundation. The Yeni Kaplica was begun in 1572 by Rüstem Paşa, Grand Vizier and son-in-law of Süleyman the Magnificent, who was the builder of the eponymous mosque at Istanbul. The most remarkable survival is the vast hot room with a central pool retaining much of its original tiled decoration after nearly half a millennium of use. Unlike the Eski Kaplica up the hill, now run as part of a Kervansaray hotel, the Yeni Kaplica remains very much part of the life of Bursa. It is not difficult to understand why the French writer Pierre Loti was drawn to the place. But it is Norman Douglas in *Looking Back* (1933) who has the last word about the city: 'There is an authentic smack of Paradise about Broussa.'

4

AIZANOI

THE ANCIENTS believed that Azan, son of King Ankas by the nymph Erato, founded the Phrygian city that bore his name. The Hellenistic city was subject, in turn, to Pergamum and to Bithynia, falling to Rome in 133 BC. The place flourished as the centre of a fertile territory, rich in the production of grain and in wood. With the rise of Christianity, Aizanoi became the seat of a bishopric. But in time her prosperity declined. The great Temple of Zeus, built during the reign of Hadrian, owes its survival to being used by Çavdar Tatars as a fortress, which in turn gave the place its modern name, Çavdarhisar. Her remote position meant that Aizanoi was unknown to European archaeologists until 1824.

The river Rhyndacus flows through the site and numerous old timber-framed houses nestle among the poplars on either bank. Of the four Roman bridges two survive. Most visitors, coming from Kütahya, cross the northernmost of these, to be confronted by a lateral view of the temple on higher ground to the south. Approached from this side, the temple looks remarkably complete: for the north wall of the cella is intact and of the original fifteen columns, ten survive. The west front also can be visually reconstructed without difficulty; it retains five of the eight columns and, behind, the portico *in antis* of the *opisthodomos*. In this respect, the design follows that of the much earlier, but less well preserved, temple attributed to Hermogenes of Priene at Magnesia on the Meander. Most unusu-

ally, the cella was raised above a vast barrel-vaulted chamber, lit by four shafts at either side and others at each end. Although some of the columns were re-erected after an earthquake in 1970, the texture of the temple, with its gold and ochre lichen, is wonderfully untouched.

The outer wall of the cella deserves detailed study. In addition to inscriptions celebrating the generosity of the local magnate M. Apuleius Eurycles, who also built one of the bridges, there are later graffiti: Byzantine crosses, some simple, one of some elaboration on a base, and numerous Tatar horsemen. Sounds from the village and birdsong emphasize the timelessness of the place. Below the temple is a small, recently excavated odeum. In the eastern section of the town, happily co-existing with the picturesque village buildings, are the ruins of a food market (*macellum*), a reconstructed section of a colonnaded street, itself built in part of reused material, and a bath. In the last there is a large mosaic pavement, with a beautiful central compartment of a maenad excited by a satyr.

North-west of the temple is a second thermal complex. Beyond this, a track leads between fields of corn and sunflowers to what is in some ways the most atmospheric monument of Aizanoi, the stadium, the further end of which doubles as the stage building of a substantial theatre. One section of the stadium has been excavated, but the whole complex remains very much as time and earthquakes have left it. Rows of seats have slumped. The front of the stage building has fallen into the pit of the orchestra, in a jumble of columns, some plain, some fluted, one spiralling. There are cornices and other decorated blocks, and a worn relief of a lion overpowering a bull. Nineteenth-century views show that the

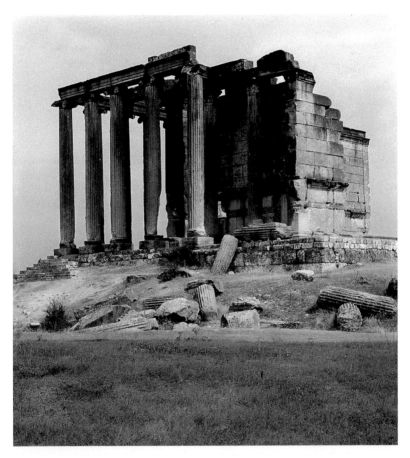

The Temple of Zeus.

central exedra had already collapsed, but that the splendid marble door to the right of this was still balanced by its pair on the left. This now has gone. But much of the structure of the theatre survives, because it was built into the hillside. As elsewhere the Romans indeed left very little to chance at Aizanoi. They had the prescience to build a dam to control the Rhyndacus when this was in spate. And the necropolises that stretch westwards from the town remind us of their respect for the hereafter.

5

SEYITGAZI

❖

THE ROAD south from the swelling university town of Eskihisar crosses an undulating plain. At length a ridge threatens to bar the way, and, before one is really aware of the modest town of Seyitgazi, the eye is caught by the domes and bristling chimneys of the monastery high on the flank of the hill to the right.

The story of Seyitgazi exemplifies the complexities of Anatolian history. Şeyit Gazi was an Arab commander in the eighth century who fell, a martyr, at the siege of Afyon. He had won the heart of Elenora, a Byzantine princess, who chose to be buried beside him. Their burial place was 'discovered', as if in emulation of the Empress Helena's discovery of the True Cross, by the mother of the Seljuk Sultan, Alaeddin Kaykubad I. She erected a türbe over the graves and this became a place of pilgrimage. A dervish tekke (monastery) constructed in the thirteenth century was largely rebuilt on a much more ambitious scale for Selim I (1512–26).

A path climbs up from the town to a stepped arcade that rises to the entrance door. Beyond, the pilgrim turns to the right up the colonnaded passage, with some finely carved Byzantine capitals, that leads up to the south end of a long tree-shaded rectangular court, which slopes upwards to the north where it is closed by a low wall. The key places of worship are on the left, west, side. At the

The tekke, with its chimneys.

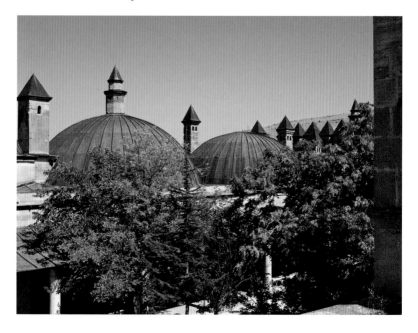

top of the colonnaded passage is the door to the Seljuk mosque, approached through a domed chamber that also gives access, though a modest door on the right, to the türbe: the sarcophagus of the gazi is some 7.2 metres/23 feet long and dwarfs that of his princess. In the mosque itself there is a handsome mimbar of grey marble. To the north is the larger Ottoman mosque, beyond which, orientated and thus approached from the garden behind, is the substantial Byzantine church. The aisles are divided from the nave by solid arches: and although it has been purged of any hint of Christian observance the building still has an unexpected muscular conviction. Before returning to look at the other buildings it is worth walking some way up the hill, a wilderness of scrub and stone, to look down over both the complex and the town, and survey the plain below and the bare ridge to the south.

The eastern range, the clustered chimneys of which are so arresting, was built to the highest specifications, as one might expect of an imperial foundation. A generous colonnade gives access to a series of domed structures. At the upper end these contain elegant rooms with substantial fireplaces: the pilgrims who used them were evidently well served. As the number of chimney stacks indicates, fireplaces are more numerous further down, the final room, the impressive kitchen, having no fewer than seven. At the southern end of the court is a very large room that was intended for those who were attached to the tekke.

Seyitgazi remains a place of popular pilgrimage. It has been beautifully restored; and the silhouette is unforgettable, as no doubt both sultan and architect intended.

6

MIDAS ŞEHRI

❖

THE COUNTRY south of Seyitgazi becomes progressively more dramatic: rocks rise up from the grassy valley floors and eroded cliffs draw the eye. This was the heartland of the Phrygians; and the rock-cut monuments left by them, and to a lesser extent by later inhabitants, deserve to be as well known as those of Cappadocia.

A few miles to the east of the main road to Afyon is the modest village of Kumbet, named after the medieval tomb that dominates this. Beyond, the road continues to Midas Şehri, the original name of which has been lost. This most striking of Phrygian sites stands on a gently sloping, marrow-shaped plateau surrounded by cliffs of varying height into which its most spectacular monuments were carved. From the centre of the village of Yazilkaya a path leads to the eastern flank of the site, and the signal monument of this, the so-called Midas Tomb, the late eighth-century BC pedimented cult façade some 16.8 metres/56 feet high, with a central doorway opening to a relatively modest cavern dedicated to Cybele. The front is perhaps most remarkable for the interlacing geometrical design carved in shallow relief, in which the eye trained by Christianity for a moment fancies it picks out numerous crosses. Worshippers would have gathered before this. To their right, at the extremity of the site, is an isolated outcrop much of which was cut away to create rooms on various levels.

An ancient path climbs the eastern cliff. But for the sightseer it makes more sense to follow the modern walkway below the northern cliffs. This passes a beautifully cut stairway which descends through a tunnel to a cistern. Then where the cliff turns, and well above the path, is the Unfinished Monument, or Western Shrine, only the upper section of which was carved. High up beside this is the cutting of a road, also apparently abandoned. Fringed by golden verbascum in the late summer, the modern path cuts across to the western cliffs, passing a Phrygian tomb. Below the extremity of the plateau, but above the valley at its foot, is a splendid group of rock-cut cisterns, all of considerable depth and reached by wide flights of steps.

From these the walkway rises to the edge of the plateau, west of the small fortress cut into the top of the northwestern section of the cliff and the small associated tower. It is easy to miss the ghost of a temple nearby. Altogether more memorable, near the centre of the plateau where this narrows, is the most eerie monument of the former city, the cult throne. This rises on three steps and bears an eroded Phrygian inscription. From here we can still sense the scale of the acropolis or upper city and survey the broken hills to the north. Further on, a path reaches the ancient 'Kings' Road', which must have been the main approach to the plateau: carefully graded, it dips gradually to the south east. A rough path to the right leads to the so-called Hyacinth Tomb, the patterned façade of which echoes the 'Midas Tomb' but on an intimate scale. Other cuttings are to be seen to the left of the 'Kings' Road' and there are numerous tombs in the eastern cliff.

A major city like Midas Şehri did not exist in isolation, and what survives of this is at the heart of a remarkable concentration of Phrygian and other rock-cut monuments. The largest group is in the Yazilkaya valley that drains to the north.

The stepped throne for a cult statue, from the south.

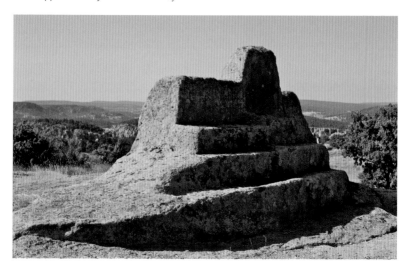

7
ARSLANTAS, AYAZIN AND ARSLANKAYA

TWO MOST evocative monuments are within easy reach of the road from Sey-itgazi to Afyon Karahisar, south of the turn for Kumbet and Midas Şehri. The first, reached by a turn to the right, is Arslantas. After a couple of miles the side road curls leftwards round a low ridge. Cut into this is a most handsome tomb with a central opening framed by matching reliefs in reverse of rearing lionesses, below which are less well-preserved carvings of their cubs. A little further on, hard by the road, are the remains of a further tomb, shattered, no doubt by an earthquake: the head of an open-mouthed lion has tumbled to confront the earth. The place takes its Turkish name from the lion reliefs.

Two miles or so further down the main road is the sign on the left to Ayazin, a sleepy agricultural village among trees. To the north is a series of cliffs into which numerous buildings were carved in successive periods. Those of Phrygian and Roman date are relatively insignificant, but the Byzantine church is both ingenious in the way the cross within a square plan was hewn from the rock and impressive in scale. Unfortunately the action of wind for more than a millennium on the relatively soft stone means that much of its has been lost.

It requires rather more effort to reach Arslankaya, which is arguably the most iconic of Phrygian monuments. Continue on the Afyon road to Gazigöl and then turn north-westwards for Ihsaniya and Doğer. There, at the turn before the rather handsome early fifteenth-century han at the heart of the town, turn right and take an eastward course, aiming for

Arslantas, the fallen lion relief.

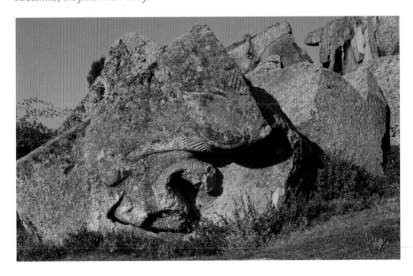

a track below a low escarpment on the right. A rock stands forwards, its base just above the valley floor. The east face is carved as the façade of a shrine to Cybele, an eroded image of whom, attended by lions, can be made out in the central niche, while the pediment above is enriched by sphinxes. It is, however, not from these but from the splendid giant lioness on the north flank of the rock that the monument takes its name. Few places are more evocative as the evening light fades, but photographers will wish to go in the morning.

The best centre for visiting these and other Phrygian sites is Afyon. And the town itself has much to offer: the İmaret Mosque, founded in 1472, with its associated buildings; a cluster of mosques in the market area; several hans and much traditional housing in the roads on either side of the spinal street that rises to the Seljuk Ulu Camii, the ineloquent exterior of which offers little hint of its rows of wooden columns. Opposite this is the path that climbs to the much-restored citadel that literally hangs above Afyon. Great efforts are being made by the regional authorities to preserve the fabric of an unusually satisfying town.

8

SIVRIHISAR

❖

APPROACHING Sivrihisar from the west it is not difficult to understand why the site was seen to be of strategic value by the Byzantines whose city of Justinianopolis was its predecessor. The town stands on an undulating platform below the dramatic Çal Daği, the highest point of which is 1,689 metres/5,540 feet above sea level, and controlled the lower ground to the south and west.

At the centre of what remains a thriving agricultural town is the Ulu Cami of 1274, which is among the finest and best preserved Seljuk mosques of the Kufa type. The bare stone exterior with tying beams offers no hint of the glowing colour of the rectangular prayer hall, the wooden roof of which is supported on five rows of hewn wooden columns, four of thirteen, while that nearest to the mihrab is of twelve because the corner of the wall of a small chamber takes the place of the thirteenth. Many of the columns stand on Roman and Byzantine bases and capitals in white marble, and others are crowned with reused capitals and marble blocks. The white of the marble stands out against the predominantly red decoration of the rafters and the roof, which is answered by the modern carpet. The effect is wholly satisfying. Above and just behind the mosque is a beautiful tomb of 1308, the Gazi Alemşah türbe, on a square base which rises to an octagon. The richly carved portal contrasts with the uncompromising simplicity of the rest of the structure. Justinian's city was in some respects the successor of Pessinus, now Balhisar, some 14.5 kilometres/9 miles to the south on lower

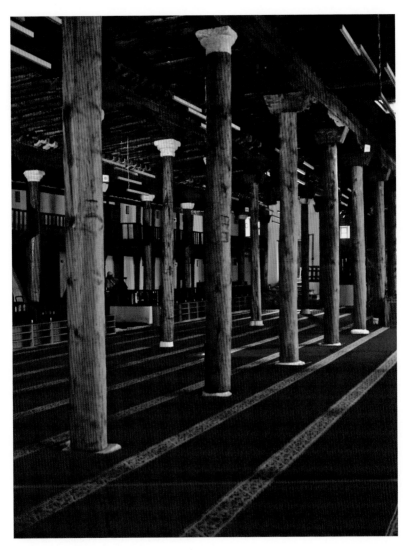

Interior of the Ulu Cami.

ground. This was an early Phrygian foundation and became a centre for the worship of Cybele, the mother goddess whose son and lover, Attis, castrated himself. Her uncompromising cult, served by eunuch priests, was maintained under the Galatians, who arrived in the area from 277 BC and chose Pessinus as a capital, and the Attalids, with whose Pergamene kingdom the city passed to Rome in 133 BC.

The road descends to cross the bed of a stream, which is almost invariably dry and was channelled between rows of marble steps and porticoes. Nearby is the excavation house. Some way to the west is what remains of the podium of the Temple of Cybele, alternatively identified as a Sebasteion and now assigned to the period of Tiberius (14–37). Below this, at the opposite end, is a wide staircase in three sections with part of a bouleuterion. A single fluted column drum serves as a reminder of what has been lost at Pessinus, which was no doubt efficiently pillaged when Justinianopolis was founded.

9

GORDION

✤

APPROACHING the modern village of Yassihüyük, it is difficult to imagine that so bare and barren a landscape could have supported the capital of a powerful kingdom. But, as archaeologists have proved, the place was settled by about 2500 BC. Much later came the Hittites and later still their neo-Hittite successors. The horse-breeding Phrygians, who reached Asia Minor in about 1200 BC, gradually secured most of western Anatolia and chose Gordion as their capital in the eighth century. Under successive kings, alternately named Gordion and Midas, Phrygia was a major power, controlling what was already a significant trade route from the east: its importance was demonstrated by the extent of the acropolis hill, which was originally defended by outlying fortresses.

Excavation has revealed part of the acropolis. The most impressive building is the eighth-century BC Phrygian Gate, approached by a ramp, which led to the sequence of four large megarons, or enclosures. These represent the great era of Phrygian domination. Under King Midas, whose wealth was legendary in the ancient world, the Phrygian kingdom was threatened by invaders from the Caucasus, the Cimmerians, who destroyed the city in 685 BC. The kingdom revived, although on a much diminished scale; but in the mid-seventh century BC Gordion fell to the Lydians, and they a century later were overwhelmed by the Persians.

Alexander wintered at Gordion in 334–33 BC, drawn by the prophecy that

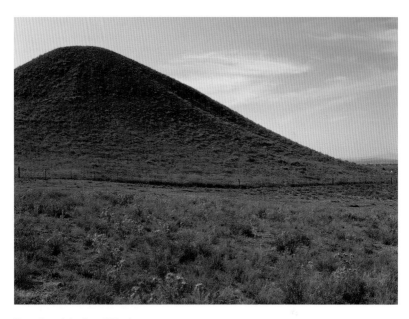

Tumulus of the Royal Tomb.

whoever cut the Gordion knot – a knot between the shaft and yoke of an ox cart – would rule Asia. He succeeded. With the sack of Gordion in 278 BC by the Galatians, the city commenced an inexorable decline, its remains gradually engulfed by the pale soil. But time could not expunge the most haunting witnesses of Gordion's former greatness, the eighty-odd tumuli, or hüyüks, that erupt out of the naked windswept terrain.

The largest tumulus, the Royal Tomb, dates from the third quarter of the eighth century BC. This is some 300 metres / 330 yards wide and was originally just under 82 metres / 90 yards high. Erosion has taken its toll, reducing the mound in height by about a third. But there is no doubt about the message the monument was intended to convey. The most re-

markable finds from the wooden tomb chamber in the centre of the tumulus – now reached by a modern tunnel – are in the Archaeological Museum at Ankara, but others are shown in the very respectable museum on the site. Hardly less interesting are the objects found in the so-called Prince's Tomb nearby, which included children's toys. The sophistication of the wooden grave goods from Gordion is matched by the elegance and originality of Phrygian pottery, which is well represented in the site museum. Neither king nor prince can be identified. But their tombs and the others that cluster about the city offer powerful evidence of the resources of the Phrygian kingdom – evidence that seems insensibly to strengthen as the shadows cast by the tumuli lengthen towards dusk.

10

ANKARA

❖

MUSTAFA Kemal Atatürk – the Gazi – transferred the capital of Turkey from Istanbul to Ankara in 1923. He did so for sound geographical reasons. Some three millennia earlier the Hittites had sensed the strategic importance of the place. They were followed by the Phrygians, to whom the name Ancyra is due. Alexander the Great came from Gordion in 333 BC. In time, his Seleucid successors were driven out by the Celts. Ancyra eventually became the capital of their kingdom of Galatia, which, renamed Sebaste, was annexed by Rome in 24 BC and remained that of the key province of Galatia with a population of perhaps 200,000. Ancyra was a major city in Byzantine times, as the citadel still demonstrates. Subjected to Persian and Arab attacks, the city was increasingly insecure and fell to the Seljuks after their victory at Manzikert in 1071. The Seljuks in turn were ousted by the Danishmendids, the Eretnids of Sivas and the irresistible Mongols. The Ottomans conquered Ankara in 1352 and although this was lost to Tamerlane in 1402, their rule was re-established by Mehmet I in 1414. Ankara's long decline continued until the late nineteenth century. The holding there of the first meeting of the Grand National Assembly in 1920 – at a time when Istanbul was still occupied by the European powers – anticipated Atatürk's selection of the city as the capital of the nation that he had revived.

What remains of Roman Ancyra has been largely engulfed by modern building. The major monument is the Temple of Augustus, built in 29–24 BC, of which the cella with facings of channelled white marble largely survives. A fallen capital with reliefs of angels near the entrance hints at the richness of the original decoration, but for the historian the monumental inscription in honour of the Emperor is of greater interest. The cella, which was adapted by the Byzantines as a church, later became the medrese of the nearby mosque. Not far to the west is the beautiful banded column which is believed to have been erected in honour of the visit of Julian the Apostate in AD 362; the capital now supports a stork's nest. Yet further to the west, across the Çankiri Caddesi, are the main Roman bath complex, built under Caracalla (211–17), and the associated palestra. The foundations of the former, in brick and stone, give an idea of its massive scale. Tenanted only by magpies and a friendly dog, the site is strangely appealing, despite being overlooked by apartment blocks. Near the entrance are arranged numerous Byzantine tombstones, many with portraits and *trompe l'oeil* doors.

The major monument of Byzantine Ancyra is the citadel that hangs above the town. Here the Emperor Heraclius (610–41) replaced an earlier fortress, building a great enceinte with polygonal towers; the citadel was enlarged on the west and to the south under Michael II (820–29). In both phases – and in later Seljuk and Ottoman restorations – much use was made of robbed material. There are numerous Roman inscriptions and sections of friezes. Near the Parmak Kapisi, the main entrance to the original citadel, are four statues of Priapus laid on their sides, and in the late fortress at the north end is what would appear to be a sacrificial altar.

The Parmak Kapisi, with two gates, the second at a right angle to the first, leads to the enclosure. On the left is the Alaeddin mosque, with a portico of reused column drums and an exceptional carved mimbar. The area within the walls, with its twisting streets of traditional timber-framed houses, has fortunately been spared from development. Many of the more ambitious old houses, some now restored as restaurants and one, bravely, as a hotel, lie between the Parmak Kapisi and the Hisar Kapisi of the outer walls. Outside the latter the ground slopes to the southeast. This was the centre of the medieval town, and later was Ankara's commercial hub.

There are several mosques. The most atmospheric is a Seljuk foundation, the Arslanhane Camii, with its associated kümbet of 1330. The mosque has a minaret with traces of tiled decoration in turquoise. The fine wooden roof of the prayer hall rests on twenty-four wooden columns with appropriated Corinthian capitals and upturned bases, their arrangement clearly inspired by the nave and aisles of a church. The walnut mimbar with patterned octagons and radiating hexagons is of 1209; the mihrab is also striking, the stucco set off by turquoise tiles and glazed lettering in black. Down the street to the west is the Ahi Elvan Camii, an Ottoman foundation of the late thirteenth century. There are twelve wooden columns, again with capitals of reused classical blocks. Here too there is a fine mimber. A diagonal route from behind the Arslanhane Camii, between more traditional houses, eventually descends to the busy Ulucanlar Caddesi.

On the further side of this is one of the least appreciated monuments of Ankara, the Yeni Camii, founded by Ahmet Paşa. His architect was none other than Sinan.

Set among plane trees, the mosque represents the quintessence of the architect's style. The tripartite portico, with domes of which that in the centre is taller than the others, stands before the higher domed prayer hall, with a minaret to the right. The cream local stone is enriched by alternate pink blocks in the arches and ribs of the portico; these were also used for the elongated triangular rays that run downwards from the top of the base of the minaret. The prayer hall is austere, the dome rising as if from an octagon; the white marble mihrab, mimber and loge are original.

From the citadel one can see not only the Temple of Augustus but also, some 2 kilometres / 1.2 miles to the south-west, the low hill used for a Phrygian necropolis now crowned by Anit Kabir, the mausoleum of Atatürk. The main approach curls upwards between trees to reach a processional way, fronted by statues and pavilions and lined with pairs of lions. This opens on to the vast central court, with, on the left, raised on a podium, the huge mausoleum with massive pilasters that houses Atatürk's tomb. The whole complex has an austere nobility that places it in the tradition of the great monuments of Asiatic rulers, yet is given a lightness of touch by the open colonnade that faces the mausoleum. In the wings, and below the mausoleum itself, is the museum. Atatürk's remarkable life and contribution to his country's development are comprehensively celebrated. The relics are oddly fascinating, ranging from swords presented to the Gazi by the Shah of Persia and the Emperor of Japan to the cigarette case Atatürk gave King Edward VIII, which the Turkish authorities purchased back in 1998. What, one wonders, did Atatürk make of the monstrous clock given to

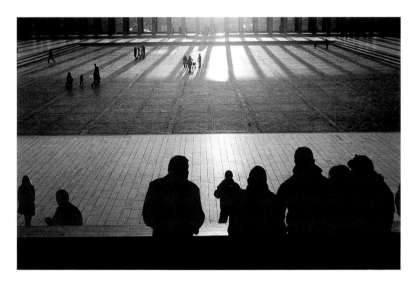

The Atatürk Memorial, the courtyard from the steps.

him by the Iş Bankasi in 1934? For his clothes imply a sense of restraint. Atatürk's 'fitness equipment' suggests his physical discipline and his library a wide range of curiosity. To an English person it is oddly reassuring to know that the great man's favourite dog, loyally stuffed, was named 'Fox'.

His memorial is the greatest monument of modern Turkey, but Atatürk has another claim on the tourist in Ankara. For he was directly responsible for the foundation of the prodigious Museum of Anatolian Civilizations, housed, most satisfactorily, in the much-restored bedesten built by Mehmet Paşa in 1458–66 and 1472–3 on the south-western flank of the citadel hill. While antiquities collected and excavated before 1923 remain at Istanbul, it is at Ankara that we can best experience the great advances in Anatolian archaeology that have been achieved since then.

The circuit begins on the right. The most remarkable of the early finds are from Catalhüyük (7000–6000 BC). These range from murals of a bull being attacked by men and of a plan of a town with a volcano erupting in the distance, to a plaster relief of two leopards. The obsidian arrowheads could still be put to use; and the pottery would be equally serviceable. From the early Bronze Age (third millennium BC) are the finds from the Hattic royal tombs at Alacahüyük: more pottery; jewellery; much gold; a gold-mounted iron dagger; and, not least, the wonderful finials of stags in bronze, many with silvered decoration. From Horaztepe there is a bronze of a breastfeeding mother and the statuette of a girl in electrum: her face and breasts are enriched with gold and she wears gold bands and anklets.

The Hittites dominate the next section. From the King's Gate at Hattuşaş comes the splendid relief of a warrior holding an axe and with a dagger at his side. His loincloth is patterned and the artist represents the hair on his chest as curls. But often it is the small objects that fascinate most: the dagger with the name of Anitta, the first of the Hittite kings; the bronze tablet of 1235 BC from Hattuşaş commemorating a treaty; or a cuneiform tablet recording a message from the wife of the Pharaoh Rameses II to Puduhepa, wife of the Hittite king. The Hittites too made extraordinary pottery, including a wonderful bird-like pair of tall libation vases and two huge bull vessels from Hattuşaş (1600–1500 BC).

The great central hall of the museum is devoted to Hittite reliefs – again from Alacahüyük – and the yet more spectacular ones from the neo-Hittite cities of Carcemish and Arslantepe. The earlier of the Carcemish reliefs date from after 900 BC. The dynamism of the designs – with chariots riding down victims lying on their backs – is matched by the spirit of the inscriptions: 'and he . . . hacked down Saparkean Tarhunzas and then overturned their gods for me'. The later reliefs from Carcemish (760–740 BC) are equally remarkable. One block shows Gilgamesh with the Animals – the ancestor thus of Orpheus; while the series from the King's Tower shows King Aras with his elder son, eight of the latter's younger brothers, two at play and two

others with a spinning top, and their mother holding the tenth boy, followed by a dog.

Back in the outer galleries are the remarkable finds from the tumuli at Gordion, which reveal so much about the sophistication of royal lives in eighth-century BC Phrygia. The bronze cauldrons and smaller vessels are of exceptional quality and the calibre of Phrygian ceramics is shown by a pair of goose-shaped vessels with painted decoration in brown. But pride of place inevitably goes to the unique wooden furniture, including two elaborately inlaid 'serving stands', to a less well-preserved table and a stool; and to the wooden toys from the Prince's tumulus: bulls, oxen, horses and lions, and – as a reminder that Phrygian princes would not have been trained to be squeamish – a lion attacking a bull.

The final section of the museum is downstairs. Here there are finds from Roman Ancyra. The finest is a wonderfully incisive bronze portrait of Trajan, clearly designed to be seen from below. From the theatre is the marble head of a woman, which preserves most of its original finish, including pigment in the hair. But the *clou*, sadly ill lit, is a late Hellenistic bronze statue of Dionysus. Found relatively recently, this was smuggled to Switzerland before being recovered by the Turkish authorities.

11
SAFRANBOLU

SAFRANBOLU is a remarkable survival, a small town with a substantial number of nineteenth-century mansions and smaller houses, built on either side of a steep valley, respectively by Turkish and by Greek or Armenian merchants, many of whose families were at one time involved in the preparation of saffron from the flowers of crocuses. The main road from Karabük curls downwards to emerge in an irregular space flanked on the right by the Kazdağlioğlu mosque, which is set back, and the fine seventeenth-century Cinci Hamami. Beyond this the road narrows to curl round to the left and double back to reach the larger central market place with, ahead to the right, the large Cinci Han of 1640–48, bristling with chimneys. Impeccably restored, this is used most appropriately as a hotel, and can also be reached on foot by a steep lane, which like so many of the streets in the town is cobbled.

Opposite the han, narrow lanes climb steeply uphill to houses perched on terraces above. The most ambitious of these is the Kaymakamlar Gezi Evi, the projecting upper two floors of which seem to hang over the town. The house has been tactfully restored and is shown as a museum, with appropriate contents and the inevitable costumed dummies. Some of the wooden ceilings have charm. Below the Cinci Han is the most beautiful of the mosques of Safranbolu, the

Izzet Mehmet Paşa Camii of 1796, a characteristic structure of the so-called Tulip period, with a slender minaret, an elegant portico and a high domed prayer hall. It is worth walking down the road below this, to look upwards to the mosque and the crowding houses of the town, and across the sunken stream to the old houses that descend the opposite bank. Here it is possible to escape the tourists, many from Turkey itself, without whom new uses could not have been found for many old buildings that might otherwise have been allowed to disintegrate.

Returning past the mosque and below the west end of the Cinci Han continue northwards, passing the porticoed Köprülü Mehmet Paşa mosque of 1661, not very happily repointed, with its charming minaret, which is in the heart of the commercial centre of the town. Above this, Hukumet Caddesi on the left leads past more old houses towards the Kent Tarihi Museum, which occupies a tall neo-classical former government building of 1904–6 in a commanding position. While most of the exhibits, which include a telescope and an early gramophone, are of limited interest, the museum offers a survey of many aspects of life in Safranbolu during the early twentieth century.

The visitor who stays in Safranbolu may wish to see the more interesting of the monuments in the vicinity. To the north, crossing the valley at Incekaya, is a handsome Byzantine aqueduct; and just over six miles to the east Yörük Köyü, with the Sipahioğlu House.

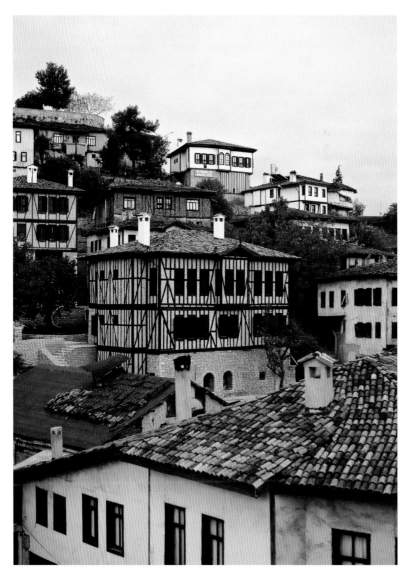

Nineteenth-century mansions.

12

KASTAMONU

THE TOWN of Kastamonu cascades down from the ridge crowned by its ruined castle to the left bank of the Gökirmak river, as it flows northwards towards the Black Sea some fifty miles downstream. The site was occupied in early times, as Phrygian tombs attest. The town became the seat of a bishopric under the Byzantines and took its name (Castra Comneni: castle of the Comneni) from the family that built up considerable estates in the area, the ancient Paphlagonia. They ruled as emperors in 1057–59 and 1081–1185, and in Alexia Comnena could claim the best informed female historian of their time. Kastamonu was an early conquest of the Seljuks, who lost it to the Dashimend Turks. Recovered for Byzantium in the 1130s, it fell to the Turkish Isfendiyaroğlu in the final years of the twelfth century, becoming the capital of their emirate. Sacked by Tamerlane in 1402, it was rebuilt by the Isfendiyaroğlu, finally falling to Mehmet II in 1459. Successive phases of its history are represented in its extant buildings.

The visitor will wish to walk up from the river to the fortress. Impressive at a distance, the Byzantine citadel was reconstructed by successive rulers, and most recently under the Ottomans. The site, a spine of rock, is commanding; enough survives of the entrance on the east side to give one a sense of the place, and there is no better vantage point to survey the town below.

Roads wind down between modest houses to the Atabey Mosque of 1273, the roof of which has been altered. Further down, and a little to the north, is one of the more ambitious Ottoman complexes in eastern Turkey, the Yakub Ağa Külliyesi. Largely constructed of pale yellow stone, the domed mosque is flanked by a medrese and a refuge for the poor with the necessary kitchen, an appropriate foundation for Süleyman the Magnificent's master of kitchens. Below this is the small Alacamescit Camii of 1715 and the substantial Cifte Hamami of 1543. The oldest bath in the town is the restored Cemaleddin Firenkşah Hamami, stated to be of 1262. There are a number of other early mosques. Almost equally important to the urban ensemble are the surviving timber-framed houses: a few are visibly in decay, but some are in reasonably good repair and others in the process of restoration.

Down by the river, the Kastamonu Museum is housed in an admirably appropriate late Ottoman building in which Atatürk announced the abolition of the fez. The archaeological collection includes a bronze rhyton in the form of a bull and a Byzantine fresco fragment. A number of Hellenistic and Roman sculptures are in the garden: a fragment of a large relief with two men in togas; funerary monuments; the lower half of a statue with unusually vigorous drapery; a beautiful, and beautifully preserved, block with the head of a bull; and a trio of rather eroded recumbent lions. At a single glance one can survey these relics of vanished civilizations, the distant castle and the quaintly nostalgic building in which the creator of modern Turkey promulgated his sartorial revolution.

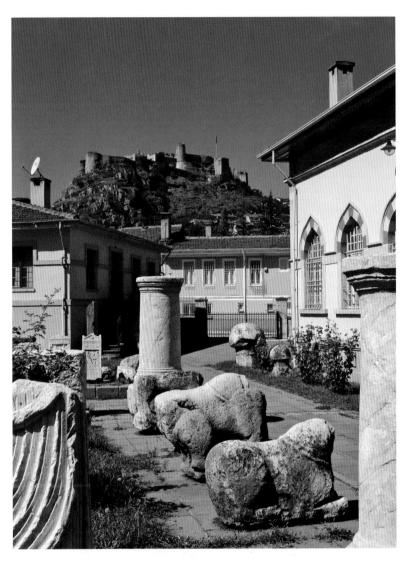

The Castle from the garden of the Museum.

13

KASABA

THE Mahmut Bey mosque at Kasaba is an enchanting survival. The road north-west from Kastramonu towards Daday runs through a gently undulating and productive landscape: after some 14 kilometres/8.7 miles, take a turn on the right for 3 kilometres/1.8 miles, before turning right and heading down to the scattered houses of the village of Kasaba Köy, passing a ruinous hamam with some original stucco that somehow holds out against the elements above a ford. Taken by surprise by this, I drove one of my front wheels into a ditch: a man came to the rescue, using a hoe to free my – or rather Avis's – car, and firmly refused my offered payment. I crossed a footbridge and walked up to the mosque with its narrow wooden minaret half-lost among trees.

The mosque was built in 1366, when the area was ruled by the Isfendiyaroğlu of Kastramonu. The bare outer walls are of stone. There is a single entrance, opening to an unexpectedly coherent space,

with a higher central section flanked by narrower aisles, with a gallery on two levels against the entrance wall. The roof is supported by four wooden columns, which retain much of their original painted decoration, predominantly a deep red. The capitals of the columns are all subtly different, for although who-ever designed the mosque had a sophis-ticated sense of space the joiners who erected this knew when to sacrifice sym-metry for their structural requirements. The great beams that rest on the columns and the rafters which these in turn sup-port are also carved and painted, in red and green and ochre. The effect is com-pelling.

At Kasaba, as in perhaps no other mosque of the period I have visited, one feels as close to the pulse of a medieval village as in any church of comparable scale in Western Europe. Moved both by the unpretentious simplicity of the place, and the harmony of its colour, I lingered. The man who had dug me out arrived after half an hour and proved to be the imam: he made no objection when I placed the note he had declined in the collection box. I left, still dazed by the radiance of a magical place.

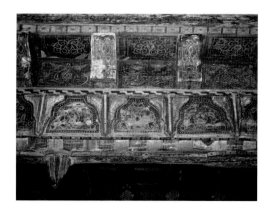

The mosque, painted decoration of the roof, detail.

14
HATTUŞAŞ

✿

HATTUŞAŞ, the Hittite Hattusha, is unquestionably one of the most remarkable sites in Turkey. On the approach from the north, by a turn off the main road from Ankara to Samsun, the land gradually rises. Ahead is the sloping hillside that the Hittites chose as their capital and guarded with a wall some 10.5 kilometres / 6.5 miles in circumference.

The place had been settled in about 2500 BC by the Hatti, a non-Indo-Germanic tribe, but the territory subsequently fell to the Hittites, who reached Anatolia about half a millennium later. Hattuşaş was destroyed by Anitta, King of Kussara, in about 1750 BC, but refounded some hundred years later. The Hittite kingdom grew in importance under King Hattusili – who took his name from Hattusha – and his successor, Mursili, who conquered Babylon. A period of decline followed. Hattusha was burnt. The Hittite power was revived under Shupiluliuma I (1350–1315 BC). King Muwatalli II transferred his capital elsewhere, but Hattusili II reinstated Hattusha. Under him and his son, Tudhaliya IV, Hattusha was considerably expanded, eventually covering an area of 180 hectares / 445 acres. Tudhaliya IV's invocation of the Hittite deities in the nearby sanctuary of Yazilikaya was powerless against wider movements of population and economic change; and his son, Shupiluliuma II, the last of the Hittite kings, abandoned Hattusha early in the twelfth century BC. Part of the site was occupied by later peoples, but the Hattusha of the Hittites faded from memory, its monuments forgotten until

1834, when Charles Texier thought he had found a lost city of the Medes.

The visitor now is confronted by a reconstruction of a section of the Hittite wall, with three towers. The effect is not convincing, but as the Hittites used stone only for the foundations and lower sections of their structures and employed mud bricks above, of which inevitably there is no trace, it is useful to have some idea of the height of these. The main monuments of Hattusha can conveniently be reached by the road from the ticket office. This turns to the right round the considerable remains of the Büyük Mahet, or 'Great Temple'. The complex is entered by a gateway with three thresholds, which leads to a paved area: on the left are storerooms, in one of which is a large green stone, once wrongly thought to have come from Egypt. Ahead is a cistern, by which the street turns into the south corner of the great platform that surrounded the temple. This was entered from the south-west front – again there were three thresholds – and had a large central court. The holes visible in many of the substantial stone blocks, drilled by turning copper tubes, were for attachments of wood for the mud brick of the upper walls. The wealth of the temple is implied both by its size and by the number of storerooms in the complex. From the precinct the low walls of a large area of domestic and other buildings to the west can be seen.

Higher up the road divides. Turn left and climb towards the royal citadel – the Büyük Kale – on a well-protected plateau which was used by the Hittites' predecessors. The ruins date substantially from the reconstruction of the late thirteenth century BC. The courtyard inside the gate, just above the turn of the modern road, is linked to three successive courts: the southern wall is particularly impressive and the views are commanding.

The road turns to cross the upper city, passing below two remarkable chambers, one of which was decorated with hieroglyphs, before reaching the walls – which continue round the escarpment from the Büyük Kale – at the King's Gate. The gate takes its name from the relief of the hairy-chested god of the left inside jamb: now in the museum at Ankara, it has been replaced by a cast. The road then follows the wall for a most splendid stretch that runs along the southern ridge. Allowing for the disappearance of the mud-brick superstructure, this is in remarkable condition. There are two enceintes, the higher on the crest of the ridge, the lower before this, both with turrets at regular intervals. The highest section at the south, the Yerkapi, is fronted by a tremendous glacis, from a gate at the bottom of which rises the celebrated corbelled tunnel that runs diagonally upwards and enters the city just below the Sphinx Gate. The gate itself is defended on the outside by the battered survivor of a pair of sphinxes which gives it its name. It is now thought that both glacis – up which there are two flights of steps – and tunnel were intended for ceremonial use.

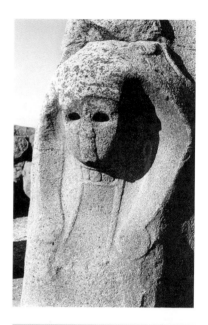

Descending from the Yerkapi, the road reaches the most satisfying building of Hattusha, the Lion Gate, a double doorway set between two substantial towers. The gate derives its name from the two battered, yet splendid, lions of the outer door. These merit close inspection: such details as the paws and hair are realized with an exacting precision. The outer section of the wall north of the gate exemplifies the exceptional calibre of Hittite masonry.

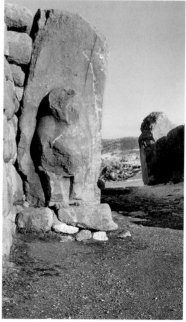

The numerous other ruins at Hattuşaş are best explored with a detailed guidebook – that by Jürgen Seeher is sold locally. The extraordinary shrine associated with King Tudhaliya IV, 2 kilometres/1.2 miles to the east at Yazilikaya, must impress any visitor, however uninstructed in the Hittite pantheon. The King's Temple succeeded an earlier one, built in front of the cliffs, and is now represented by no more than scant foundations. A ceremonial route led to a large, but irregular, natural inlet in the cliff, some 30 metres/98 feet deep, known as Chamber A. The left wall of the rock face was carved with some sixty-six representations of deities, of whom the largest, at the extremity of the cleft, are Teshub and Hebat, who is attended by their son Sharumma. On the opposite, south, wall, which never catches the sun, is King Tudhaliya himself.

A few metres to the south of this shrine is a narrow gully, artificially widened, which leads upwards to a second enclosure in the rocks, Chamber B. The reliefs here are fewer in number, but unusually well preserved. On the right there is a sequence of twelve armed men who appear to be running: these are guards of the underworld. On the opposite wall is a large relief, apparently of Nergal, god of the underworld, whose shoulders and arms are represented by lions; to the right is a compartment in which King Tudhaliya is embraced by his patron, the god Sharumma. It is suggested that the chamber was dedicated to the King's memory by his son and successor, Shupululiuma II, before he withdrew from Hattusha.

No visit to Hattuşaş is complete without a detour to Alacahüyük, some 20 kilometres/12.4 miles off the approach road, which was discovered by W. J. Hamilton in 1836. Settled occupation of the city began in about 3500 BC, and late in the third millennium BC it became the base of the Hatti, whose sophistication is established by their grave goods, which are among the most striking of the early Bronze Age. Their civilization failed long before the advent of the Hittites, to whom the major monuments of Alacahüyük are owed. While the finest reliefs from the site are in the museum at Ankara, the Sphinx Gate through which the complex is entered is very impressive, although it is to be regretted that new buildings have been allowed on the line of the central axis. Both sphinxes remain in situ; on the side of that to the right is a double-headed eagle, a motif that had reached the Hittites through the Assyrian trading colonies that were so important in Anatolia early in the second millennium BC. Beyond the gate on the left are the footings of a number of storerooms; on the lower ground behind these are the walls of the thirteen royal tombs of the Hatti, the treasures from which are also at Ankara, though some finds are in the small museum nearby. The other excavations are really only of interest to the specialist, but it is appropriate that a tree growing in the small temple to the south has in turn evoked a spiritual response and been decorated with ribbons to express the wishes of a different age.

Opposite, top: Alacahüyük,
the Sphinx Gate, detail.
Opposite: the Lion Gate.

15
AMASYA

❖

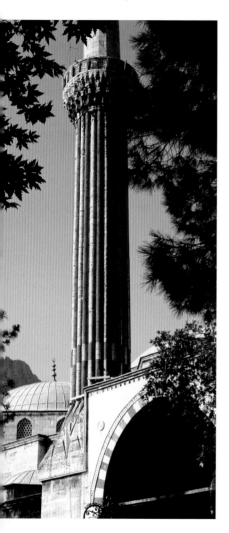

The Mosque of Sultan Beyazit II, minaret.

AMASYA has suffered much. Flanking the river Iris, now the Yeşilirmak, as it bursts northwards from the Pontic range, the site was settled by the Hittites. In 302 BC the place was taken by Mithridates, who proceeded to found the kingdom of Pontus, which would survive until his descendant, Mithridates VI Eupator, rashly took on Rome, courting defeat by Pompey. Strabo, the great geographer, was born at Amaseia in c. 64 BC, within four years of the Roman conquest. Rome was succeeded by Byzantium. And as a result of the Byzantines' crushing defeat at Manzikert, the Seljuks arrived in 1071. Later the Mongols cut their destructive swathe. Beyazit I conquered Amasya in 1392 and under his Ottoman successors the town enjoyed a long prosperity.

The city is divided by the river. To the north is a relatively narrow stretch of ground, backed by the great hill that served as the acropolis of ancient Amaseia. Five spectacular pedimented tombs of the kings of Pontus are carved into the cliffs below this. The original marble facings of these have gone, but their blank façades – the tallest some 12 metres/40 feet high – hang over the town that has so constantly been remodelled at their feet.

Seljuk and Ottoman monuments abound. The more distinguished are south of the river. A circuit from the west would take in the Seljuk Gök Medrese Camii – with its türbe and some original turquoise tiles – founded in 1366, which now houses the Archaelogical Museum; the unusually large porticoed Sultan Beyazit II Camii built in 1486 by Beyazit's son, Prince Ahmet, who was governor of Amasya; the only slightly less ambitious Kileri Süleyman Uğ Camii, begun in 1485; and, on the bend of the river, the unexpectedly substantial lunatic asylum built in 1308 under the Il-Khanid Mongols, the Birmahane Medresesi. Further north, the Seljuk Kuş Köprüsü, or Bird Bridge, the finest of Amasya's five bridges, overlooked by the mosque built by Mehmet I's vizier, Beyazit Paşa in 1419, leads to the vast octagonal Büyük Aga Medresesi of 1488, which has now been restored.

There are numerous türbes in the town. Of these, that of the Danishmendid vizier, Halifez Gazi, datable to 1145–46, is the most elaborately decorated. Lining the north bank of the river are many of the traditional timber-framed houses that used to be such dominant features of the Ottoman townscape. Even at Amasya, too many such buildings have been destroyed, but others have been energetically restored. One of the largest has been arranged as a museum; many now serve as boutique hotels. Few, if any, are still inhabited by descendants of their original proprietors. None the less, it is to the survival of these domestic buildings that Amasya owes its enduring charm. No visitor will forget this or the drama of the backdrop, the acropolis hill with its royal tombs.

16
TOKAT
❖

TOKAT deserves to be more widely known. Its jagged fortress rock dominates a town that may have been relatively modest in the eleventh century, but was much enlarged under the Danishmendid Turks. The latter were followed by the Seljuks and, in 1326–52, by the Mongol emir Eretna, whose main base was Sivas; later it was controlled by Burhan ed-Din of Sivas, whose lands passed to the Ottomans in 1400. It flourished as a key station on a branch of the trade route to and from Persia, traders on which approaching from the west were served by hans at Pazar and Mahberi Hatun, and on leaving Tokat and crossing the Kizilinişgeçidi Pass by the Çiftlik Hani. Tokat was also a considerable industrial centre.

The early town, like its successor, covered a considerable area, its main monuments concentrated on two intersecting roads. One ran southwards from a bridge of 1250, now restored, across the Yeşilirmak. On the right, incongruously incorporated in a house, is the beautiful portal of the Sünbül Baba Zaviyesi of 1291–92. Further on, also on the right, is the outstanding monument of Seljuk Tokat, the Gök Medrese, formerly used as the museum: this has an elaborately carved frontispiece and elements of its rich decoration survive. Beyond is the very large Voyvoda Han of after 1631. Opposite these, across an open area, are the Hatuniye mosque and medrese, built in honour of his mother, Gülbahar Hatun, by Sultan Beyazit II Yildirim ('Thunderbolt') in 1485 and separated by a substantial garden. The decoration of

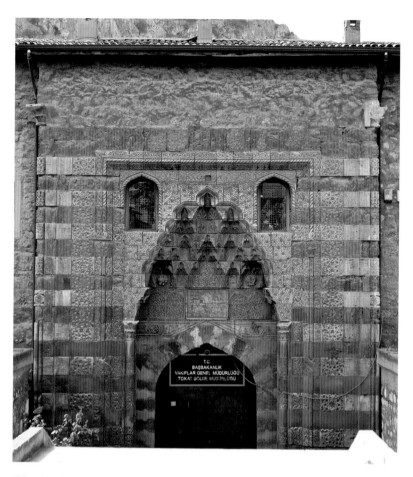

Tokat, the Gok Medrese, portal.

the portico of the mosque is particularly satisfying.

Narrow roads behind the Voyvoda Han climb upwards below the fortress towards the Ulu Cami, rebuilt in 1679–80. That south of the han leads to the second of the key streets, that runs east–west, emerging opposite the very accomplished Ali Paşa mosque of around 1570: the seven shallow domes of the portico – which extends beyond the body of the prayer hall – echo the dome. To the east is the massive Paşa Hamami, built for Yurguç Paşa in 1424–25 and well restored. The road rises gradually to the west. A little way up, to the right, is the beautiful Ali Tusi Türbe of 1233–34, decorated with turquoise tiles. There follows the Sulu Han, formerly used for dying cloth; the Bedesten, to which the archaeological museum has been very successfully transferred, and the Kazancilar Mescidi. Across the street from this is the Çukur Medrese, a Danishmendid foundation, beyond which is a bath built for Beyazit II in 1489–90. Further west is a han of 1751, behind which is a contemporary hamam. Returning to Tokat after a quarter of a century, it is hugely encouraging to see how much has been done to preserve and consolidate both the major monuments and some of the nineteenth-century domestic buildings in the town.

17

SIVAS

✿

SIVAS boasts a wonderful group of thirteenth-century Islamic buildings, but the name derives from its Byzantine and Roman past. Originally called Megalopolis by Greek, or Greek-speaking, settlers, the place was renamed Sebasteia in the reign of Augustus. In the early fourth century, during the Emperor Licinius's campaign against Christianity, the Forty Martyrs of Sebasteia were frozen to death, while, according to a later legend, the city's Bishop Blaize was beheaded. In their honour the city became a major place of pilgrimage. Persian and Arab incursions followed, and the town was subsequently exchanged by the Byzantines with the Armenians, who repopulated it, only to be driven out by the Seljuks after the rout at Manzikert in 1071. The extant monuments of medieval Sivas are due to the Seljuks and the Mongols, who in turn supplanted them. A Mongol governor, Eretna, established a dynasty that lasted until 1380. Sivas was largely destroyed by Timur (Tamerlane) in 1402 and has only recovered in importance in relatively recent times.

The mound of the citadel that lay to the south-west of the medieval town is now a garden. On its flanks are a number of old houses and below, to the east, is the outstanding monument of Sivas, the Gök Medresesi. The Seljuk vizier who built this in 1271 was a serial architectural patron, also ordering a mosque at Konya and a medrese at Kayseri. The façade is a masterpiece. The central portal is richly detailed, with stylized animal heads as well as the more usual plant motifs. This is flanked by boldly decorated buttresses that support the paired minarets above: the tiled decoration in a pale turquoise has a numinous quality. The turrets at the outer corners of the front are also elaborately carved. The gate leads to the courtyard, where the detail on the entrance façade is also exceptional. The mosque is to the right, its dome memorable for the inscription in black lettering on a blue ground. The lateral ranges are beautifully balanced, with central iwans between the students' cells. The use of tiles in the northern iwan is particularly ingenious.

North of the citadel mound is a group of almost equally remarkable buildings, also of the Seljuk period. First comes the splendid hospital constructed for the Sultan Kaykavus in 1217–18. The gate opens through a deep entrance hall that leads to the medrese-like courtyard with lateral arcaded porticoes: the domed tomb chamber is on the right. Like other structures built for the Sultan, the hospital impresses with its scale and restraint. Opposite is the façade, which is all that survives of the Çifte Minare Medresesi, built in the same year as the Gök Medresesi by the Il-Khan's vizier, and in evident competition not only with this but also with the contemporary Muzafer Bürüciye Medresesi north of the hospital. As Sinclair observes, the portal of the lat-ter is 'comprehensively' decorated and the same is true of its counterpart. Both are exquisite in their modulation of patterns, yet perhaps lack the dramatic energy that is so striking in the Gök Medresesi. Muzaffer Bürüciye, who came from Persia, was not, it seems, a powerful official, but he was clearly a man of considerable wealth. He was buried in the beautiful tiled chamber to the left of the entrance, where an inscription preserves his name.

The mosques of Sivas are inevitably outshone by the wonderful Seljuk medreses. The Kale Camii, built by the Ottoman vizier Mehmet Paşa in 1580, is opposite the Muzafer Bürüciye Medresesi. The Great Mosque, to the south-east, has a fine early minaret. Further east is the han of Behram Paşa, built in 1573, flanked by the Kurşunlu Hamami of 1576, also built by Mehmet Paşa, who was no doubt fully aware of architectural developments at Istanbul. Some way to the north – and not easily found without a map – is a fascinating monument of Mongol Sivas, the now-truncated Güdük Minare ('truncated minaret'). This was the türbe of Eretna's son Hasan, who died in 1347–48. The father's princely ambitions were eloquently expressed in the scale and elaboration of the structure.

The Gok Medresesi, paired minarets, Sivas, towards dusk.

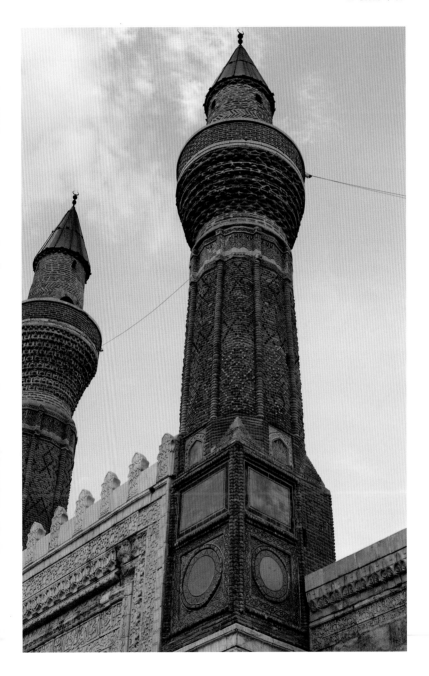

18

DIVRIĞI

THE Ulu Cami at Divriği is one of the most original and inventive Islamic buildings in Turkey. It is set in a remote valley carved by the Çalti Cagi, a tributary of the Euphrates. Far from the main arteries of modern Anatolia, the town, despite recent building nearby, still has the air of an overgrown village, with timber-framed houses on the steep slopes of the valley. And those who attend the weekly market still have a traditional generosity to the visitor. On my first visit, in a moment of inattention, I allowed my car to fall off the narrow road and down a steep grassy bank.

Twelve men, whom I had just overtaken in their trailer, hauled the motor up, amazingly unharmed, with evident amusement.

As Tephrike, the town was a Byzantine redoubt. But in the ninth century, the Muslim rulers of Malatya permitted a sect of Christians who were anathema to the Orthodox, the Paulicians, to settle there. Byzantium only recovered Tephrike in 969, banishing the Paulicians to Thrace; from there the contagion of their Manichaean belief in the balancing powers of God and the Devil helped to inspire the Albigensians. After the Byzantine rout at Manzikert in 1071, Divriği fell to the Seljuks, who installed the Mangujakids. As their capital, Divriği flourished. The Mangujakids were in turn inevitably swept away by

The Ulu Cami, detail of the portal of the hospital.

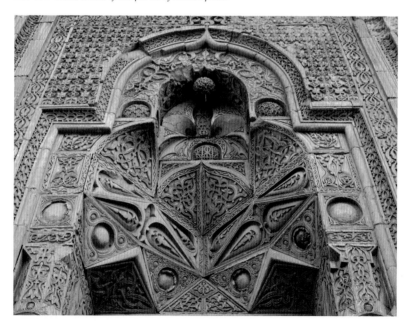

the Mongols, whose victory over the Seljuks at Kosedag in 1242 completely changed the balance of power in eastern Anatolia. Later Divriği was subject to the Eretnids of Sivas, falling to the Ottomans in 1516.

The fortress of Divriği is on a high promontory between the main valley and that of a tributary, north-east of the modern town. The original Byzantine defences have been rebuilt and patched in successive campaigns, and are most remarkable in any case for the views they command, to the great cliffs above and over the monuments of the former city and the valley. In 1180, the Mangujakid Seif ad Din Şahanşah built the mosque that is the most prominent building within the fortress. His architect was Hasan bin Firuz of Merga. The prayer hall is barrel vaulted, while the aisles both support two domes. As so often, the most lavish decoration is on the doors, and the use of turquoise brick introduces an additional element of colour. The balcony for the shah, itself something of a departure in the area, suggests the confidence of the dynasty.

On a terrace at a lower level, southwest of the citadel, are the Great Mosque and Şifahane (hospital) of 1226–29. These are said to have been designed by Hurran Şah, who came from Ahlat on Lake Van. They were built for the Mangujakid Emir Armed Şah and his wife, Melik Turan. The two institutions were placed in a single block: the mosque with a main entrance at the north end and a subsidiary portal on the long west façade, to the left of that of the şiferhane. Externally the most remarkable elements are again the portals, here carved with immense vigour: the double-headed eagle the Seljuks had adopted is used with falcons and plant motifs, as well as elaborate geometrical patterns. No other Seljuk buildings are so richly eclectic, and the designer was clearly aware not only of Armenian sources but also of the sophisticated stucco decoration of Persia. The interior of the mosque is also magnificent, with a central nave flanked by aisles. The niche of the mihrab is carved with the energy one has by now come to expect, and the carved mimber of 1241 has the distinction of being signed by Ahmed Bin Ibrahim, who came from Tiflis in Iran. Some of the celebrated carpets, which must have contributed so splendidly to the visual richness of the mosque, are exhibited in Istanbul. The şifahane, entered from the west, is planned like a medrese, with four iwans round a roofed court, which is lit by an oculus above the central pool: the columns on the left are of octagonal form, those to the right cylindrical.

Below the mosque, among the scattering of timber houses on the slopes above the modern town, are a handful of substantial tombs. That nearest the mosque, the Kamareddin Türbesi of 1196, has a pyramidal-roofed dome. The octagonal Sitte Melik Kümbeti of 1196, below the citadel, with a richly patterned façade, was originally built for Seif ad Din Şahanşah. Happily these tombs have not been encroached upon by recent buildings. Indeed, its rural character is one of the pleasures of Divriği.

19

KEMAH

THE Mangujakids were instinctive builders, as their monuments at Divriği attest. The family held two other emirates to the east, in the valley of the Upper Euphrates, at Kemer and at earthquake-shattered Erzincran. Kemah, at the confluence of a minor tributary, the Tanadzor, with the Euphrates, just before this carves its passage between sheer cliffs, and on the late Roman road along the valley, is a spectacular site. A major Zoroastrian centre, it became the capital of the Armenian principality of Daranaghi, and was from the early tenth century the seat of the Byzantine bishopric of Mesopotamia, passing about two centuries later to Mangujak, whose successors retained it until 1228 when it fell to Seljuk control.

Set back from the left bank of the river is an isolated plateau, protected on the west by high cliffs carved in the past by the Euphrates and by the somewhat less precipitous cliffs above the Tanadzor to the east. So formidable was the position that it did not require a complete circuit of walls. The Mangujakid town lay within the citadel: its successor is on the lower ground to the south-west.

The main approach is from the west, up a partly excavated ramp. In the seventeenth century Çelebi saw three gates, of which only two survive. The lower one is faced with carefully cut blocks of varying shades of brown, unquestionably intended for visual effect. The less impressive upper gate is roughly at the centre of the cliff. The plateau slopes upwards to the right (south), protected by a fragmentary wall, clinging to the crest of the cliff. Further on a narrow shelf extends towards the southern tip of the plateau. Recognised as a weak point

Tower above the town.

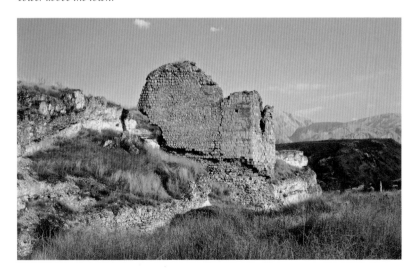

in the defences, this was controlled by a substantial tower with a projecting prow-shaped outer face. A larger tower of the same form protected the yet more vulnerable salient to the east, where the subsidiary landward entrance to the citadel was routed through partly rock-cut tunnels, probably of Mangujakid date, from the bottom of the gorge below. Such precautions availed little when Timur (Tamerlane) took Kemer in 1402. What is assumed to have been the governor's residence is at the northern end of the plateau, where recent excavation has clarified the functions of a number of other buildings, including a hamam. But striking as the ruins on the citadel are, it is the views from this that are etched in the memory. The Euphrates bends majestically downstream; and a fine medieval türbe is perched above the cliff to the north.

The modern town surrounds the Gölabibey mosque, apparently founded in 1454 but probably subsequently altered and with a mihrab of 1765–66. The satisfying prayer-hall is supported on twelve wooden columns. Nearby is the hamam, tactfully restored as a tea-house-cum-ethnographical museum. On the right bank of the river, in sight of the town, is the notable early thirteenth-century Mausoleum of Abu'l Fath Saljukshah which was subsequently claimed to be that of the founder of his line, Mangujak. Beside this is the associated zaviye. Nearby is a fourteenth-century türbe, with an elaborately decorated brick portal.

20
ŞEBIN KARAHISAR

❖

ŞEBIN Karahisar is not a place the sightseer is likely to chance upon by accident. I was drawn to it by Sinclair's account. Some 93 kilometres/55 miles south of Giresun on the Black Sea and well to the north of the subsidiary of the major trade route from the east that branched off west of Refahiye for Niksar and the north-west, the Byzantine Koloneia was by the ninth century the command post of a theme, or military district. The looming rock on which the citadel sprawls, which indeed looks black ('kara') from a distance in a landscape predominantly green, lent itself to defence; and a town grew up on the slope that descends to the west. No invader could afford not to take the place: it fell to the Danishmenids and Mangujakids in 1074 and became part of the Ottoman empire in 1473. The alum ('şebin') mines to the north meant that the town was also of considerable economic importance. It had a substantial Armenian population and was one of the few places where a stiff resistance was attempted during the First World War.

The route up through the town passes the main mosque and a ruined han, built against the hillside. Above, a paved path clings to the flank of the slope, climbing, in places up ancient steps, to a gate in the Byzantine defensive wall, which may at least in part have been built under Justinian. This originally enclosed the very considerable area above the cliffs, with the main, western, summit, the ridge above the cliff that runs to the east, the extended spur to the north-east, and the ground between these. The gate is faced

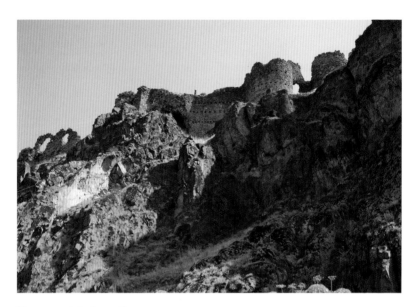

The approach to the castle.

with blocks of purplish stone and flanked by round towers: a well-preserved stretch of wall runs westwards. The path above the cliff to the right leads to what remains of the Byzantine defences at the eastern angle of the rock. The Byzantine wall then turns, descending to follow the line above a series of low cliffs and screes, before cresting the north-east spur. The masonry is eroded and the line is incomplete. But one can only admire the efficiency with which the Byzantine engineers sought to complement the natural defences of the rock.

Higher up, near the centre of the site, there is a fine rock-cut cistern to which a flight of steps descends. Above this is the main path to the striking upper citadel, which is of the Ottoman period. The irregular courtyard, entered through a gate flanked by two towers which are complemented by two angle-towers, is dominated by the commanding octagonal tower embedded in the opposite, south, wall. The observant traveller, Evliya Çelebi, likened the citadel to a 'galleon without masts' in 1647, and recorded that there were then seventy bastions. Time and an earthquake of 1939 have taken their toll: a citadel that once secured the caravans that bore their loads of alum to Trebizond, for export to the west, or by way of Sivas and Konya, is now, for practical purposes, no more than an amenity for the inhabitants of the growing town at its foot. Turkey boasts innumerable fortresses. Many are better preserved and of greater architectural sophistication than that of Şebin Karahisar. But few are more visibly dominant of their terrain. '

21

TRABZON

❖

THE Turkish Trabzon – two harsh sylla-
bles – conveys little of the romance of
the earlier forms, the ancient Trapezus,
founded in the seventh century BC, or
the medieval Trebizond. And the sightseer today has to allow the thriving
modern city time to yield the evidence of
the past. Zenophon's exhausted army
reached Trapezus in 400 BC. Hadrian
came in AD 129. The city controlled
access to passes leading through the
Pontus mountains and was the most
important port at the eastern end of the
Black Sea. When Byzantium fell to the
Franks in 1204, two brothers of the Comnenus family founded an empire at Trebizond, and their line would outlast the
restored empire at Constantinople, surviving until 1461.

The modern city is a more provincial
entrepôt, despite the unexpected hu-
mour of its shop signs – the Levi store
called 'Keep Out' and the 'Crazy Inter-
net' nearby. To the south of the main
artery, as one heads west, is the small
Byzantine church of St Anne, on a road
that leads upwards to the domed church
of the local martyr St Eugenia, now the
Yeni Cuma Camii. The structure survives, an impressive space transformed
in character by white paint. From vantage points nearby there are fine views of
the citadel to the west. This stretches up
a ridge that rises inexorably from sea
level, protected on the east by a deep
valley, now invaded by gardens, and
commanding lower ground on the west.
The citadel is a patchwork of ancient fortifications and more recent buildings,
including late nineteenth-century man-

sions, whose original owners no doubt
fled in the exchange of populations that
followed the First World War. The neo-
classical former town hall is on the Uzun
Yol, or long street, which crosses from
the central metropolis. Near by, dominating a narrow square, is the Panagia
Chrystokephalos, the tenth-century cathedral where the Comneni were crowned
and which they dignified with a proud
dome in the thirteenth century. When
Mehmet II conquered Trebizond in 1461
the cathedral became a mosque, the Fatih
Camii. But the fabric was respected: the
balcony where the emperor presented
himself to the people survives and some
of the lavish marble decoration of the
apse is in place.

A road, the Içkale Caddesi, follows the
spine of the citadel ridge. Towards the
highest point of this, the Elflatun Kanak
on the right leads to what survives of the
palace of the Comneni. Admirers of Rose

The Fatih Camii, the former Cathedral.

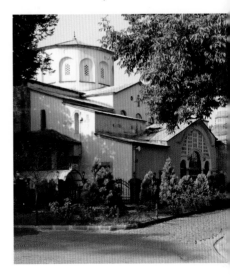

Macaulay must lower their expectations. For the towers are not very remarkable, and it is all but impossible to conjure up a vision of the sophisticated court recalled – perhaps with the rose-tinted vision of age – by Cardinal Bessarion, most civilized of prelates, who was born at Trebizond. Later buildings have encroached on the walls, but one can still see a considerable hall that rises above two deep basement rooms, with three fine windows, two with mullions. The fortress is not impressive. Yet there is the magic of old stones, spared the indignity of repointing that disfigures so many well-meaning restorations and set off by the charm of the small, irregular gardens, the green fig trees and vegetable plots and the innocence and honesty of a place where shopping is left outside every door.

The western flank of the citadel still expresses something of its former strength. Below is one of the purest Ottoman buildings of eastern Turkey, the Gülbahar Hatun mosque. This was built in 1512 by Selim I the Grim, in memory of his mother, Ayşe Hatun, born a princess of the Comneni, who had married Beyazit II. For the Ottomans, like the Comneni in their day, understood the use of matrimonial alliances.

Trabzon has long since burst beyond its early boundaries. The urban sprawl marches westwards, but mercifully does not completely engulf the greatest monument of medieval Trebizond, the wonderful church of Haghia Sophia. This and the associated tower are set among trees on a level platform above the sea raised originally for the temple Hadrian dedicated to Apollo. The original basilica was transformed under the Emperor Manuel I (1238–63) into a great domed cruciform building, preceded by a narthex. Much masonry was recycled from earlier buildings. Externally, decoration is concentrated on the south porch, with an eroded frieze of scenes from the life of Adam, divided by a keystone with the Comnenus blazon, an eagle. The church was appropriated as a mosque and was subsequently in use as a store.

As a result of a programme directed by the great English Byzantinist David Talbot Rice, for Edinburgh University from 1957 onwards, the remarkable murals of the interior have been responsibly restored. The busy narratives of the narthex, which the pilgrim would have seen first, are of fine quality. Much more impressive is what remains of the decoration of the dome, with animated tiers of angels, a crucifix so intelligently placed that the lateral perspective works and such well-observed details as the peeling stucco on a wall behind one of the four Evangelists: unfortunately, as the building has now been re-commissioned as a mosque, these are now concealed from view by screens. The murals of the apse must have been of equal distinction, as is seen, for example, in the subtle modelling of the legs of the Apostles in *The Miraculous Draught of Fishes*. The floor under the dome, now covered, is of *opus Alexandrinum*, in which both mosaic and marble are used; and the dome itself is supported on four huge columns of Proconnesian marble, which must have been brought by sea through the Bosphorus.

The best time to visit Haghia Sophia is the morning, when sunlight catches the smooth blocks of the exterior of the apse. The empire of the Comneni depended on trade – and the exactions that could be levied on this – and there are scratched drawings of dozens of the ships that

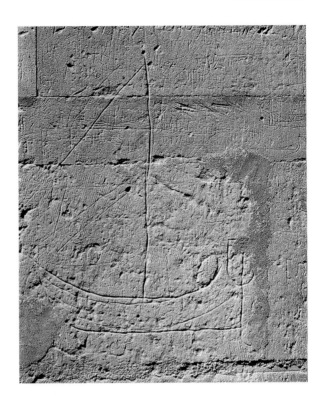

Haghia Sophia, graffito of a galleon on the external wall of the apse.

plied the Black Sea, galleys and galleons, sails unfurled. Studying these, aware of the sounds of sea and birds, but now also of the motorway below, one literally turns one's back on the excrescences of the encroaching concrete sprawl.

Haghia Sophia has been responsibly looked after as a museum. Alas, the same cannot quite be said of another church with notable murals, which is equally near the centre of Trabzon, although less easily reached. Kaymakli is on the east flank of Boztepe, the hill south-east of the town. Below this, 46 metres/50 yards separate industrial sprawl from rural Turkey. An unmarked track curls up from the busy main road heading south and doubles back. The place was a

significant Armenian monastery. This endured until 1915, and then a relatively small church, or chapel, was put to service as a hay store. As a result, the murals survived, partly spared from the wanton obliteration of faces from which so many others have suffered. The earlier, fifteenth-century, scenes are in the apse. On the west wall is a later, but visionary, depiction of *The Last Judgement*, imaginative both in composition and detail. In 2003 the roof had fallen. Protests to successive Turkish ambassadors in London elicited a letter implying that the authorities had other priorities. I despaired. But within a few weeks the roof was replaced; and the murals will thus continue to bear witness to the rich plurality of Christian art in the territory of modern Turkey. The farmer who lives in one of the monastic buildings has the key.

The monastery of Sumela, untainted in the official mind by Armenian associations, 46 kilometres/29 miles inland, has been intelligently preserved. The position is spectacular. The visitor climbs steeply up the side of a wooded valley. The monastery is first seen from below, the walls built into the cliff. The monks chose the place as a retreat from the world, but, as the approach reveals, the site also offered protection from the casual marauder. The buildings are not architecturally remarkable and the murals are late and relatively undistinguished. It is for the setting that tourists go – and in impressive numbers.

Less accessible and very much more atmospheric is what remains of the smaller monastery of Vazelon to the west of the main road to the Zigana Pass. A side road at Kiremitli, south of the turn for Sumela, leads after some 4 kilometres/2.5 miles to a fish farm. Follow the track on beyond this, turning right at a fork, after which Vazelon comes into view. The monastery of St John is on the south flank of the valley, partly built, partly rock cut. In the small detached chapel are the abused, yet still eloquent, survivors of what must have been a particularly vigorous cycle of sixteenth-century murals. Their robust design is matched by a strength of colour. There is no guardian and, even since Sinclair's photographs were taken, the process of deliberate vandalism has continued.

22
TERCAN

✣

BEYOND the largely rebuilt city of Erzincan, the road to the east follows the Upper Euphrates. After some 17 kilometres/10.5 miles there is a turn on the left to the key Urartian site of Altintepe, the remains of which, with a palace and a temple on a low hill, have been partly excavated. The most important finds are in the Archaeological Museum at Ankara. Some 68 kilometres/42.25 miles further on, the road cuts eastwards up the valley of the Tuzla. After 13 kilometres/8 miles, this skirts the unassuming town of Tercan, notable for a large caravansarai and a türbe of 1192, of altogether exceptional elegance, which is one of the most beautiful buildings of its date in Anatolia.

The mausoleum of Mama Hätun, which is by Sesi Muffada ('the squinter') from Ahlat and commemorates a princess who was evidently a key ally of Saladin when he annexed the area, consists of an octagonal türbe with curving convex sides on a square base, set in an enclosed court surrounded by a circular wall with twelve internal recesses. The entrance to this is through a magnificent decorated portal. A flight of steps to the right of this leads up to the top of the wall, from where we can see the subtlety of the roof of the central türbe, with its eight compartments rising from the curved faces of the monument. The tomb itself is on the lower floor of this, while above is the small prayer chamber of octafoil plan, reflecting the form of the structure. The decoration thoughout is of the most consistent quality.

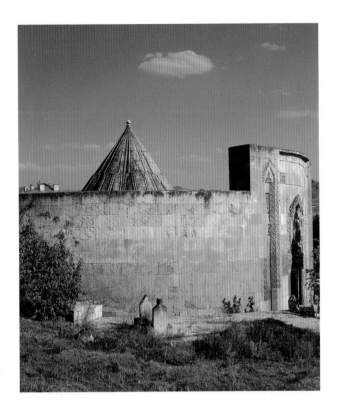

The Mausoleum of Mama Hätun.

Immediately to the west of the mausoleum, and coeval with this, is the large caravansarai; the internal arrangements were considerably modified in three successive stages during the Ottoman period. The great gate opens to a passage with raised and recessed lateral bays. From this, a portico leads to the central courtyard with three iwans opposite, and at either side rows of five small rooms, each with windows and hearths, and at the west ends single small iwans. Behind these, and approached from either end of the portico, are two long vaulted rooms, of which that on the left

runs the length of the south front, lit by openings in the roof: these were evidently for the use of those travellers and merchants who could not aspire to use the more intimate rooms flanking the courtyard.

While the caravanserai does not compare with the great Seljuk examples of the ensuing century, it and the türbe are both very impressive. And if the modern traveller does not have to share the former with his horses and camels, Tercan continues to be a halting place on one of the high roads of eastern Anatolia.

23

ERZURUM

EVEN by Anatolian standards, Erzurum has a complicated history. The area was inhabited in early times, and by the fourth century was already of some importance. Its position, at a point where a key trade route from east to west was intersected by roads to the north and south, explains both Erzurum's enduring prosperity and its political vicissitudes. It became known as Theodosiopolis, after Theodosius II who fortified it, and fell to the Persian Sassanians in 502. After its recovery, the Byzantines renamed it Anastasiopolis; to the Arabs, who arrived in 655, it became Qaligala. Byzantium recovered the city in 751, but in 961 it passed to the Georgian Bagratid kings of Tao, and was known as Karin from 994 to 1000, before returning to Byzantine rule. After their victory at Manzikert in 1071, the Seljuks took the city, calling it Arz-er-Rum ('Land of the Romans'). The Saltukid dynasty was followed by a succession of independent Seljuk princes. The Mongols arrived in 1242. Timur conquered Erzurum in 1400, using it as the base for his campaign against Sultan Beyazit I; and it was only in 1515 under Selim I that the city passed to the Ottomans.

Early descriptions are numerous. In Ibn Battuta's day, 1333, the place was in ruins because of local rivalries. The bibliophile Robert Curzon gives a detailed account of life in Erzurum during the winter of 1843 in his *Armenia*, published in 1854. Brief occupations by the Russians in the nineteenth century and in 1916–18 have left relatively little trace. But serious earthquakes in 1939 and 1983 caused lasting damage – and as a result the turfed roofs that Curzon described have almost disappeared. None the less, Erzurum still boasts a very substantial number of early buildings.

The citadel is not the most important monument of Erzurum. The site, to the east of what is now the centre, was chosen as the highest within the city and there is no better vantage point than the clock-tower at the south-western angle. To the south is what has to be the most beautiful monument of the city, the Çifte Minare Medresesi of 1255. The façade is splendid, with a gate flanked by the two minarets from which the building takes its name. The detail of the decoration deserves careful study. The builder was Sultan Alaeddin Keykubad II: the no less splendid Hatuniye türbe at the further end of the courtyard was intended for his daughters. The contemporary impact of the building is suggested by its evident influence on the design of the Gök Medresesi at Sivas. Behind the medrese is one of the most arresting sights of Erzurum, the Uç Kümbetler, a group of three kümbets. Traditionally attributed to Ali Ibn Saltuk, who established the Saltukids as the rulers of Erzurum in the late eleventh century, these are in fact of rather later date.

Next to the medrese is an earlier and much less lavish Seljuk foundation, the Ulu Cami of 1179. This was apparently built for Melik Mehmet, Saltuk's grandson, but has been substantially reconstructed. The design of the iwan hall reveals a knowledge of Sassanian building. The efficient sobriety of the mosque epitomizes one aspect of Seljuk architecture. The Ulu Camii is on the main thoroughfare, Cumhuriyet Caddesi, which runs east to west. To the west, on the opposite side of this at the junction with

Menderes Caddesi, is the Lala Mustafa Paşa Camii. This was completed in 1562 for the then governor of Erzurum, who was subsequently to conquer Cyprus for the Ottomans. His taste was clearly metropolitan, and the building is so faithful to the style of Sinan that it has been attributed to him. Following Menderes Caddesi northwards, there is another major Ottoman monument commissioned by an influential official, the bedesten of Rüstem Paşa, the Grand Vizier to Süleyman the Magnificent, who also ordered major buildings in both Istanbul and Bursa. On the other side of the street is a sixteenth-century Ottoman hamam, which is still in use.

North-west of the Lala Mustafa Paşa Camii is the second of the great monuments of Erzurum, the Yakutiye Medresesi. This was built from 1308 for Khwadja Yakut, who ruled the area for the Il-Khans. The doorway is richly carved with such motifs as lions and eagles. The beautiful turquoise-glazed decoration of the minaret clearly reflects the taste of the Il-Khans' Mongol homeland. The interior, now appropriately used as a museum, is of equal refinement. The Archaeological Museum is to be found south-west of the town centre.

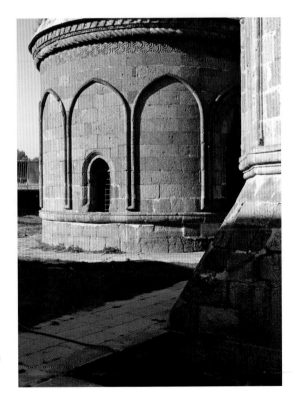

Uç Kümbetler: kumbets south of the Çifte Minare Medresesi.

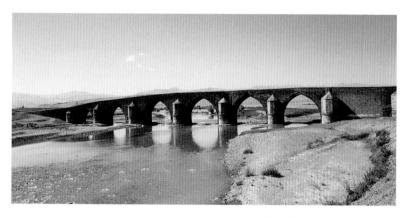

24

THE ÇOBAN KÖPRÜSÜ

❖

The bridge from the north-east.

ANATOLIA abounds in beautiful bridges, but few impress more than the Çoban Köprüsü. The main road eastwards from Erzurum climbs through a strangely remorseless upland, before sinking into the verdant and visibly productive valley of the Aras, whose name preserves its ancient form, the Araxes.

The first town of importance is unrewarding Pasliner, near the Hasan Kale rebuilt by the Ak Koyunlu Uzun Hasan in the mid-fifteenth century. Some 55 kilometres / 34 miles from Erzurum the road passes the Çoban Köprüsü, which with its seven arches spans the Aras and originally served the important route to the south-east. Those who pay too much attention to guidebooks would have every excuse to be puzzled: two describe the bridge as Ottoman and record that it has been claimed for Sinan; another asserts that it is Seljuk; while a fourth states that it is the finest medieval bridge in Turkey. With this, it is difficult to disagree.

Sinclair considers it 'likely but not certain' that the bridge was constructed in 1297 by Choban, a Mongol in the service of the Il-Khans. It was restored in 1727, in 1872, in 1946–48 and in recent years. The ground to the south of the river is lower than the north bank, and the design took this into account: the bridge rises gradually from the south to the fifth arch, levelling off for the next, before going downwards over the seventh and final arch, now blocked. The piers are unusual. The beaks facing upstream are of hollow masonry and can be reached from staircases inserted in 1946–48. Downstream the buttresses rise in three stages to pyramidal tops. The transitions between these stages are defined by mouldings, some of which are decorated with geometrical patterns.

Beautiful whether by morning or afternoon light, the bridge is an eloquent witness to the strategic ambition and administrative efficiency of the Il-Khans.

25
OŞK VANK AND IŞHAN

✤

THE Georgian churches are among the lesser-known marvels of Turkey, monuments that largely owe their survival to their remote positions in the wild valleys south of the Pontus. The Georgians were a determined people, staking claims to a wide territory from their capital of Ardanuç (see page 78). Their brief-lived kingdom of Tao-Klardjeti stretched far to the west of their original heartland.

The road north from Erzurum follows the valley of the Tortum Çay which cuts through a series of ravines. At Tortum, dominated by a Georgian fortress, the valley briefly opens out. A few miles to the north a restored Ottoman bridge on the left leads to a side valley up which is the fine church of Haho, founded by King David the Great, now in use as a mosque. It is worth trying to secure the key, as there are fragments of murals in the apse and the right transept. But if the imam is away, one can still enjoy the charm of the walled enclosure, the serenity of the church and the crude vigour of the external sculpture. A visit to Haho is an appropriate prelude to seeing its much more imposing neighbour up a larger valley further north.

The great cruciform church of Öşk Vank, completed in 961, was built for King David and his brother Bagrat – whose line would end nearly a millennium later with the Russian Princes Bagration. It now stands at the heart of a modern, and of course non-Christian, village, but this does not diminish the visual impact. For the church is impressive, both in size and detail. The great dome is still supported on the skeleton of

its piers. The series of reliefs on the external walls of the choir includes portraits of the two donors in full Byzantine dress; another, of the Virgin, has been displaced. Most unexpected perhaps is the structure attached to the right side of the nave, with proto-gothic pointed arcading and remarkably ingenious capitals and vaults created by craftsmen as obsessed with their trade as the sculptors of the Rosslyn Chapel; sadly the most elaborate, which included a portrait of the architect, has been wilfully damaged since Sinclair's photograph was taken. One of the pleasures of visiting Öşk Vank is the way the village flows by, taking only polite notice of a persistent sightseer: women with donkeys, the odd lorry.

Öşk Vank, the south portal.

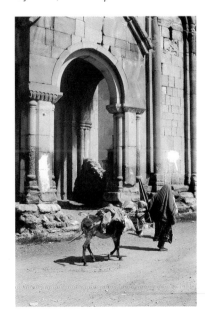

Öşk Vank is roughly halfway between Erzurum and Artvin, about 7 kilometres/5 miles to the west of the main road. This continues northwards. The Tortum valley is incredibly beautiful, with the almost lurid greens of the fields and trees, and hills that vary from pink or salmon to a golden yellow and near-whites. But, alas, there has been a gradual invasion of concrete. The İşhan turn is some 30 kilometres/18.6 miles from that for Vank. The modern village is on this side road; but for its predecessor a road twists and turns up the pale hillside, the eye drawn to the lush vegetation high above.

The church, half-hidden among poplars and orchards, is set on a shelf below rising ground. The apse with a semicircle of pillars remains from the original early seventh-century Armenian structure, which was apparently altered in about 828. But it was only in 1032 that the church was reconstructed on a Latin cross plan, with the long nave and the majestic dome. The outside of the building is liberally decorated, with elaborate window frames and long inscriptions in Georgian. On my first visit, I was followed on my circuit by a boy, who firmly asserted that an eagle was a fish, and by a puzzled young soldier, evidently bored with his companions.

Rich as is the exterior, it is the bare interior of İshan that is unforgettable. Considering that it hung on its four piers alone, the dome is a miraculous survival, with its mural of a bejewelled cross on a blue sky, brighter at the centre and supported by four tremendous angels whose wings and raiment, blue and green with pink, suggest the drama of their movement. Other wall paintings survive, plausible portrait busts in four window embrasures and a group of Apostles of classical inspiration, visibly swarthy. In the nave, which was used as a mosque until relatively recently, the blind arcade is decorated with *trompe l'oeil* motifs, including rosettes and acanthus, while high on the west wall there is a startlingly realistic head. The arrival of a large party of German visitors made me hope in 2003 that the resources that will be necessary to preserve so beautiful, yet vulnerable, a building might be forthcoming: happily a full restoration, including the reinstatement of the roofs, was almost complete in 2015.

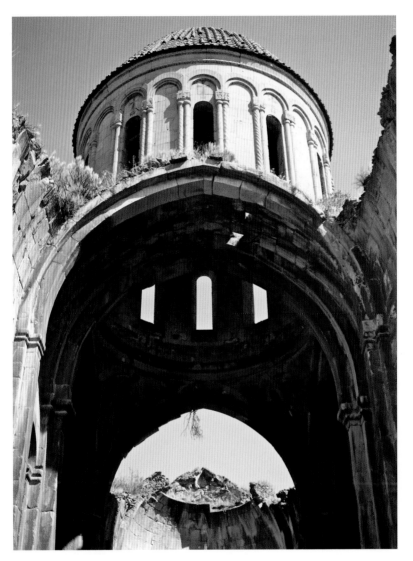

İşhan, the dome, before restoration.

26

DORTKILESI AND BARHAL

THE growing town of Yusufeli on the fast-flowing Barhal Çay, just above its confluence with the Çoruh, is a convenient base from which to visit two other fine, and closely related, Georgian churches. It makes sense to see these in chronological order.

The bridge in the town leads to the route that follows the Çoruh valley to Ispir, still dominated by its castle, and reaches the main road from Erzurum to Trabzon at Bayburt, the vast citadel of which has been energetically reconstructed. After some 5 kilometres/3 miles the road passes below a spectacular and ostensibly inaccessible outcrop, crowned by a Georgian fastness and a small church. A little further on, a turn on the right climbs up a side valley. High up near the stream, noble in isolation, is Dortkilesi. This spectacular monastic church apparently dates from before 961, when David the Great succeeded to the Georgian crown. The substantial building to the west of the church was added to it in King David's reign.

My first sight of Dortkilesi was unforgettable. The sheer volume of the church impressed. And so did its fragility. What havoc a hurricane or an earthquake might wreak. Time has eroded, and vegetation encroached upon, the walls; and it seemed almost miraculous that much of the tiled roof had somehow defied the rules of gravity. It is equally miraculous that enough of the tiered murals of the time of King David survive to give some sense of the intended character of the towering interior. Had the church, like its smaller neighbour at Barhal, been appropriated as a mosque, the murals would almost certainly have been destroyed, but the fabric, with its elaborately decorated arcades and windows, might have been preserved. One can only hope that Dortkilesi, like Ishan, will be rescued before it is too late.

From Yusufeli a narrow road rises bravely up the valley to the north, passing a castle high on the left before reaching the village of Serigöl: Barhal is some 13 kilometres/8 miles further on. The steep valley is well wooded and modest houses are scattered on the left bank of the stream. The church is on a shelf a little way above, and to the right of, the road. The monastic foundation was built by 973, the date of the Barhal Gospel, now at Tflisi. Like the church at Haho in the Tortum valley to the south, that at Barhal has survived substantially intact as it was put to service as a mosque, as indeed it still is. The builder took Dortkilesi as his model, but what Barhal lacks in originality is balanced by its architectural coherence. The blind arcading of the exterior is particularly satisfactory, not least in sunlight when the shadows this casts gradually lengthen or diminish. The carved detail, particularly on the east front, is of crisp quality; and as at Osk Vank and elsewhere red paint was used to supplement architectural detail, for instance above some of the upper windows, and for inscriptions. It is usually necessary to find the muezzin, who lives at some distance in the village, to see the austere domed interior.

Above the west wall of the church is what must be one of the most charming pansiyons in Eastern Turkey, with a tree-shaded veranda. On my recent visit I was served a singularly delicious breakfast.

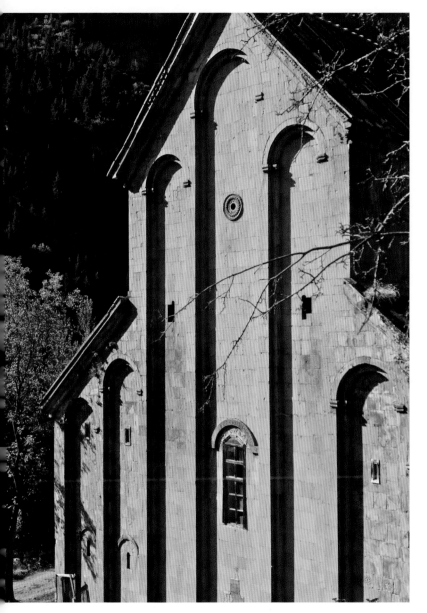

Barhal from the east.

27

ARDANUÇ

❖

ARDANUÇ was once on a major trade route linking Kars and distant Persia beyond the Yalnizçam Pass with Artvin and the road to Trabzon and the Black Sea. This explains why the place was chosen in about 820 by the Georgian ruler Ashot the Great as the capital of his realm of Upper Iberia, controlling the mountainous territory from Erzurum to the Euxine. Georgia's Bagratid rulers, kings from 888, always had to contend with local rivals and with more powerful neighbours, Byzantine, Arab and Turk. The outstanding Georgian king, David the Great (961–1000) did not control Ardanuç. The power of his successors fluctuated, with periods of revival under Queen Tamara (1184–1213) and Giorgi the Brilliant (1318–27), who early in his reign won the trust of the local Mongol ruler. In 1465 the Jakeli, feudatories of the Bagratids in Upper Iberia, seceded from the Georgian kingdom. Their successors became uneasy vassals of the Ottomans in the early sixteenth century. Ardanuç was taken by siege in 1551 and, although the Ottomans were driven out in 1588, they returned in 1625.

The road from the north twists through a spectacular gorge, defended on the west by the cliff-top Georgian castle of Ferhatli, with walls of coarse masonry that exploit every projection of the outcrop. The valley that opens out beyond the gorge comes almost as a surprise. The modern town of Ardanuç is a modest, ordered place on the valley floor. Little remains of its predecessor, set on higher ground to the west of the eponymous river. But few fortresses are

more majestically placed than the great early ninth-century citadel that protected the town and was itself defended by prodigious cliffs and precipices. An unmetalled road climbs to the old town, where a few new houses are interspersed with the ruins of their predecessors. A boy pointed out to me a path to the northern tip of the rock, where steps and two ladders, one wooden, the other of metal, reconstruct the original approach to a recessed arch hanging on to a pinnacle of rock.

Within the walls, the ground slopes steeply downwards to the east. There are substantial remains of the southern and south-western sections of the walls, a well-preserved postern and a very ruinous church. Water must always have been precious, and an area of rock was carefully smoothed to catch such rain as fell. There is a scattering of fig trees, and by late September desiccated plants are hung with small snail shells like substitute seeds. A metal silhouette of Atatürk's head is so placed as to be seen from the valley, presiding over the former Georgian heartland, with the old town and its türbe below and the inexorable drama of the hills, cliffs that Mantegna would have relished and grey eroded slopes on which trees have now been planted. The late afternoon's sun emerges from cloud to light up distant ranges and gild the precarious Georgian walls.

For those who are not too fussy, Ardanuç is a well-placed base from which to visit some of the most appealing of the Georgian churches. About 24 kilometres/15 miles south-east is the tenth-century church of the monastery of Yeni Rabat, which was founded by St Gregory the Illuminator and became a major centre of manuscript production.

The setting is beautiful: a natural platform on the flank of the valley, with tillage below and the occasional house on the slopes above. The church is among old chestnut trees. When I was there, unexpectedly a cab was waiting and another car was being repaired: a team of archaeologists from the University of Aarhus were on the second day of a comprehensive survey. Dressed blocks have been robbed from the more reachable levels of the façades, but enough survives to give some notion of the original richness of these: functional pilasters and a majestic double window on the south, other decorative elements to the west. The scale of the church is most easily appreciated inside, with the massive piers of the crossing, the beautifully controlled apse and a confident dome.

Equally accessible from Ardanuç or from Artvin are two churches north of the road eastwards from the latter towards Savşat. That of Dolishane (called Hamamli in *The Blue Guide*) served for many years as a mosque and is thus well preserved. When this is closed, it is possible to see the fine and rather bare cruciform interior from the chancel window. Further east is Porta. A sign from the road points to a vertiginous path that strikes steeply out of the valley. After walking for twenty minutes an old building reassures that one is on an ancient route – in a world of oaks and brambles and butterflies. After passing above more houses, the path rises and turns round some rocks: and suddenly the dome of Porta is in sight. The path, now hemmed in by the staked fences of the village, passes a small chapel by a spring, above which there is a battered cross. The church itself is preceded by a belfry. The dome was, almost miraculously, still in place, but in urgent need of attention. One can only hope that restoration won't disturb the magic of the place, the beauty of the twelfth- or thirteenth-century masonry, the unaccountable charm of the few trim houses of whose inhabitants there is neither sight nor sound or the timeless efficiency of their flimsy aqueduct of hollowed-out trunks. As reluctantly I leave, voices break in on this idyll: men who have been collecting the red berries of which I had been suspicious rest in dappled light by the spring, and on my descent four others pass with their Sunday picnic.

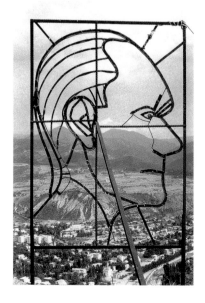

View from the citadel, with a profile of Atatürk.

28

KARS

❖

NO OTHER town in Turkey is quite like Kars, whose formidable citadel on a high ridge long controlled the valley of the eponymous river and thus one of the main routes to Anatolia from the east. Its early history is obscure, but from 928 until 961 Kars was the capital of the Bagratid kings of Armenia, becoming that of Musbegh's kingdom of Vanand in the later year. Bagratid rule endured until 1065, when the place fell to Alp Arslan. From 1207 until about 1335 Kars was held by the Georgians, who were ousted by the Kara Koyunlu, the black sheep Turkomen: they in turn were defeated in 1534 by the Ottomans. The fortress was of crucial importance in ensuing campaigns against Persia and was substantially rebuilt in 1579. None the less it failed to withstand a Persian assault of 1604. In the nineteenth century

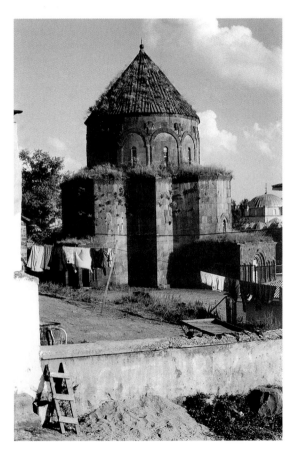

The Cathedral of the Holy Apostles.

imperial Russia was the threat. Kars was attacked in 1828 and fell to Russia after a prolonged blockade in 1855 during the Crimean War, only to be returned to the Ottomans at the ensuing peace. In 1877 the Russians again conquered Kars, retaining it until 1918, when they were driven out in the wake of the Russian Revolution, leaving their 'modern' town, built on a grid with chastely classical houses, many of which happily survive.

Despite a long history, the fortress of Kars, so imposing from a distance, does not reward too close an inspection, although it is usually possible to walk up the impressive ramp and wander round. Little survives from before the Ottoman reconstruction of 1579, and most of the original towers were dismantled by the Persians in 1604, only to be rebuilt. Much of the existing structure is of the nineteenth century, partly postdating the heroic defence of 1854–55 described so compellingly in Colonel Lake's *Kars and Our Captivity in Russia* of 1856. Protected on the west – at the high point of the shelf – and to the north by the gorge carved by the river, the ridge was vulnerable only from the south and the east.

The great monument of Kars is below the citadel and not far from the river. The Cathedral of the Holy Apostles was begun in 930 under King Abbas I (928–51) and is of impressive size. It is square in plan but with apses at the centre of each wall, the deepest to the east: there are squinches at the corners of the square and the internal space thus reads as an octagon. This supports the dodecagonal drum, which is decorated externally with blind arches and rather coarse figures of the Apostles. The survival of the cathedral is due to its appropriation as a mosque in 1579. In 1877 it was converted to use for the Russians' Orthodox rite, with a screen across the narthex to the west and low additions to the apses.

South of the cathedral is the recently restored Evliya Camii, built in 1579 by Lala Mustafa, the pasha responsible for the contemporary work on the citadel. Other Ottoman mosques are nearer the river. There is a handsome bridge of 1725 and beside this a domed hamam. Old houses nearby incorporate material from earlier buildings, and the occasional sculptured block can be found, including one with a cross on a road eastwards to the modern commercial centre. Development threatens, sooner rather than later, to overwhelm the measured rhythm of the Russian garrison town; but none the less the tourist can still sense something of the fascination Kars held for Orhan Pamuk, who describes the town in forensic detail in his novel *Snow*. This, as it happens, was not the first novel to be set in Kars: that distinction is held by *Ayesha*, published in 1834 by James Morier, who had a wide knowledge of the local tribes.

29

GEÇVAN

GEÇVAN, the Latin Artogerassa and Armenian Artagers, was a stronghold of the ancient kingdom of Armenia, drawing its wealth from the productive valleys of the Aras and its tributary, the Kötek Çay. During the Persian invasion in the 360s, the royal treasury was taken to Geçvan, where Queen Parantsem held out for a year. When the town eventually fell in 368, the defenders were massacred. The place subsequently dwindled in importance, only to revive under the Bagratids by the eleventh century. It remained a significant Armenian centre until after the Ottoman conquest.

Geçvan is south-west of Kars, reached from a turn after some 39 kilometres/24 miles on the road to Kağizman. After 10 kilometres/6 miles one is confronted by a promontory of rock, protected on the north by a basalt gorge and by a deep valley to the south. The road follows the southern side of this, climbing to turn to reach the western side of the town. This was the most vulnerable section of the position. A massive wall with a fine gateway and rounded towers runs from the cliff above the gorge and then turns to take advantage of the slope to the south, continuing to the cliffs towards the eastern end of the site. The masonry is medieval, but may follow that of the original Armenian enceinte.

Behind the western wall is the modern village, with turf roofs, haystacks and stands of manure for the winter's fuel, and ancient and less ancient agricultural implements. I was there on a Friday, the day of prayer, so many children were about, watched by an elegant patriarch in matching trousers and waistcoat. A younger man insisted on escorting me up through the houses to the end of the town proper and then across a further ravine to the final outcrop. This too was defended by walls, most of which have been lost. Yellow hollyhocks and carpets of small pink flowers wave in the wind. The vertiginous drop to the gorge contrasts with the gentle cornland to the east and the flowing contours of the distant hills. No more dramatic position could have been chosen for the small Armenian chapel, apparently constructed with reused material in the fourteenth or fifteenth century. As so often, much of the more accessible masonry has been robbed. But enough survives for one to be left in no doubt of the calibre of the architecture. The narrow external niches complement the rounded mouldings of the corners and the centrally placed blind arches, one of which frames a narrow window set in an elaborately interlaced frame. Lingering beside this unexpectedly moving building, one can only be impressed by the enduring ingenuity of a people whose artistic resilience was not tamed by political misfortune.

The walls from the south-west.

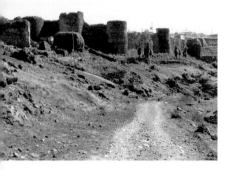

30
ÇENGELLI

❖

A LARGE photograph in the museum at Kars aroused my curiosity. For although Çengelli is not particularly remote, the place is ignored by most guidebooks: even Sinclair's account is restrained. Some 20 kilometres/12.4 miles south of the turn for Geçvan, a road leads to the west, rising towards a settlement. The surface is rough and progress slow. Beyond a village the road continues to climb. After 20 kilometres/12.4 miles, one reaches the outskirts of the sprawling village of Çengelli, a scattering of houses. The inhabitants are Kurds, their economy agrarian: stacked hay and drying dung with piles of brushwood remind the visitor that preparations for the winter can never be neglected in these unforgiving uplands.

The great rectangular domed church floats above the flimsy structures that surround it, a dark silhouette against the sky. Like its earlier Georgian counterparts, the church survives in part because it lay so far from the main centres of eastern Anatolia. The building is held by Sinclair to be of the late thirteenth century, but can never have any pretension to represent the vanguard of metropolitan taste. It is a solid, indeed a stolid, structure. The masonry is spare, the stone cut with precision. There is a minimum of external decoration. Within, a number of elements recall the great church of İşhan. On entering the building, the eye takes a little time to grow accustomed to the dim light, for the win-

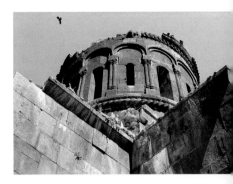

The dome of the church.

dows are both high and small. A beam of sunlight cuts across the dome. The glory of Çengelli is that this remains intact.

I had assumed that it would be necessary to retrace my route. But two helpful youths implied otherwise, with typical Kurdish courtesy. They directed me to a yet narrower and more uncertain road to the west. After 1.5 kilometres/1 mile or so this turned steeply upwards. I paused at the top, on what proved to be the lip of a small volcanic crater with a circular lake, the Deniz Gölü, as beautiful as it was unexpected, at my feet. The road clung below the rim, before climbing again to the west. At the highest point the young men asked to be set down, pointing out the route I was to follow. This turned precipitously downwards. Heavy rain and agricultural vehicles had taken their toll; I was thankful not to be struggling uphill, and thankful too that so imposing and complete a monument from the Christian past still seems, however unaccountably, to dominate its setting.

31

ANI

ALTHOUGH it is no longer necessary to secure a permit to visit Ani, the 47-kilometre/29-mile drive from Kars seems more of an expedition than it is. The road strikes straight across the plain; herds and obsolescent tractors take precedence. At length the formidable walls of the city come into view.

Ani occupies a promontory that is roughly triangular but 'waisted', like a primitive trumpet, the longer flanks protected by the deep canyon of the Arpa Çay, now the border not with Russia but with Armenia, and the less steep valley of the tributary Alaca Çay. Two lesser streambeds determined the line of the walls to the north.

Although the site had been occupied in the second millennium BC and there was a fort in Byzantine times, the development of Ani was due to the Bagratid kings of Armenia, descendants of Ashot Bagratuni, whose rule over his countrymen was recognized in 806 by the Caliph Haroon Ar-Raschid. His namesake, whose claims were endorsed by both the Abbasids and the Byzantines, was crowned King of Armenia in 885 as Ashot I. Ashot III the Merciful (952–77) transferred his capital from Kars to Ani in 961, occupying the citadel on the high ground where the promontory widens to the south. To the north of this, at the point where the level ground was at its narrowest, Ashot III built his defensive wall, of which little survives. Under his successors Ani grew exponentially, benefiting both from being the capital of a rich polity and from the fact that this lay astride key trade routes, access to which

must have been helped materially by the Bagratids' links with both Baghdad and Byzantium. The city expanded to the north, where new walls were constructed under King Smbat II, who died in 989.

The long reign of Gagik I (989–1020) was followed by the division of the kingdom under his joint heirs, Ani falling to Hovhannes Smbat, who bequeathed this not to his nephew, the future Gagik II, but to the Byzantine Emperor Basil II, in 1040. The Armenians defeated Basil's army outside Ani, but Gagik II was tricked into visiting Constantinople and imprisoned. Under Byzantine rule from 1045, Ani remained the regional capital. It fell to the Seljuks in 1064 and eight years later was made over to a Kurd, Minuchihr, who retained it until 1110; his Shaddadid heirs held out, despite two brief Georgian incursions, until 1199 or 1200, when Ani became part of the Georgian kingdom, under the Mkhargrdzeli, who although of Kurdic origin were Armenian Christians. The Mongols who arrived in eastern Anatolia in 1237 left the Mkhargrdzeli in control, as vassals of their client kingdom of Georgia, and they held Ani until at least 1320. The Il-Khans owned Ani by 1335, retaining it for a generation, to be succeeded by the otherwise obscure Djalayrids, who in turn were expelled by the Kara Koyunlu in c. 1380. Although major work on the Church of the Redeemer took place in 1348, Ani had by then ceased to be a town of more than local importance. Trade had drained away and the population dwindled. Under the Ottomans, who occupied Ani in 1579, this was no more than a modest town. In the nineteenth century, Ani was rediscovered by the French explorer Charles Texier, and serious excavation took place during the

Russian occupation, which ended in the aftermath of the First World War.

The walls of Ani are by any standard impressive. The most vulnerable section was that between the two natural ravines, which is protected by an outer wall. The circuit was laid out by Smbat II, but was extensively restored under the Shaddadids – to whom much of the ornament is owed – and subsequently reinforced for the Mkhargrdzeli, to whom their present character is largely due. The Kars Gate is flanked by the tallest towers of the enceinte: both are well preserved. As Sinclair notes, an unusual feature is the arch before and at a higher level than the upper wall. Further east is the Aslan Kapisi ('Lion Gate'), reconstructed and redecorated under Minuchihr. Minuchihr may also have been responsible for the relief of two dragons separated by a bull that runs across a semi-circular tower further east. The easternmost gate was restored by the Shaddadid Shahanshah (1164–99).

From the three gates streets converged towards the citadel. The domestic and commercial structures that lined these were of rough construction and have left little recognizable trace. Readers of the mid-fourteenth-century *Travels of Sir John Mandeville* who expect to see a thousand churches at Ani will be disappointed. But those that do survive are impressive enough. Nearest the Kars Gate is what remains of a small Georgian church of 1216. To the west is the Church of St Gregory, built by the architect Trdat for King Gagik I and completed in the millennium year, 1000. The circular design was bold, indeed too bold, as the building shortly collapsed; what survives was excavated by the Russians in 1906.

More substantial is the Church of the Apostles, built by 1031, to which the splendid hall, or gavit, was added before 1260. The vault of this is remarkable for its use of polychrome masonry and the east wall is richly decorated. To the south-west is one of the marvels of Ani, the mid-tenth-century Church of St Gregory (Abughamrents) perched above the drop to the Alaca Çay. The externally polygonal structure rises to a circular drum. This rested on the walls between the extensions that radiate from the circular central space. Inscriptions establish that the church was associated with the powerful Pahlavuni family. South-east,

The church of St Gregory (Abughamrents).

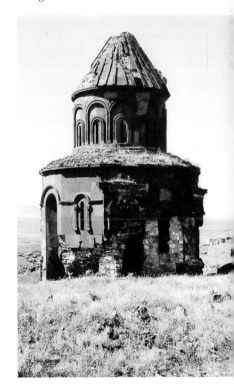

at the eastern end of Ashot III's wall of 964, is the mosque built in the eleventh century by Minuchihr, which hangs over the gorge of the Arpa Çay. The prominent octagonal minaret bears an inscription in Kufic. Because of sensitivities about the border, the tourist is not permitted to go beyond the mosque. This is thus the best vantage point from which to take in the citadel hill on which defensive walls of differing date survive, as does a chapel of 622, which must have been associated with the Byzantine fortress. Beyond, on a rise at the tip of the promontory, is – or was – the ruined church of a monastery that was inhabited as late as 1735. Looking down to the river, the abutments of a medieval bridge can be seen.

Two hundred metres/656 feet to the north-west, set well back from the escarpment, is the cathedral, began under

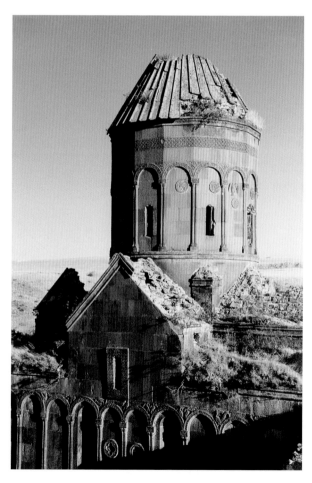

The Church of Tigran Honents.

Smbat II and finished by Gagik's wife Katranide in 1010. This is a massive rectangular structure. The façades are memorable for the rhythm of the blind arcading, so perfectly calculated for visual effect in a land of strong sunlight. Broad piers supported the drum and dome, the last now lost; and the apse is flanked by two chambers reached from passages off this and directly from the body of the church. The interior must always have seemed somewhat ponderous.

This could never be said of the Church of Tigran Honents some 400 metres/437 yards to the east on a shelf just below the plateau. This was finished in 1215. Approached through an elaborate but incompletely preserved arcade, the church is of 'domed rectangle' type, with a narthex opening on to the main domed area, beyond which is the apse, flanked by the customary paired chambers. The church was extensively decorated with murals and much of the scheme can be made out: two roundels of heads on the outer arch of the apse are particularly well preserved. The exterior is memorable not only for the inventive carving of the blind arcade and the squinches within this, but also for the assured relationship of the dome to the structure this crowns.

Nearby a signpost reads 'Silk Road'. Tourists are not encouraged to pass it and descend the still partly covered stairway to the small but particularly beautiful Church of the Convent of the Virgin perched above the ravine. Like other churches at Ani, this is in urgent need of sympathetic attention. The fragility of such buildings was demonstrated by the collapse in 1957 of much of the circular Church of the Redeemer, which is not far from the edge of the plateau to the northwest.

Ani now casts a profound spell with the drama of the walls; the distinction of the extant monuments; and the beauty of their context – the undulating turf, the wide horizons and the sense of *frisson* inspired by the watch towers across the frontier. In our age, when religions coexist so awkwardly in the Near East, it is sobering to sense the cultural vitality of the Christian Bagratids, who had the support of the Caliph, and the Mkhargrdzeli, who were endorsed by the Mongols. The Turkish authorities have, at length, recognized their responsibility for this inheritance by repointing the city walls; it is to be hoped that a newly independent Armenia does not allow development that could damage the setting of the capital of its medieval predecessor.

The visitor should spend as long as possible at Ani. He or she will be discouraged by the authorities from following the road to the east for the remarkable monastery of Horomos. This was founded in 931–36 in a remote position in the ravine of the Arpa Çay and thus antedated Ashot I's decision to transfer his capital to Ani. A less demanding excursion on the way back to Kars is to the Kizil Kilise, a tall domed cruciform church of 1228, built of an unusually red stone, which was restored rather too vigorously by the Russians. The village has a certain charm in the afternoon light, with its prosperous farms and their noisy gaggles of geese.

32

THE İSHAK PAŞA SARAYI

❖

DOĞUBAYAZIT is not a prepossessing town. But, as the last place of any importance before the Iranian border on what has long been a major route across Anatolia, it has an obvious strategic importance. The approach from the north is dominated by the snow-capped peak of Mount Ararat, which hangs above a high table land. This is the domain of Kurdish shepherds, whose flocks fan out across the landscape in the morning and whose dogs aspire to savage passing traffic (I passed the corpses of several).

In the late eighteenth century the area was controlled by the Çildiroğlu family, whose wealth was, of course, due to the duties they levied on the merchandise that passed from east to west and vice versa. The extent of this passing trade is attested by the extraordinary palace successive generations constructed on a hill 7 kilometres/4.3 miles south of the town, the İshak Paşa Sarayi. Begun about 1785, the complex takes its name from the İshak Paşa who was vizier of the area in 1790–91, and was, it seems, completed by his son, Mahmut Paşa. The Çildiroğlu had local roots – whether Armenian or Georgian or Kurdish is debatable. And their honey-coloured palace reflects a number of styles: Ottoman, Georgian and Seljuk.

A road curls up the hillside below the complex, now unhappily lined with lampposts, leading to the richly decorated main entrance on the south side. This opens on to a considerable courtyard, with stabling and other structures, from which the inner court is reached. The men's apartment, the selamlik, is on the north side, and beside this is the relatively well preserved domed mosque. At the north-west angle of the inner courtyard is the türbe of İshak Paşa and his wife, with steps leading down to their tomb. Near the türbe, decorated with lions, is the door to the harem. The entrance hall of this is memorable for the contrasting decoration of basalt and sandstone blocks. The rooms that follow are most rewarding for their views to the north, with the white cone of Ararat floating in the distance. Unlike its near contemporary, the Brighton Pavilion, the sarayi was not an anachronism. Its builders were working within traditional formulas, striving at once for comfort and for effect, but without a thought – as Western architects of the time would have had – for originality of design. And it is for this reason that the extravaganza is so compelling.

To the east of the palace is the much higher outcrop on which it seems that the Urartians, perhaps in the eighth century BC, constructed a fortress. An eroded Urartian relief and a cuneiform text can, with some difficulty, be made out. The fortress was reinforced in turn by the Byzantines, by the Seljuks and in the Ottoman period. And on a platform at its foot is a mosque built under Selim I the Grim. He, one suspects, would never have allowed the Çildiroğlu to attain the quasi-independence of which the İshak Paşa Sarayi is so ostentatious a statement.

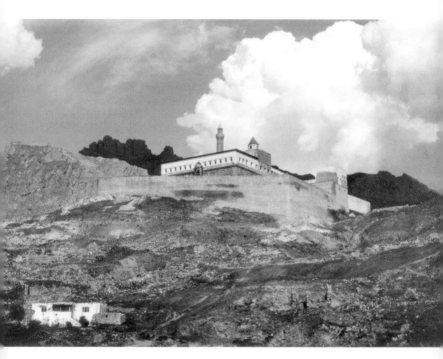

View from the west, under gathering clouds.

33

VAN

THE ancient city of Van grew around a spine of rock on the eastern shore of Lake Van, which is set among mountains 502 metres / 1,648 feet above sea level. Van is first recorded, as Tushpa, in Assyrian reliefs of the ninth century BC, when Sarduri I (c. 840–830 BC) established a kingdom over the Urartians. It was at Van that he was buried, as were his successors, Menua (c. 810–786), under whom the kingdom reached its zenith, and Argishti I (786–764). To Menua is due the 50-kilometre / 31-mile-long canal that brought water to Van and is still partly in use. The Assyrians made inroads in the reign of Rusa I (735–714), and by the late sixth century BC power had passed to the Armenians, who acknowledged the supremacy of the Achaemenids of Persia. In 66 BC Tigranes I submitted to Pompey and thus Van became, in time, part of the Roman Empire. The city was in the tenth century AD the capital of the Armenian kingdom of Vaspurakan, but was recovered by the Emperor Basil II for Byzantium in 1021, only to pass to the Seljuks after the defeat at Manzikert in 1071. Occupation by the Kara Koyunlu, or black sheep Turcomans, and destruction by Timur followed. Subsequently the area was controlled by Kurdish emirs. In 1534, with Süleyman the Magnificent's defeat of the Persian Safavids, Van – and thus control of the south-eastern bastion of Anatolia – passed to the Ottomans. Much of Van's wealth was in the hands of Armenians, and their support for the Russian troops which took Van in the First World War explains – if it does not perhaps excuse – the destruction of the ancient city after the Russian collapse.

Van is an eerie place. Where the early town used to be, a few Islamic buildings preside uncomfortably over a bare wasteland: above, to the north, on a dramatic outcrop, is the great fortress to which Urartian, Byzantine and Turk in turn contributed. To the west is the wonderful expanse of the lake. The modern town, further inland, is in fact of some antiquity but had little to commend it, serviceable hotels and spirited carpet vendors apart, even before the recent earthquake. The small museum, however, does deserve to be visited. In the forecourt are numerous inscribed blocks and a notable basalt relief of the god Teisheba from Adilcevaz. The archaeological section includes excellent Urartian material from Çavuştepe, Awraf and elsewhere, as well as a series of primitive stelae with stylized figures in relief of between 1500 and 1000 BC, found near Hakkari in 1998. Wisely the ethnographical section has been purged of a display that grated on my first visit in 1990 when, under a banner inscribed 'GENOCIDE', there were photographs of members of a Turkish family who were murdered by Armenians.

The fortress of Van stretches along a ridge 2 kilometres / 1.2 miles in length. On the south there are cliffs, up to 183 metres / 600 feet in height, that no attacker could hope to scale, but the gentler drop to the north had to be strongly fortified. The so-called Madir Burcu, a massive structure of cyclopean blocks, was clearly intended to defend the western end of the ridge. Inscriptions in the cuneiform the Urartians learnt from Assyria celebrate King Sarduri's responsibility for the construction. On the climb upwards there are innumerable steps cut in the rock for the footings of walls that have disappeared. Near these is the narrow platform from which steps, now fenced off, descend to the tomb of Argishti I, the entrance to which has a spectacular inscription in cuneiform commemorating the achievements of his reign. The substantial main chamber is flanked by subsidiary rooms which the Ottomans put to service as magazines. The ridge climbs to what remains of the Ottoman barracks and of a mosque erected after Süleyman's conquest. Further on, a precipitous and partly eroded path leads down to the platform before the vast chamber tombs thought to be of Kings Menua and Sarduri I, the former facing south over the cliff face. Below the north-eastern flank of the ridge, and most easily approached from the road, are two niches, each with a stela celebrating the reign of Sarduri II (764–735 BC).

The views from the fortress down across the former town are haunting. Within the circling walls, of nineteenth-century date, every domestic building has gone and the churches are in advanced decay. Only the minaret and scattered walls survive of the Ulu Cami, which was built in the fifteenth century for the Turcoman Kara Yusuf and inspired by Persian example. The Hüsrev Paşa mosque of 1567 and the associated tomb of the pasha have been restored, as has the nearly contemporary Kaya Çelebi Camii to the east. But the near-obliteration of the town makes these monuments, until recently degraded by modern graffiti, seem oddly insignificant, as one walks between them, looking up at the great, and ostensibly inaccessible, trilingual inscription of the Persian King Xerxes I carved into the towering cliff above.

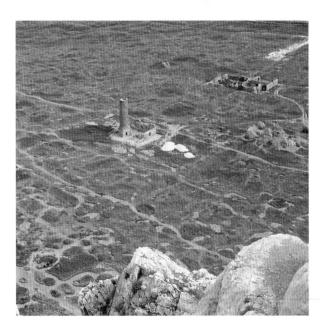

Islamic monuments in the former town, from the citadel.

34
ÇAVUŞTEPE AND HOŞAP

❖

CONTROL of the route from Van to the south-east has long been prized. The Urartians built their great fortress of Sardurihinli, now Çavuştepe, some 28 kilometres/17.4 miles from Van, in the time of King Sarduri II (764–735 BC). The site is above the modern road, dominating the valley. The lower fortress is at the western end of the ridge. Storerooms can be seen and the remains of a temple in which there is an altar with a dedicatory inscription on finely cut basalt blocks. In the upper, eastern, fortress there is a larger temple with a rock-cut platform. The surviving Urartian masonry is of superlative quality. To the east, the upper fortress is defended by a formidable ditch that cuts it off from the higher ground beyond; in May there is a scattering of white irises on the hillside.

Further east the country becomes perceptibly wilder. There is much pink in the eroded hills and nature is tamed only by the road, an artificial lake and the inexorable power lines. Hoşap first appears as a jagged excrescence, jutting between the nearer hills. When it was built in 1643 by the Emir Süleyman Bey, the castle effectively blocked the approach to Van. Except for the lavishly detailed entrance, the masonry is not of remarkable quality. But from the southeast, reflected in the water of the river, Hoşap still seems formidable. The internal arrangement of the fortress with a mosque and a small bath complex suggests the wealth of the builder. And no one looking downwards from the castle can be left in any doubt of the ruthless efficiency with which the Bey's Mah-

moudi tribe exacted customs dues from the passing caravans and controlled the resources of the valley that descends from the mountains to the south.

The castle replaced a Seljuk structure, blocks from which were evidently re-used for the round tower. Behind the castle are the dissolving mud walls of the associated settlement. But in the friable soil within these, early shards are as numerous as those of later periods. Below the castle is the fine bridge built by a seventeenth-century Mahmoudi, Zaynal Bey. On the opposite bank, beside the modern road, is the commercial centre of the village: a row of shops protected from the sun by awnings, and three tea shops. Are these both political and commercial rivals, like, for example, Quadri and Florian on the opposite sides of the Piazza San Marco? The spectator quickly understands something of the tensions of the place. For in 1990, soldiers and police apart, many of the men carried guns and cartridge belts, under licence, as I later learnt in Van, from the authorities. A trio of boys walk by, suited and in ties, followed by their weather-beaten and more casually dressed elders; lorries pass, including one from distant Nevsehir decorated with a Turkish echo of a willow-pattern landscape, oddly appropriate in a place that has always drawn much of its wealth from Asia's passing traffic. In 2008 guns were less evident. While I waited for tea, my only fellow customer announced in strident tones that Turkey is not a democracy. As he did so, the proprietor of the shop toyed with his television, switching for my benefit from a 'Mesopotamian' service to a French channel that, however improbably, showed a couple rowing to the lugubrious strains of the Eton Boating Song.

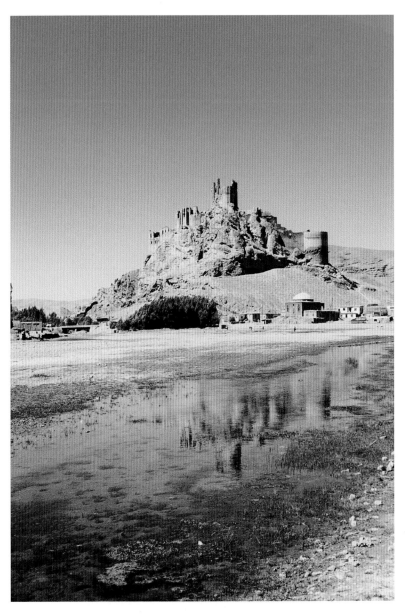

Hoşap: the castle from the south.

35

ALBAYRAK
AND SORADIR

❖

BEYOND Hoşap the main road rises to a pass and then gradually descends towards the valley of the Great Zab that flows southwards though the Hakkâri country and eventually drains into the Tigris. The first proper road to the left, well before the town of Başkale, cuts to the north-east, offering commanding views over the fertile valley to the rugged hills across this that mark the frontier with Iran. It is 10 kilometres/6.2 miles to Albayrak, a sprawling village by the river, now of course in Kurdish occupation. The occasional reused Armenian inscription or piece of redeployed masonry hints at the patterns of the past. On a platform to the north, until recently incorporated in a military post, is one of the most ambitious Armenian churches in Turkey, the Monastery of St Bartholomew.

The scale of the rectangular church, predominantly in a pale brown stone, is evidently due to the erroneous belief that the saint died at Albayrak. The existing structure has been dated to the late thirteenth century, but was extensively restored as late as the nineteenth, remaining a place of pilgrimage into the twentieth. An earthquake of 1966 dealt harshly with the place. The façades are articulated by pilasters which divide these into tall compartments. The tympanum above the west door, with a horseman riding down a vanquished enemy, is considered by Sinclair to be a reused Sasanian block: what remains of the upper tympanum, probably of the fifteenth century, shows the lower part of a large figure of God the Father with a lion and a bull below and pairs of stylized angels in flight at either side. There are decorated panels on the east façade. Within, the vault of the zhamatun has fallen, although the pillars and pilasters that supported this are partly intact: the walls are incised with innumerable crosses. The dome of the church proper

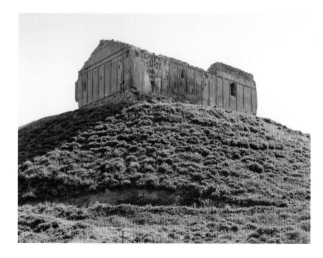

Albayrak, the Monastery of St Bartholomew.

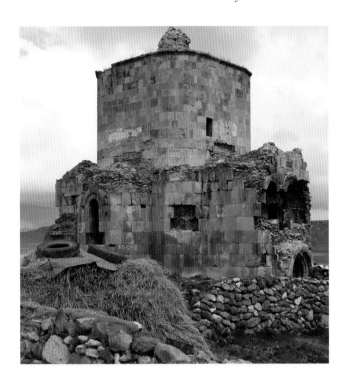

The church at Soradir.

has collapsed and not been cleared.

A road below the church runs northwards up the valley for some 18 kilometres/11 miles to Soradir, the former Armenian Etshmiadsin. Dominating a scattering of farmhouses is the beautiful church of the Monastery of Karmir Vank ('Red Monastery'), so named no doubt from the warm colour of the stone. The cruciform building, the east and west arms of which are longer than the others, is surmounted by a solid sixteenth- or seventeenth-century vaulted crossing tower with a small central lantern. This replaced the drum and dome of the original church, of which the lower level survives, variously dated between the sixth century and the ninth. Decoration is applied with restraint, notable above the windows of the west and east fronts. There are numerous incised crosses, and others can be found on some of the stones used for a boundary wall a little to the east.

Like other Armenian churches Soradir owes its survival in reasonable order to being used for storage by the villagers. At some 2,362 metres/7,750 feet, it commands the headwaters of the Great Zab and remains the focal point in a productive valley that offers no hint of the dramatic gorges through which the river has carved its way to the south. Always a frontier post, Soradir is now disturbed by nothing louder than a veteran tractor or more menacing than bursts of gunshot celebrating a local wedding.

36

AGHTAMAR

AGHTAMAR, on its island 2 kilometres / 1.2 miles from the southern shore of Lake Van, was not the most ambitious or innovative of Armenian churches. But it is without question the most lavishly decorated. H. F. B. Lynch wrote, in his pioneering *Armenia, Travels and Studies* of 1901, that it looked like 'the work of a jeweller rather than an architect'. It does indeed resemble an outsize casket. There had been a lesser monastery on the island from Byzantine times, but in the early tenth century the place was favoured by King Gagik I Artsruni (908–43). He built a major palace of which no trace now survives, and caused the church, dedicated to the Apostles, to be built on a south-facing shelf opposite the mainland.

Boats cross from a pontoon by the main road to a landing stage below the church. Built between 915 and 921 by an architect called Manuel, this is of a pinkish sandstone. It is not large. Indeed, the original building, to which the gavit, or narthex, and belfry were much later additions, is no more than 11.5 metres / 38 feet wide and less than 15 metres / 49 feet in length. But the visitor is immediately aware of the richness of the external decoration, which is true not only of the west front, now masked by the gavit, but also of the lateral and eastern façades. The most significant of the reliefs, showing Gagik offering his church to Christ, is on the west front. The Old Testament scenes on the south side include the story of Jonah – with a well-observed ship – and David about to dispatch Goliath, a subject of obvious relevance to a people always confronted by powerful neighbours, while Adam and Eve are seen on the north. Some way to their right is a beautiful rendering of Daniel in the lions' den, in which the two animals lick the prophet's feet. To English eyes it is less appealing that St George's charger rears over a prone man. Higher up, above the level of the lateral windows, is a continuous frieze with animals, birds and humans set among vine leaves. Below the line of the roof is a second frieze, with more animals, including lions, dogs, gazelles and hares respectively hunting or being hunted; birds and grimacing faces punctuate the chase. More faces and animals are carved under the eaves of the church. The sculptors were clearly aware of the way strong sunlight would emphasize their work.

The plan of the church was of course determined by Armenian custom, in a form sometimes compared with a four-leaved clover. The main entrance is on the west, but there are subsidiary doors at the sides. The square at the centre of the church is crowned by a drum with eight windows, supporting the pyramidal roof. The sanctuary is raised and there is a gallery for the king in the south apse. The walls were muralled. Exposure for nearly a century has taken its toll, but many of the subjects can still be made out. The style is linear and rather crude. Its energy is best sensed in the relatively well-preserved *Raising of Lazarus* and *Triumphal Entry to Jerusalem* of the western apse.

With the exception of the apse of a subsidiary chapel, the monastic buildings to the south of the church, visible in old photographs, have largely disappeared, but a number of finely carved tombstones survive to the east. It is sobering to remember that the mona-

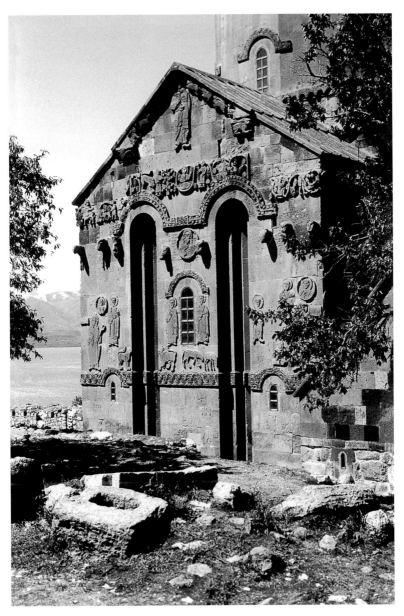

The church: the apse from the north-east.

stery remained in commission until less than a hundred years ago. We know the fate of the last few monks, for when, in 1952, Derek Hill travelled with Freya Stark, the boatman he hoped to hire could without any embarrassment state that his own father had killed them. Luckily the fabric proved sufficiently robust to survive in the decades that ensued before the Church of the Holy Apostles' potential as a tourist asset was recognized. The exemplary recent replacement of the doors and windows should now ensure the preservation of the murals.

At Gevas, 12 kilometres/7.4 miles to the east, near the shore of the lake, is a notable Islamic monument, the mausoleum of the Kara Koyunlu Halime Hatun, built in 1358, set in a graveyard surpassed only by that of Ahlat and backed by the rugged Artos Dağ. Almost unbelievably, a vast apartment block has been built beside this most elegant of medieval tombs. In the village to the south-west is an admirably restrained mosque of before 1446.

37
AHLAT

THE kümbets and cemeteries of Ahlat on the north side of Lake Van are among the most moving sights of Turkey, survivors of a city that developed under Arab rule and was in the twelfth century the capital of the Turkish Shah-Arman principality. The Shah-Arman dynasty, founded by a former slave, Sukman, endured until 1207, controlling the whole littoral of the lake and profiting from the trade with Persia and Mesopotamia. Ayyubid control was followed in 1229 by that of the portentously named Khwarizmshah Jelal ad-Din Manguberti: the Seljuks followed, to be supplanted by the Mongols, under whom in the 1260s prosperity revived. This declined when the Il-Khan empire disintegrated in the fourteenth century, but a notable kümbet was built later under the Ak Koyunlu, the white sheep Turkomen. Ahlat was conquered in 1534 by Süleyman I, but largely destroyed by the Persians in 1548. Although the Sultan recovered it within months, Ahlat never fully recovered.

The visitor at Ahlat should start in the small museum beside the main road. There are some interesting finds from the site, of which the finest is a large jug with representations of half-length women. But more useful is a large map showing the locations of the surviving monuments, and those that have been excavated. If time allows, the most satisfactory way of seeing Ahlat is to follow the main road eastwards and take the first turn on the left, passing the spectacular Bayindir Bey Kümbeti and the northern end of the rocky outcrop in the

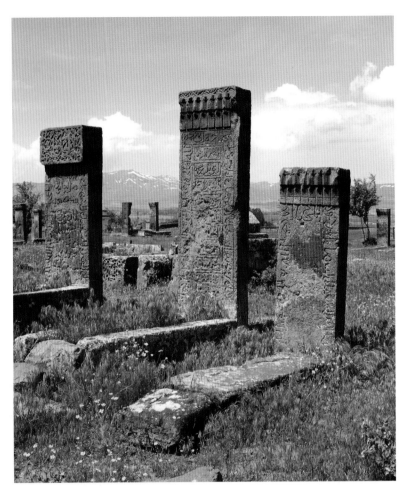

Clustered Seljuk gravestones in the cemetery.

valley beyond, to make south to the spectacularly placed, although much restored, Hasan Padişah Türbesi of 1275. There are views southwards towards the lake and northwards over the ridge in the valley that was a natural fortress.

The only visible traces of the city walls are built on this and there are numerous rock-cut structures in its eastern flank. To the south is a fifteenth-century bridge, and to the east a ruined hamam. To the east of the ravine, on a great natural platform that was almost certainly within the walls, are most of the kümbets – tombs on square bases, rising to drums of dodecagonal form with small mosques –

for which Ahlat is celebrated. Nearest, on the right of the road, is that of the Ak Koyunlu Bayindir Bey, who died in 1481. The builder was clearly influenced by the earlier kümbets at Ahlat, but the arcade of ten columns in the upper tier is a unique feature: below the columns are lavishly decorated panels. Take the road opposite the kümbet. Three other relatively late tombs follow. Beyond these is the Keşiş Kümbeti, probably of between 1350 and 1450, plain to the point of austerity. This eminently picturesque group is completed by two kümbets, each with twelve decorative panels, the nearer of 1279, the second of 1281. These commemorate respectively Hasan Temir and his daughter, and the former's father Buğatay Ağa and his wife. The finest of the tombs, the Ulu Kümbeti, is over 1 kilometre/0.6 miles to the south-west. There is no evidence as to whom this commemorates, but a date in the late thirteenth century is clear. The carving, whether of the blind arcade or the conical top, is of a high order, emphatically Seljuk in descent, although aspects of the structure, for example the tall niches, echo Armenian architecture.

Between the Bayindir Bey Kümbeti and the museum is the main cemetery, with a scattering of some two hundred carved gravestones: many of these are clustered in small groups. The earliest may be of the late eleventh century. As Sinclair and others have shown, the designs of the stones at Ahlat evolved in the twelfth and thirteenth centuries and reached an apogee in the fourteenth. Subsequently standards fell off. Interesting as such distinctions are, the charm of Ahlat is the way the stones arrange and rearrange themselves as one walks among them, and the contrast of their reddish stone with the vegetation – lush green in the spring, a scorched gold in the late summer – and with the subtle turquoise of the lake in the distance.

After Süleyman I recovered Ahlat, he built the substantial fortress that stretches down to the shore 1 kilometre/0.6 miles east of the museum. Much of the facing stone has been pillaged. But the two Ottoman mosques below the inner citadel have recently been restored. One is flanked by small fields fringed with cow parsley; and the sounds of water and of rooks in the overhanging trees soothe the spirit.

Many visitors to Ahlat also go to see the prodigious volcanic cone of Nemrut Dağ to the west, with its three lakes. Adilcevaz, some 20 kilometres/12.4 miles east of Ahlat, also deserves attention. There is an unusually fine Ottoman mosque below the walled citadel of the medieval town. On a high cliff-protected promontory 3 kilometres/1.9 miles inland from this is Kefkalesi, a walled Urartian town. The setting is splendid: orchids and daphnes thrive, and the basalt bases of a sequence of palatial rooms in the citadel answer the lingering snows on Şüphan Dağ, another extinct volcano. Below the cliffs is the husk of a late Armenian church.

38

HASANKEYF

❖

NO medieval Islamic site in Turkey has quite the magic of Hasankeyf; and none is in more immediate danger. Control of the Tigris must from early times have been considered a strategic prize. The exposed cliff of the wedge-shaped outcrop on which the upper city was constructed rises abruptly from the river, dominating the low ground on the opposite, northern, bank. The main town stretches to the south: the low cliffs opposite are pigeonholed with early rock-cut houses. The prodigious piers of a great bridge stride across the Tigris; and it was across this that the all-important traffic from Diyarbakir to Cizre and Mesopotamia passed.

The citadel was apparently fortified by the Romans, but Hasankeyf's great moment followed its capture by Sukman, son of Artuk, in 1102. As vassals of the Ayyubids, whose empire ran from Syria to Mesopotamia and Egypt, the Artukids controlled a fluctuating tract of Anatolia, centred on Hasankeyf (Hisn Kayfa) and the Tur Abdin, until 1232, when the town fell to a cadet line of the Ayyubids. Prosperous in the fourteenth century, Hasankeyf suffered from incursions of the Ak Koyunlu and a prolonged siege in 1462. The Ak Koyunlu finally prevailed about 1495, but were in turn ousted by Kurds. The place gradually declined, although the caves and other rock-cut dwellings in the citadel hill only began to fall from use in about 1960.

The most spectacular approach to Hasankeyf is from the north. The cliff towers above the Tigris and a great stair,

The bridge over the Tigris, with the upper town.

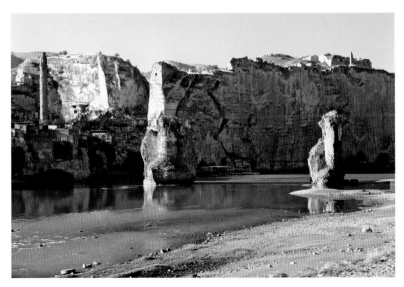

now inaccessible from below, zigzags upwards from near the splendid remains of the bridge, built in 1116, shortly after Sukman's death. Early visitors seem to have thought this the most striking monument of the place. North-west of the bridge is the beautiful tomb of Zaynal, who died in 1473. Much of the original glazed decoration in dark blue and turquoise, has gone, and the exceptional stucco of the domed interior is in precarious condition; but the tomb is unquestionably the most sophisticated of its date in Anatolia and vies with any building of the type in Iran.

The new bridge crosses to the modern township. To the east of this is the substantial Sultan Suleyman Camii, which takes its name from the builder of the çeşme of 1416, but was in fact largely constructed for his father, Ghazi, in 1356. There are two domed mausolea and a prayer hall with a spectacular unrestored stucco dome; the minaret, built for Ghazi in 1407, is particularly fine. This was taken as the model for that of the Cami-ar-Rizk, which Sultan Suleyman erected in 1409 near the great bridge. The elaborate carving of both these minarets merits close inspection.

Stairway from the upper town to the Tigris.

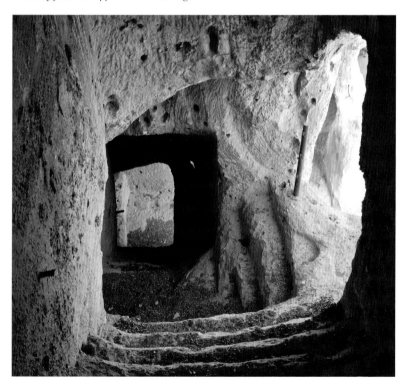

The main lateral street, lined with tourist shops, rises beyond the Cami-ar-Rizk into a narrow valley between the citadel rock and the promontory to the east. The ancient way to the citadel hairpins up the flank of the outcrop. There are three decorated gateways. Numerous rock-cut rooms are passed on the climb. On reaching the crest, turn right and make for the 'Little Palace' – near which is the upper entrance to the great stairway seen from across the river. This can be entered, but is blocked near the bottom. Keeping to the clifftop walk, one comes to the larger palace, now very ruinous. Behind this is the austere Ulu Cami, dated to the mid-fourteenth century by Sinclair, who fairly compares the decoration of the mihrab with that of the Sultan Suleyman Camii.

Some 200 metres/218 yards beyond the mosque, recently blocked, is the only postern gate of the citadel, controlling the approach from a cleft rising from the ravine to the west. The steep cliffs meant that much of the perimeter of the citadel did not need to be fortified, but towards the landward end of the outcrop, some 500 metres/545 yards to the south, are the remains of an apparent defensive system of considerable ingenuity. The most unusual element is a rock-cut ditch, originally crossed by a bridge and fed by cisterns and a channel that can be followed for some distance to the east. The ground in front falls away and then rises to the tip of the outcrop, on which there is a small tower, possibly late Roman like the ditch, but with Artukid extensions.

But why was so sophisticated a ditch called for when no enemy had a realistic chance of scaling the cliff?

Returning to the main entrance along the eastern cliff, look across to the opposite hill, the final section of which, hanging above the lower town, is cut off from the higher ground by a deep rock-hewn ditch. If time permits, it is worth walking past the entrance up the ravine. There are numerous excavations in the cliffs at either side. Below the Roman tower, a wide flight of steps is cut through the rock. And opposite this, the sides of a narrow gorge have been cut away, presumably to create a cistern. One can continue round the scarp. Where the valley narrows towards the river, the streambed has been cut to a rounded channel and an associated flight of steps takes one down to the bank of the Tigris; turning to the right, another stair in the cliff, now inaccessible, is passed. When the water is low, one can walk back to the town.

Hasankeyf is a place of exceptional fascination, rewarding by day and strangely atmospheric at night, when care is of course called for, and dogs bark their warnings. Tragically, future generations will almost certainly be deprived of the experience of seeing it. For if a controversial dam project is realized, not only the bridge and the tomb of Zaynal, but also the mosques and minarets of the lower town will be destroyed. Turkey's unique historic inheritance is too precious to be sacrificed for mere commercial gain.

39

THE TUR ABDIN

THE Tur Abdin is a place apart, a territory of undulating hills and ridges stretching from Midyat, its natural capital, towards the right bank of the Tigris to the east. Here, as perhaps nowhere else in Turkey, ancient religions co-exist, Syrian Christians, the Syriani, and Muslim Kurds, while until very recently a smaller number of Yezidi survived in a handful of villages. But civil wars do not respect minorities and these suffered grievously at the hands of both the PKK, the Kurdish Workers' Party, and the Turkish army in the early 1990s.

Midyat, still a mainly Christian town, enjoys a gentle prosperity. Although of traditional design, the numerous stone houses are of relatively modern date. And so are the several churches. A little to the north of Midyat, a side road strikes eastwards for Kerburan across the heart of the Tur Abdin. From high ground there is an unexpected prospect, with hilltop villages dominated by churches, that recalls certain parts of Italy or southern France.

Seven kilometres/4.3 miles from the turn, a minor road on the right leads to Arnas, with a late seventh-century church, where much of the original decoration survives in the apse. Six kilometres/3.7 miles or so to the east is the closely contemporary church of Mar Azaziel at Keferzi, in a commanding position above the village. I have twice been unable to find the custodian. Eight kilometres/5 miles further on is the village of Hah. Once a town of some consequence, this was the seat of the bishopric of the Tur Abdin until 613 and

again in the late eleventh and twelfth centuries.

The town, like the modern village, radiated from a low hill, approximately oval in plan, around which no fewer than six churches survive. By far the most remarkable is that of the Virgin, to the right of the approach. Set within a modern enclosure, the seventh-century structure is rectangular, with a narthex from which three doors open to the body of the church. The central square section of this is domed and leads to the main, apsed, sanctuary, which is flanked by smaller sanctuaries, the principal entrances to which are from the aisles. The decoration is of a high order. The use of rich acanthus capitals and intricate mouldings between, and in the arches above, endow the interior with an exceptional visual coherence. The exterior of the dome is enriched with a double arcade, of which only the lower tier is original. The church exudes prosperity. This is due to the support of Christians from the area who have settled in Germany. The other churches at Hah are ruinous and with the exception of Mar Sovo, a large sixth-century structure, difficult to find.

From Hah it is easy to cut through a gentle valley to the Kerburan road. There is another church at Zaz, the compound of which is still inhabited. But it is more rewarding to make for Salah, now known as Barıştepe, taking a road opposite the Arnas turn. On low ground beyond the village, set in a compound, is the substantial monastic church of Mar Yakub. The monastery was founded by Yakub, who died in 421, but the impressive church is of the sixth century. This has recently been restored. The narthex was originally porticoed; and there is a single portal to the unexpectedly large

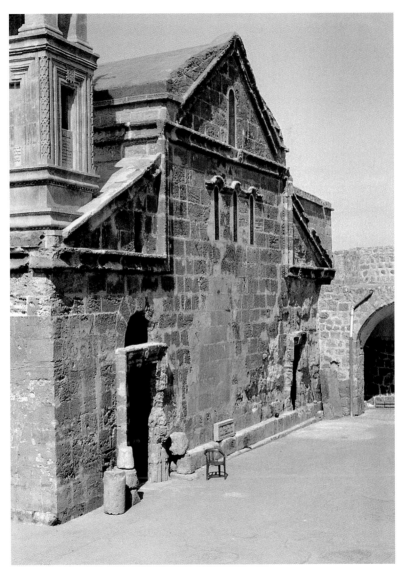

Salah, Mar Yakub, south elevation.

but dark transverse nave, from which the three sanctuaries are reached. The pilasters supporting the arch to the central sanctuary are enriched with birds and with vines rising from basins in which pairs of birds drink; traces of original paint survive. The barrel vaults of both narthex and church are decorated in patterns of tiles, laid side by side and augmented by paint. There are numerous inscribed blocks in the narthex and high on the external walls. The lateral elevations of the church are admirably austere: the way the gable ends of the nave are echoed by the lower roof lines at either side, admittedly at a somewhat less acute angle, oddly anticipates the pedimented design Palladio adopted for some of his most successful church façades. By the entrance to the compound is the smaller church of Mar Barshabo, also with a decorated ceiling. To the north, outside the compound walls, other early monastic buildings are being excavated. The monastery now serves as a seminary: in 2003 there were nine novices, and one can only hope that recent work on the structure will prolong its ministry.

Mar Gabriel, 20 kilometres / 12.4 miles south-east of Midyat, is unquestionably the most important monastery of the Tur Abdin. Already in the fourth century there were 400 monks, and from 613 until 1088 Mar Gabriel was the seat of the bishop. What imperial donations did for the construction of the complex, subventions from the United States and Canada have done for additions from 1955 onwards. Both the eastern and western emperors, Arcadius (395–408) and Honorius (395–423), contributed to Mar Gabriel: their example was followed in 409 by Theodosius II, and in 512 Anastasius despatched the craftsmen who were responsible for the decoration of the main church. Flanking an irregular courtyard, this has a porticoed narthex – the model no doubt for that at Salah – and a barrel-vaulted nave. The central sanctuary was richly decorated in mosaic, the walls with symbols of the Sacrament, and the vault with a Greek cross and vines growing in jars set at the corners.

A door at the north end of the courtyard opens to the long corridor that links the components of the monastery. A narrower door opposite leads to the fifth- or sixth-century domed octagon, presumed to have been the baptistery, which was later put to service as a kitchen. At the far end of the corridor is a small court before a further portico. From this are reached two other fifth-century structures: to the left the windowless Church of the Virgin, and to the right the burial chamber below the Church of the Forty Martyrs.

Despite substantial twentieth-century additions to the upper storey, Mar Gabriel is now much smaller than it was in its heyday under Byzantium and during the centuries of Arab rule. It lacks something of the charm of Hah or Salah, but happily remains a vibrant centre of the Syrian church.

40
NUSAYBIN AND DARA

❖

SOUTH of the Tur Abdin, the hills fall
away towards the Mesopotamian plain.
The border between Turkey and Syria
follows an arbitrary line some kilometres
beyond the escarpment. This has always
been frontier territory, contested by regional powers and caught up, as it were,
on a natural fault line between both civilizations and religions.

Nusaybin is a few kilometres from the
former town of Nasibina recorded in
Assyrian inscriptions. Founded as Antiochia Mygdoniae by the Seleucids, the
place passed successively, as Nisibis, to
Rome and to the Parthians. Retaken by

Trajan in AD 115, Nisibis became the capital of the province of Mesopotamia. In
the fourth century the city was unsuc-
cessfully besieged by the Sassanians,
only to be surrendered to them by Julian
the Apostate's luckless successor, Jovian.
In the sixth century Persian control was
challenged by the Byzantines, but even
so accomplished a general as Belisarius
failed to capture the city. Taken by the
Arabs in 640, Nisibis fell to the Ottomans
in 1515. The frontier with Syria now runs
through it. In view of this turbulent history it is remarkable that the unprepos-
sessing modern town still boasts one of
the most beautiful of early churches. The
original cathedral to which this was
attached has gone, but the baptistery
built in 359 is a remarkable structure,
enriched internally with a lavishly deco-

Nusaybin, the Baptistery of 359, south elevation.

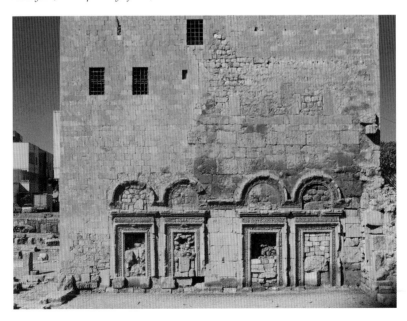

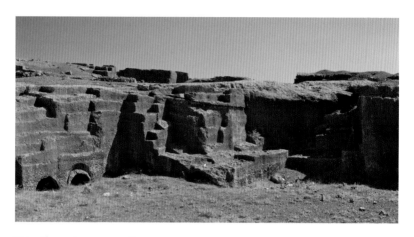

Dara, the western necropolis.

rated frieze and Corinthian capitals; the narthex and the dome were rebuilt in 1872. Between 713 and 758 a church was added to the south of the baptistery. This too is elaborately decorated, although much restored. Recent excavations by the University of Diyarbakir have revealed more of the complex.

A number of other Christian buildings survive on or below the escarpment to the north of Nusaybin. There is a substantial medieval church, long since abandoned, in the ruined town of M'arre in a valley to the north-east. And 1 kilometre/0.6 miles further east, perched high above the plain, is the abandoned monastery of Mar Augen. This is said to have been founded in the fourth century. When Gertrude Bell visited it in 1904 it was still in use. The last monk left in 1974, yet, on the steep approach, one almost imagines that the place is still inhabited. The wooden door swings open. Beyond a modest cloister is the church, reconstructed in 1271, solemn and unexpectedly high.

Dara is some 25 kilometres/15.5 miles north-east of Nusaybin. The city was built quite specifically to challenge Persian control of the latter at breakneck speed in 505–7 under the Emperor Anastasius. Strengthened in 530, the place fell to the Persian King Chosroes I in 573; it was recovered by the Emperor Maurice in 591 and finally fell to the Sassanians under Chosroes II after a nine-month siege in 604. Under Arab rule from 640, Dara remained a place of some importance until the thirteenth century.

The site was carefully chosen to control movement below the escarpment. But as one approaches from the west, passing quarries and necropolises, many of great interest and recently cleared, for a kilometre the ingenuity of the defences is not immediately obvious. The city is divided by a stream and the line of the walls exploits two low hills to the west of this and a longer sloping ridge opposite. Within the city the most substantial monuments are a large cistern, the barrel vaults of which have largely fallen, near the western angle of the wall; a partly rock-cut granary of considerable size; and the prodigious underground cistern which originally supported a church, part of the apse of which survives. South-east of this is a small bridge, rutted by many centuries of wheeled traffic. Beyond is a relatively well-preserved section of the walls, and a substantial tower which defended the vulnerable salient to the east of the riverbed.

The best-preserved stretch of the walls is to the north-east, running from the tip of the ridge – where an artificial moat reinforced the defences – to the flank of the northern hill. Many of the towers are intact and most of the wall survives to nearly full height. Particular ingenuity was called for where this crossed the stream, which of course after the winter rains becomes a torrent. The contemporary historian Procopius records that the Emperor Justinian realized, evidently at about the time of the Sassanian siege of 530, that a dam should be constructed upstream to control the flow of the water; and part of this survives. The wall was carried over the stream on two narrow arches. These were defended from assault by iron bars, fitted into holes that can still be seen. Crouching under the arches, one begins to understand why the Sassanians needed 23,000 cavalrymen and 40,000 infantrymen supported by 120,000 labourers to take the city in 572.

Sightseers to Dara will themselves be under siege from an excited mob of children if they arrive out of school hours, as I learnt on my first visit. But to find the way about the village a guide can be helpful: the mukhtar's engaging son, waiting to do his military service, leaves one in little doubt of the impatience of a television-influenced generation with the traditional constraints of village life.

41
RABAT KALESI

RABAT KALESI is the perfect site for those who do not like to be encumbered with specific information. We don't, it seems, know who constructed the fortress, although it seems to be of the fourth century. We can, however, guess that the builders' intention was to defend the high ground west of Mardin, which in turn controlled the route from east to west that followed the margin of the Mesopotamian plain. And, without the benefit of a pre-Islamic name, we have no historic reference to the place. But for Sinclair's excellent account, and impeccable directions, I would have never have found my way there.

From Mardin take the road south-west for Kiziltepe – where the noble mosque is worth the detour – and then turn at Derik, to make for the scattered village to the south-west of the high promontory on which the fortress stands. A day earlier I had been plagued by children at Dara, so it was a relief on my first visit to arrive during school hours. A man in need of a cigarette pointed to the best path.

The ground rises steeply. As one heads up the lower part of the slope, a stretch of wall with five towers of regular honey-coloured masonry comes into view. This is in fact secured from the attacker by a deep ditch cut into the rock. The towers are best seen from the opposite side of this, but to enter what is in fact the lower section of the fortress it is necessary to retrace your steps. I came on two graves and the excavated footings in the rock of a puzzling building before

making for the ditch, to enter by a postern. The area of the lower enclosure is roughly square. That linking the towers apart, a continuous wall was hardly necessary. There are precipices at either side, commanding the plain on the right and a narrower valley to the west; ahead, the enclosure is cut off from the ridge by a second, and almost equally impressive, ditch, gouged from the rock and now filled with debris from the massive wall that defended the upper enclosure. The remains of towers continue to the natural rampart of the cliff on the east. One small section is of unusual interest: the rock footing has been cut to match the regular blocks of masonry above this. There are cisterns and numerous houses, partly rock cut, with holes for posts, recesses for storage and so forth. And towards the far end there is a fragment of the arcade of a church. The entrance ramp beyond is much eroded – and it is difficult to imagine that the third ditch, dividing the upper enceinte from the hillside to the north, was really necessary.

Rabat Kalesi is not on a tourist trail. As I returned, a balding man was at work on one of the half-dozen tilled plots on the valley floor. The sight of a stranger aroused his curiosity. In the village two equally curious and very hostile dogs were driven off by a woman who did not acknowledge my expression of gratitude. A kilometre and a half or so down the road, flashes of unexpected colour caused me to stop the motor. Dozens of birds, perhaps hundreds, were taking off as if in relays from the telegraph wires, flashes of blue and yellow which made me grateful for my field glasses. I watched, spellbound, for half an hour. It was only later that I learnt that these magical apparitions were bee-eaters.

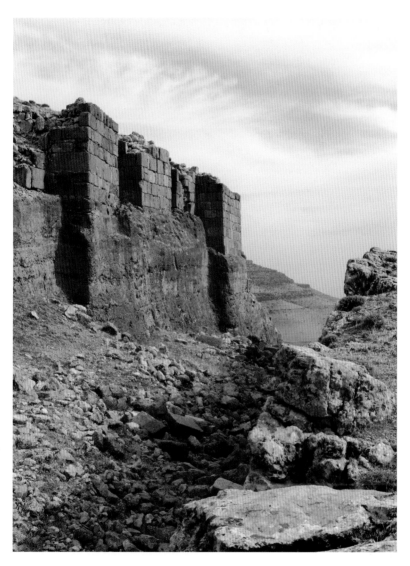

The southern wall of the fortress.

42

MARDIN

APPROACHED from the plain, Mardin makes an unforgettable impression. The city spreads out on descending levels below the cliff of the citadel ridge. Easily defended – and still in use as a radar base and thus inaccessible to the tourist – this must have drawn early Arab settlers to the place. Under the Artukid dynasty established here in 1107 by Il-Ghazi, Mardin became a regional power, controlling tracts of territory to the west, including Harran, Birecik and Silvan. Aware of the importance of trade and tolerant of their Christian subjects, the Artukid sultans coaxed the Syrian Orthodox patriarch to nearby Deir Zaferan, and built the first of the two great medreses that are the outstanding monuments of Mardin. The Artukids held Mardin until 1409; after a generation of rule by the Kara Koyunlu, the city fell to the Ak Koyunlu in 1432, serving as the capital of the emirate of three rebel members of the clan. With the Ottoman ascendancy, Mardin lost its independent status.

The centre of the town is notable for the number of its substantial stone mansions. Few are earlier in date than the nineteenth century, yet one has the impression of a medieval city, a Mesopotamian Gubbio. Many of the larger houses have belfries attesting that their builders were among the Syrian Orthodox minority that must have contributed so signally to the prosperity of Mardin. The central square is the obvious point of departure for a circuit of the town. To the north is the well-arranged Archaeological Museum; below is the substantial

Latifiye Camii, begun in 1371 by a slave of the Artukid Sultan Dawud: the minaret is a replacement of 1845. Further east, below the main thoroughfare, is the Ulu Cami, another Artukid foundation, largely restored in the nineteenth century. The elaborately decorated minaret, originally of 1176, is a prominent feature of the townscape. Behind is the Kayseriye Bazaar, built before 1500 by the Ak Koyunlu ruler, Kasim Padişah, better known for his medrese. Further on, up a side street below the eastern slope of the citadel, is the Hutuniye Medresesi, attributed to Sultan Kutbeddin Il-Ghazi (1176/7–84/5): the beautiful carved mihrab in the domed türbe has recently been relieved of an unfortunate layer of paint.

Up on a side street north of the Ulu Cami is the Sultan Isa Medresesi, built for the penultimate Artukid sultan, who was killed in 1407. The splendid – and partly unrestored – doorway at the east corner of the south-facing façade opens to a corridor. From this a longer corridor leads on the left, past the domed mosque, to the lower courtyard, on the south side of which an open portico offers views over the town; beyond this is the domed mausoleum. A staircase at the junction of the corridors rises to the upper floor, with rooms for the students and a terrace overlooking the courtyard below.

The medresesi was evidently the model for the Kasim Paşa Medresesi, built against the slope of the hill to the south-west of the town. Here a richly carved portal of pink stone enriches the white façade. The passage behind leads to a corridor to the mosque on the left, while a narrower passage opens on to the two-storeyed colonnaded courtyard. The entrance is flanked on the west by

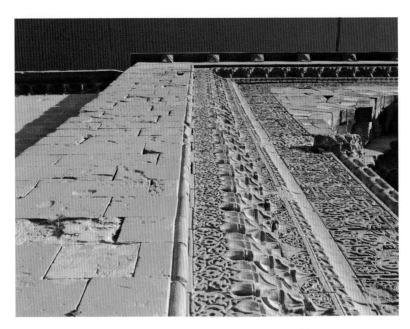

The Sultan Isa Medresesi, detail of portal.

three cells and on the east by a fourth: there are five matching cells on the opposite wall. At the centre of the north wall is a deep iwan with a fountain that flowed to the central pool: as in the Sultan Isa Medresesi there is an open portico to the south, of five bays. At either side, reached through the lateral colonnades, are matching domed rooms, perhaps intended as türbes. From the roof – or from the slope above it – there are spectacular views over the complex with its domes, and downwards towards the plain, which is framed by ridges at either side; but the advent of the bypass means that development will inevitably continue to encroach upon the lower ground.

The bypass is one sign of changing times. When I first visited Mardin, in 1991, it seemed almost forgotten. Four years later, as Turkey contended with the PKK, there were soldiers on point duty at every street corner. In 2003 the administration of a popular mukhtar had brought hope, and a degree of prosperity. Historic buildings were being restored. Yet the evidence of the recent past was never far from the surface. I walked into a tea shop on the main street. It was full – a party of a dozen or so youths talking excitedly in German. They proved to be Syriani living near Hanover, who had returned to see the Christian villages from which their parents had come, talking excitedly of their plans to visit Hah and Ayn Vert. By discriminating against such people, and denying them the right to be taught in their own language and about the religion of their choice, Turkey did itself a signal disservice. In 2013 it was encouraging to see that Mardin has become a magnet for Turkish tourists.

Some 3 kilometres/1.9 miles from Mardin, on the Nusaybin road, is the great monastery of Deir Zaferan, an imposing complex rebuilt late in the nineteenth century that incorporates a sixth-century church and mausoleum. The atmospheric interior of the church, with apses on three sides, is notable for the richness of the Corinthian capitals and decorative frieze; but it is irritating that the tourist is no longer able to see properly the remarkable external frieze with animals and birds. The mausoleum adjoins the church: the entrance wall with the dolphin-adorned doorway is of particular interest.

For a brief period under the Artukids in the twelfth century Deir Zaferan was the seat of the Syrian Orthodox patriarchate; the patriarchs returned under the Ak Koyunlu in the fifteenth century and remained until 1924. The monastery continues to thrive. There are other, abandoned, monastic sites in the circling ridge to the east. The most spectacular is Mar Yakup, excavated into the top of the cliff. Neither the main church nor the lower 'secret church' is of particular architectural interest, but the place has a strange charm, with views down towards Deir Zaferan with its neat fields and eastwards across wilder country, still happily untamed.

43
DIYARBAKIR

DIYARBAKIR, the Byzantine Amida, is unquestionably the most splendid city of eastern Turkey, equally memorable for the spectacular girdle of the black basalt walls and for the exceptional interest of the mosques and churches and large areas of traditional housing that survive within these. In retrospect it seems surprising that the site, a natural platform above a bend of the Tigris, well placed for communication in every direction, was not occupied until the Roman era. The early town, first walled in 354, is overlaid by the later citadel. This occupied the most readily defensible position, on high ground above the cliffs overlooking the river, but none the less was captured by Shapur II of Persia in 359, only to be recovered by Julian the Apostate after a second siege. From 363, as a result of the treaty that followed Rome's defeat by the Sassanians and the forced evacuation of Nisibis, Amida grew exponentially. Within a few decades new walls were built, of which a circuit of 5.5 kilometres/3.4 miles survives, as does much of the plan of the Byzantine city.

Initially defended by a legion, Amida became the hub of the Byzantine defensive system in eastern Anatolia. The Persians took Amida again in 503 and slaughtered 80,000 of its inhabitants. The city returned to Byzantine rule and the walls were reinforced under the Emperor Justinian II (527–65). The last great Sassanian warrior, the Emperor Chosroes II, took Amida, but once again the Byzantines recovered it under Heraclius. The balance of power was, however, totally changed by the Arab victory at the Yarmuk in 636. Amida fell to the Arabs, and was granted to the Beni Bakr, whose name it retains. Omayyad rule from Damascus followed from 660 until 750, when the Abbasids of Baghdad took over. Later Diyarbakir was ruled by a Kurdish dynasty, the Marwanids, who in turn were succeeded by the Seljuks in 1085. The Inalids won the city in 1096, retaining it until 1183, when Saladin expelled them. Until 1232–33 Diyarbakir was governed by the Artukids of Hasankeyf. The Mongols followed in 1259; in the next century, the Ak Koyunlu controlled the city, which was taken by Selim I in 1515. Four centuries of Ottoman rule ended in the aftermath of the First World War, when the Western Allies planned that Diyarbakir should become the capital of a Kurdish state, but were forestalled by the Turkish resurgence under Atatürk.

The most dramatic approach to Diyarbakir is from the south, by the old Mardin road which runs close to the river and passes the west end of the successor of the great fifth-century bridge across the Tigris. The surviving structure was undertaken in the time of Nasr ad-Dawla and completed under Nizam ad-Dawla Nasr in 1065: although much restored, it leaves one in no doubt of the power and sense of purpose of the Marwanids. Two kilometres/1.2 miles upstream, the black walls of the city loom 100 metres/328 feet above the river.

The walls largely follow the Byzantine circuit, but were reconstructed and strengthened in successive campaigns during the Middle Ages, notably under the Marwanids, the Inalids and the Artukids. The line of the walls had been carefully chosen. To the east they crown the steep bluff above the river, and to the south the alignment follows the contour

The bridge across the Tigris.

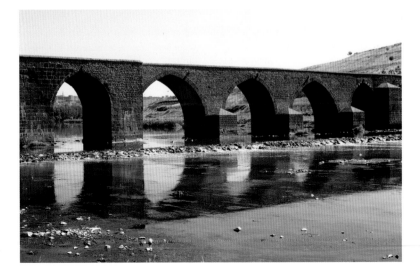

of the plateau to take advantage of the fall of the ground. But from just south of the western Urfa Gate to the citadel in the north-east angle, the ground was level and consequently the defences had to be particularly elaborate. The northern Harput Gate retains its Byzantine form, but was rebuilt in 909, when earlier inscriptions were retained. To the west of this a section of the wall has been destroyed, but there follows a stretch with thirteen towers, defended by a lower outer wall which runs to the Urfa Gate, an Artukid reconstruction of 1183. This is enriched by reliefs of an eagle and a dragon.

It is particularly rewarding to follow the section of the walls to the south. After four more towers, the line circles inwards and then turns to run out at a salient to the Ulu Badan, a massive tower of 1208–9, the outer wall of which bears an inscription surmounted by a double-headed eagle flanked by lions with human heads. The alignment turns sharply to the south-east, and after a series of seven smaller towers, one reaches the Yedi Kardeş, an even wider variant of the Ulu Badan: both were built for the Artukid Sultan Masud (1200–22). The tower that follows, reconstructed by Seljuk Malik Shah in 1089, is remarkable for its reliefs. Further on, beyond a series of polygonal towers, is the southern Mardin Gate. This was rebuilt in 909 and, on its east tower, has a relief with two lions. To the east is the projecting Keçi Burcu ('Goat Tower') which, in its present form, is of 1029–37. Beyond is a particularly attractive section of the wall, with numerous towers. Fragments of two Greek inscriptions are built into the outer face, and there is a stretch of the original Byzantine construction. Further on, where the ground slopes more

steeply, the cliff below the wall is cut away to form an outer defence. The eastern section of the walls was partly rebuilt under the Ottomans, and so was much of the citadel. Within this is the surviving fragment of what must have been a most sophisticated Artukid palace, now under restoration. A huge domed room, now open to the sky, leads to an exceptional oval chamber. Roman and Byzantine columns were put to service in both and the processional relationship of the two spaces is evident. The window at the far end looks out across the Tigris valley.

The Ğazi Caddesi, which runs north–south from the Harput to the Mardin Gate, clearly follows the cardo of Roman Amida. The most important church in the Byzantine city was dedicated to St Thomas. And it is tempting to suppose that the Ulu Cami to the west of the street occupies its site, and indeed that some of the material reused in this beautiful complex belonged to the church and its dependencies. The main entrance opens to the magnificent courtyard, in the centre of which is a striking sadirvan of Ottoman date. On the south is the very substantial prayer hall, the façade of which was built in campaigns of 1091–92 and 1155–56, although the central section is of Ottoman date. The east and west ends of the courtyard are remarkable for the intelligence, and indeed sympathy, with which the Byzantine elements – columns, capitals and friezes – are deployed. People of every age and condition cross the courtyard; and there are few more perfect places to pause and sense the pulse of the living city.

There are some notable sixteenth-century mosques in Diyarbakir. South of the citadel is the Fatih Paşa Camii, built in 1518–20 by Biyikli Mehmet Paşa, the soldier who had conquered the city for the Ottomans. The beautiful portico is of seven bays, and the dome of the prayer hall is borne on four columns. South-west of the intersection of the Gazi Cad-desi with the Melek Ahmet Caddesi that runs to the Urfa Gate is the Behram Paşa Camii of 1572. Preceded by a double por-tico, the prayer hall is notable for the cal-ibre of the tiled decoration. Other good tiles can be seen in the Safa Camii, north of the Melek Ahmet Caddesi, and in the Melek Ahmet Paşa Camii nearer the Urfa Gate.

In the south-western quarter, half-lost in a maze of narrow streets in one of the many areas where traditional houses predominate, is the Meryemana Kilise of the Syrian rite. This was a sixth-century foundation, but what survives, much restored, is only the eastern section of the original church, including two splendid capitals and small portions of the associ-ated cornice. Yet the very fact that the church exists at all is remarkable and there are indeed few more compelling Christian sites in Turkey. On my penulti-mate visit a not particularly generous contribution to its funds led to an invita-tion to a tea party, at which the bishop and his Christian guests from Midyat conversed in Aramaic.

Diyarbakir had of course a large Armenian community. Their vast nine-teenth-century church is in the eastern part of the city. The roof had nearly fallen in at the time of my first visit: the debris has now been cleared away, but one wonders how long the spindly columns that supported the ceiling will last. The small community has withdrawn to a

Yedi Kardeş, rebuilt by Malik Shah, 1089.

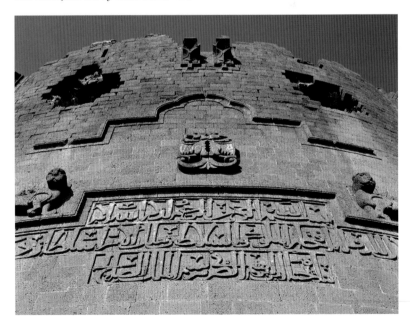

smaller chapel of no particular interest. The neighbouring church of the Chaldeans, of whom only one family remain, is usually closed.

In recent years the population of Diyarbakir has grown dramatically. The modern city to the north-west of the walls has been greatly enlarged. Inevitably there has been development in the old city also, but this remains a place of unusual fascination, as the sightseer searches out the two most handsome Ottoman hans – one now a comfortable hotel, the other most suitably a bazaar – and the many religious buildings. But for most visitors it will be the walls and the great bridge that linger longest in the memory.

44
EĞIL

❖

THERE are few stranger places in Turkey than Eğil, the successor of Carcathiocerta. This, in the second and first centuries BC, was the capital of the Armenian kingdom of Sophene, which at its zenith controlled much territory between the Tigris and the Euphrates. Although Eğil can be reached on a dirt road from Ergani, the easier route is from a point some 23 kilometres / 14.3 miles north of Diyarbakir, where a side road, long marked by a smashed car suspended from a stand as a warning to the motorist, runs north-eastwards for just over 20 kilometres / 12.4 miles. The modern town is a quiet place: shalwar, the traditional Kurdish trousers, predominate, and no woman is in sight. The stranger is watched with a certain wariness and the police are in strong evidence. Beyond the village is the western end of the citadel rock. Fairly described by Sinclair as a 'narrow table', this is a massive promontory carved on its northern side by the Tigris and flanked to the south by a deep valley. The original town was in the lower section of this, beside the river. The eye is first caught by an Assyrian relief of an axe-bearing king, high on the western cliff. The walls of the citadel were largely rebuilt by the Kurds, but on the southern side sections of Hellenistic masonry survive, with bevelled blocks laid with an exacting precision.

On my first visit, I followed the southern defences and then worked my way towards the end of the outcrop, only too aware how greatly the Dicle Dam had affected the place. For the site of the town has been lost beneath the sullen waters of the lake, which has of course also partly flooded the gorge cut by the Tigris. The kings of Sophene were buried in a series of cylindrical tombs with pointed tops cut from outcrops of the rock. I feared that these would also have been submerged – and it was only from the tip of the ridge that I could see them far below, just above the present water-line. To clamber down demanded patience: one path failed, but a series of ancient hand- and foot-holds cut in the sloping rock brought me down to the level of another. I passed two tombs, and then reached the spectacular group of three, all circular but one on a rectangular base. These rise above a natural shelf, submerged in the spring, but in the autumn just 9 centimetres/3.5 inches above the waterline. Armed with my torch, I entered the low passage to the chamber of the easternmost of the tombs: a startled bat and thick dust cooled my interest after the first bend. Cut into the rock behind the central tomb, and presumably coeval with this, is the schematic outline of a life-size man, timeless in design, which came as a surprise. The place is strangely eerie, the sullen waters shadowed by the citadel rock from the afternoon sun that beats upon the barren boulder-strewn hills opposite.

I made back upwards, grateful again for the handholds. The views from the citadel are spectacular and there are a number of points of interest: cisterns; a group of long rooms, hewn from the bedrock; and at the highest point, where the ridge is honeycombed with cuttings, an ambitious staircase which is blocked after a descent of 13.5 metres/15 yards. The other staircase at Eğil, carefully described by Sinclair, has evidently now been flooded. Before leaving, it is worth

taking the road north of the citadel, which zigzags down to a ferry, where boats to the tombs can be hired. The cliff towers above the swollen waters of the Tigris, and it is not difficult to understand why Eğil was chosen as the capital of a kingdom.

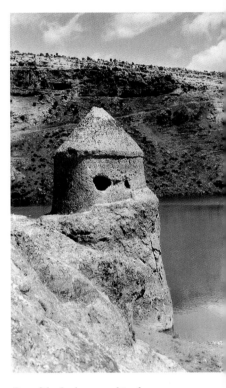

One of the Sophene royal tombs.

45
ARSEMEIA ON THE EUPHRATES

ARSEMEIA ad Euphratem, Gerger Kale, is less easily reached than its better-known namesake, Arsemeia ad Nymphaeum. South of Karaduc take the Gerger turn and head eastwards; ignore a sign 'Gerger Kale' and continue for a further 7 kilometres/4.3 miles, to turn right across a river, then left at the first 'proper' junction; the site is on the left-most outcrop of the ridge ahead. The road passes a pylon and a ruinous minaret and circles round to below the northern tip of the rock.

The place commanded the ancient route along the Euphrates and can be seen from a considerable distance – from Siverek to the south-east, and from Nemrut to the west, serving indeed as the eastern sentinel of what was evidently the spiritual heartland of the kings of Commagene. To the east the ground falls away vertiginously to the waters of the great lake created by the Atatürk dam. An ancient path is partly cut into the western flank of the rock. Where this descends towards a tunnel turn and look upwards to see the large relief hewn into the rock of King Antiochus I advancing to the left, in conscious emulation of equally inaccessible reliefs left by the Hittites and other early rulers of Anato-

lia. Little but the relief and the path survive of Antiochus's town, which must have spread over the ground below the rock. The Romans seem not to have occupied the site, but it was subsequently taken over by the Armenians and became of some importance to the Mamelukes, who refortified the citadel that crowns the rock, and was to some extent maintained under the Ottomans as the truncated minaret reminds us.

From the southern end of the tunnel an obvious but in places steep path turns the flank of the outcrop to reach a substantial, if ruinous, Mameluke gatehouse with a vaulted guardroom within, supported on piers of beautifully aligned blocks. The path continues upwards, the rock to the left, the ground plunging towards the lake on the right. There are sections of a wall, and, where the route narrows, a long inscription in Greek. Above this the ground opens out to the level area, sloping downwards to the north, of the inner enceinte. The protection of the cliffs meant that walling was hardly necessary. There is a cistern near the centre and a number of crumbling buildings cluster at the southern end, one with a partly extant barrel vault. Gerger Kale is remarkable not for these, but for the prodigious views over the former course of the Euphrates, views that help to explain why such ingenuity was given to fortifying the site by Antiochus and those who subsequently occupied it.

Cliff, with relief of King Antiochus I of Commagene.

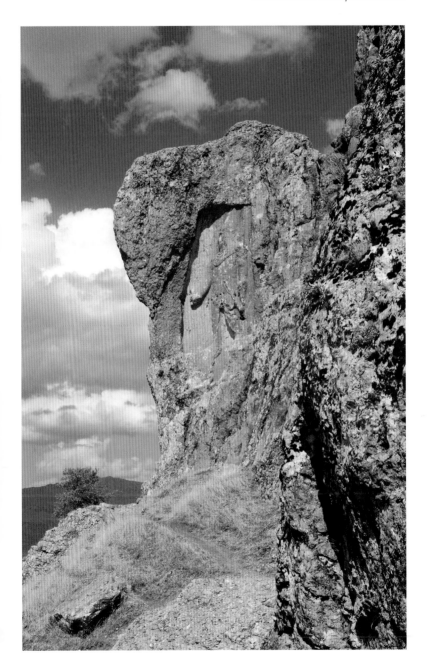

46

NEMRÜT DAĞ

❧

NEMRÜT DAĞ is unquestionably the site in eastern Turkey that exerts the strongest spell on most tourists. It is indeed a most remarkable monument to the aspirations of an otherwise unremembered king of a realm that itself achieved only a transitory power.

The kingdom of Commagene was neither very large nor inordinately rich. From its capital at what is now Samsat, it controlled the territory of the former neo-Hittite kingdom of Kummah under a line of kings founded by Aroandus, a commander in the service of Artaxerxes III of Persia (405–359 BC). The heartland of Commagene was the rough mountain territory that fed the Euphrates – which marked its southern boundary, a territory crossed by trade routes and one that had a clear strategic importance at a time when Rome sought to impose her rule on Asia Minor. Early in the first century BC the kingdom was ruled by Mithridates I. His son, Antiochus I (c. 70–36 BC), was evidently a man of prodigious vanity, only too aware that he was named after his maternal grandfather, the Seleucid King Antiochus VIII Grypus. Antiochus I chose the highest and most visible mountain top in the area centring on the town of Arsemeia ad Nymphaeum, which was clearly of particular importance to his family, as the site of his own tumulus and shrine. The construction of this can only have drained the kingdom's resources at a time when Commagene was also claimed by the king of Armenia, who was, however, conveniently vanquished by Pompey. But the Roman alliance was

won at an ultimate cost. Antiochus II was executed in Rome in 29 BC. The kingdom reverted to his brother and was finally absorbed by Rome in AD 71–72.

Getting to Nemrut Dağ can be something of an adventure. My first attempt seemed to be doomed. Approaching the ferry across the now-flooded Euphrates, I braked sharply to avoid a fearless tortoise – and only when it had been taken to safety realized that my hireling was billowing smoke. So I spent a day at Siverek, where two of the Kurdish mechanics who rescued me insisted on being photographed in front of a tomb to an aunt who had been killed in the custody of the police. And a day later my first experience of Nemrut was not improved by the September bus groups. As I later found, it is more satisfying to go in the spring.

The logical place to begin the circuit is Karakuş, north of Kâhta. This great tumulus is 30 metres/98 feet high. Six columns were arranged in pairs at the south, north-west and north-east of the mound. Four of these survive and an inscription on one of the extant northeastern pair establishes that the tumulus was built by Mithridates I in honour of his mother, sister and daughter; the inscription on the surviving north-western columns is a dedication to Antiochus I's sister, Laodice, Queen of Parthia, and thus implies that the tumulus continued to be used for female members of the family. Its Turkish name ('black bird') is due to the eagle on the south column. Strangely moving in evening light, the place is in sight of Nemrut Dağ.

Eight kilometres/5 miles beyond the tombs, the Cendere Suyu is crossed where it emerges from the hills by a Roman bridge. Built by the XVI Flavia Firma legion in AD 198–200, this must be one of the most beautiful of all buildings of the kind. The single arch has a span of some 34 metres/79 feet; and the carriageway is flanked by elegantly stepped parapets. A pair of columns stands at the south end, but one of the two to the north has been lost. Otherwise the structure is remarkably complete.

Beyond the bridge the road turns east. Ahead is the spectacular Yeni Kale, built on a narrow spine of rock above the gorge of the Kâhta Çay, originally part of the defensive system of the Commagene town of Arsemeia ad Nymphaeum. The later castle that clings to this was an outpost of the crusader county of Edessa, but later passed to the Artukids of Hasankeyf and Diyarbakir. But much of what survives was built under the Mameluke Sultan Kaloun, whose contri-

butions, including the outer gate and that of the upper ward, use large bossed blocks. A stair descends the cliff face to the Kâhta Çay. Originally vaulted, this led to a tunnel under the river, excavated to ensure communication between the two sections of Arsemeia ad Nymphaeum in the event of a siege.

The heart of ancient Arsemeia was to the east of the river. This was a major religious centre. A processional way cuts up the mountainside. Associated with this is a series of monuments. The visitor comes first to a relief of Apollo on a freestanding rock. Higher up is the entrance to a staircase descending to a tunnel which is no less than 158 metres/518 feet long. There is a long inscription in Greek and nearby a remarkable relief of a king, presumably Mithridates or Antiochus,

Karakuş, the tumulus.

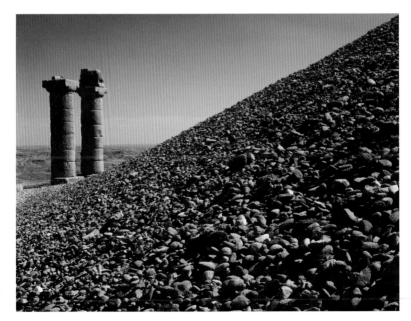

shaking hands with Hercules. The relief was clearly inspired by earlier Hittite and neo-Hittite ones, but by being represented on the same scale as the deity the king proclaimed his equal status. A path continues to the summit of the hill on which Mithridates may have been buried. Excavation has shown that the site was still occupied in the medieval era.

Narince is the last settlement before the turn for Nemrut Dağ. There are a few pansiyons and it made sense for me to settle for the furthest of these. Knowing that a snowplough had been up, I set off at dawn, little realizing how thick the drifts would be. Eventually, ice on a steep curve defeated my car. I slid ignominiously backwards and then walked. Others had been before and the snow was far from virginal.

The summit of the mountain is crowned with an immense tumulus of small stones, under which the king was to be buried. To the east is a wide terrace. This was backed by a series of statues of seated deities over 9 metres / 30 feet high, carved in sections in blocks of ashlar. Some of the heads lie below the still impressive trunks of these monster statues. In the centre is Zeus-Oromasdes: to the left Commagene, the female deity of the eponymous kingdom, followed by Antiochus I; to the right two other deities. At the ends of the row were two statues of a lion with an eagle, of which only the base of that on the north survives. The terrace was flanked by stelae commemorating Antiochus's ancestors and there was an altar to the east, overlooking the tremendous panorama of hills cascading downwards to the valley of the Euphrates. The prospect would

have inspired the German painter Caspar David Friedrich, so it is appropriate that the place was discovered by a German engineer, although not by that architect of Prussian military expansion, von Moltke, who discovered the site of Arsemeia ad Euphratum some 30 kilometres / 18.6 miles to the east.

Spectacular as the east terrace is, the west terrace, set at a somewhat lower level, is in some ways more satisfying. The pattern repeats that to the east. Here again the heads have been dislodged. These remain where they fell: Antiochus himself; the beardless Mithras, whose cult was to pervade the Roman Empire; Commagene, with her headdress of corn and fruit; the bearded Hercules in a conical hat; Zeus-Oromasdes, also bearded; and two eagles. Near by, there are four reliefs of Antiochus and the gods with whom he sought to identify himself: Zeus, Apollo, Hercules and, inevitably, Commagene. Equally remarkable is the large relief of a lion with a crescent moon at his neck, the background of which bears nineteen stars, of which the three largest are identifiable as Jupiter, Mercury and Mars: this may refer to the configuration of these planets on 7 July 62 BC.

Nemrut Dağ is extraordinary at any time of the day or season of the year. Ideally it should be seen both late in the afternoon and soon after dawn. To see the great heads emerging from the winter's snow is an unforgettable experience. Yet one cannot help wondering what the not unsophisticated sculptors he employed really thought of the king they served and his titanic ambition for immortality.

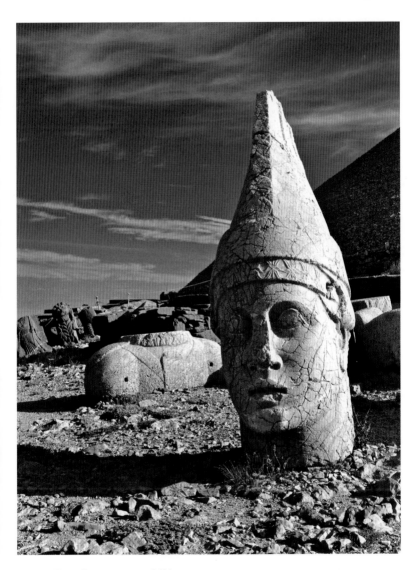

Nemrüt Dağ, the west terrace, Mithras.

47

URFA

❖

URFA, formerly Edessa, which may occupy the site of the Hurrian and Hittite city of Ursu, was founded by Seleucus I Nicator at roughly the same time as his capital, Antioch, in c. 300 BC. With the eclipse of the Seleucids, Edessa became a small kingdom, which endured for some three hundred years; King Abgar VIII became the first monarch to convert to Christianity. Rome took control of Edessa in AD 215. Fought over by the Byzantines and Sassanians in the post-Roman period, Urfa was controlled after the Arab conquest of 637 by the Marwanids. Sold to the Byzantines in 1030, it was seized in 1083 by an Armenian, Sombat,

whose successor, Thoras, called in the crusaders. Their county of Edessa, founded by Baldwin de Bouillon in 1098, held out until 1144; two years later Nur ad-Din of Aleppo sacked the town. Urfa's subsequent history was equally charged: Ayyubid rule was punctuated by a Seljuk incursion of 1234; two Mongol phases were interrupted by a Mameluke occupation; and although the Ottomans won Urfa in 1516, it was lost to Persia from 1623 until 1637. The modern adjunct to the name, Sanli, celebrates Urfa's resistance to the French after the First World War.

So turbulent a history explains why the citadel on the ridge above the city remains the dominant building. From afar, the two honey-coloured Corinthian columns of King Abgar's winter palace stand out against the skyline. But the

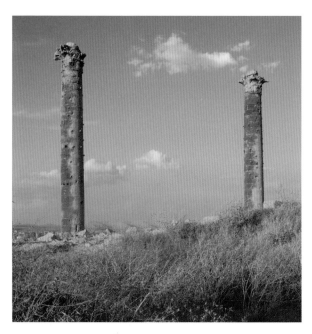

The columns of King Abgar's palace on the citadel.

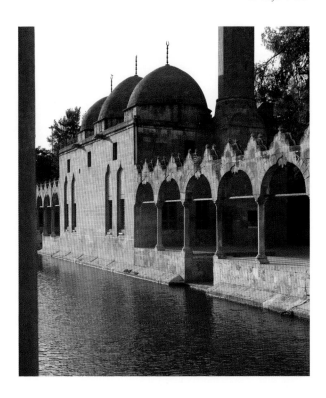

The Birket Ibrahim with the Abdürrahman Medresesi.

most impressive thing about the castle is the great moat, gouged into the rock, which cuts it off from the ridge, except on the northern side where the ground falls away. The strength of the position is best understood by walking round the moat, but such detritus as murdered puppies and innumerable plastic bags may discourage some visitors. The bases of the towers were cut into the rock and a shaft was left near the south-western corner to support a drawbridge. The large stone blocks of the lower courses of the built walls may be of about 812, when the city was rewalled. The Mamelukes tended to use smaller stones, while the Ak Koyunlu Uzun Husan in his rebuilding campaign of 1462–63 imitated the original masonry. The Ottomans made further repairs, and more recently the northern walls and towers have been much altered by restoration.

Below the citadel, on the course of a river that has long been since diverted, is the celebrated fish pool, the Birket Ibrahim. This is lined on the north by the enchanting Abdürrahman Medresesi, the mosque of which was built in 1717: the builder clearly knew how effectively his delicate forms would be reflected in the water. To the south-west of this is a complex of different structures. The oldest is an Ayyubid minaret of 1211–12, evidently inspired by a Christian belfry. To the east, beyond the large modern mosque, is an elegant one attributed to

Uzun Husan, and, further on, a very satisfying souk. This centres on the Gümrük Hani, with a square courtyard, stated to have been built in 1566 for Behram Paşa. How slowly taste evolved in such building types is shown by the nearby vaulted souk of 1887, now used by metalworkers.

The Divan Caddesi, the main street of modern Urfa, runs north from the eastern end of the souk. A little way up on the left is the Ulu Cami, with a striking octagonal minaret and a spacious courtyard fronting the arcaded façade of the prayer hall. Austere and much restored, this was begun in or soon after 1146; opposite, beside the minaret, is a section of the arcade of a Byzantine church. Both on the higher ground to the west of the mosque and across the Divan Caddesi to the east, significant areas of early housing survive. A straightish street across the Divan Caddesi from the mosque runs to the back of the best surviving section of the city wall, the Bey Kapisi ('Lord Gate'), which may incorporate part of the Byzantine enceinte. Wander back, taking side streets to the north if there is time. The numerous large stone houses, with corbelled and bracketed projections, are a closed world to the tourist. But some sense of their character can be gained at the Haçi Hafiz Efendi house on the Divan Caddesi, a large if late traditional mansion perhaps too energetically restored, now used as an art gallery.

A number of fine carved doors and shutters – labelled 'window wings' – salvaged from earlier houses are displayed with rather less appealing plaster statues of Christ and various saints in the excellent ethnography section of the Archaeological Museum in the northern part of the town. Most visitors make naturally for the earlier exhibits, which include an Assyrian relief from Harran, finds from the recent rescue excavations necessitated by the Atatürk Dam and, not least, the remarkable material from Gobekli Tepe. The pottery in particular is very remarkable. Less expected, in the garden of the museum, were two carved voussoirs of almost naked couples embracing, discreetly unlabelled – relics presumably of Christian Edessa rather than Muslim Urfa, which have now been moved. The museum is relatively modest in scale. This cannot be said of the huge structure built to display the remarkable Roman mosaics found relatively recently on the low ground to the west of the old town. There are some fine excavated tombs in the necropolis on the slope above this, between the town and a major road. To the north of the old town, recently restored, is the medieval aqueduct that brought water from the higher ground to the north.

48
GÖBEKLI TEPE

GÖBEKLI TEPE is surely the most remarkable archaeological discovery of our time. A reference to flints in a census of Byzantine sites led Klaus Schmidt to visit the site on a hill north-east of Urfa in 1994. As a geologist he immediately recognized that the top thirty metres of the hill was artificial: he quickly realized that he had found a major early site, and, when he left, turned back to see innumerable flints caught in the low evening light. He would work with a team of archaeologists at Göbekli until his death in 2014, excavating part of what is by far the earliest major cult site to have been found, originating in the ninth millennium BC.

Göbekli Tepe is reached from a turn off the main road east from Urfa. To the right of the entrance is an area of levelled bedrock with shallow grooves which originally anchored narrow pillars and were surrounded by an oval wall of small stones, bonded in clay. The hunter-gatherer builders, who worked with their flint implements, would after a time have filled in the shrine. This footprint does not entirely prepare the visitor for what is to be seen further on, at the cen-

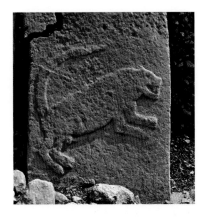

Relief of a lion.

tre of the complex. Here, where the excavations are now protected by a wooden structure with a curving walkway, are a series of better preserved oval shrines of differing scale and at varying levels. Many of the substantial pillars survive in situ, as do the flimsy walls surrounding the groups of these. The largest of the stones is some 3 metres/10 feet high. Most remarkably, many of the stones are carved, with animals, including lions and snakes, and in some cases with stylized arms, the hands bent round the sides of the blocks. Some are set into carved bases, of which the most remarkable, below and to the left of the walkway, shows a row of seven ducks.

Relief of ducks on the base of a pillar in the central area of the excavation (detail).

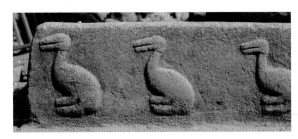

Because the shrines were filled in once these had served their purpose, the reliefs have not suffered from exposure. No comparable body of reliefs of their type is known.

After crossing the main excavation area, the path turns to the highpoint, marked by a wishing tree and a group of graves. From here is is more obvious why the hunter-gatherers were drawn to the hill: there are sweeping views to the uplands to the north and southwards down the Harran plain. A number of other shrines, also now covered, can be seen to the west. Further on, on the north-western flank of the hill, not yet open to the public as work proceeds, is an area in which more shrines have been cleared. These are more modest than those in the central area, but here too there are a number of exceptional reliefs: a fierce lion on a block, now split, and an ambitious composition with fish, serpents and birds.

Schmidt's discoveries at Göbekli have changed our understanding of the origins of civilization and organized religion in the Near East. No equally ambitious monuments of the ninth millennium have been found. But what is almost equally remarkable about the site is that it continued to be built over for many thousands of years. As its discoverer Schmidt takes his place with the great pioneering archaeologists of the past, and we can only regret that his death in 2014 deprives posterity of his definitive account of Göbekli Tepe.

49
HARRAN
❖

HARRAN, the city of the Caliph Marwan II, is hardly 45 kilometres / 28 miles from Urfa. The road south makes across the level ground, with low hills to the west. Irrigation is changing the character of what was an almost empty landscape, fringed to the south-east by the distant range of the Tek Tek Dağı. The Syrian border is only 30 kilometres / 18.6 miles away; and it is of Syria that one is reminded in Harran with its clusters of mud-brick beehive structures like those in the desert south of Aleppo.

Harran is mentioned in the book of Genesis, because Abraham stayed there on his return from Ur of the Chaldees. For well over two millennia, despite successive Assyrian, Babylonian and Roman occupations, it was the centre of a planet cult, dedicated to the moon-god Sin. Julian the Apostate worshipped at his temple and the cult endured until as late as the eleventh century. Harran was taken by the Arabs in 639 and Marwan II (744–50) chose it as his capital. His city, oval in plan, built round an isolated hill, was girdled by walls which largely survive: the road from Urfa reaches the relatively well-preserved north-western section, with a fine gate, recently excavated.

The citadel is at the south-east extremity of the enceinte, built on the site of an earlier and presumably redundant moon temple. Part of the surviving structure is of no later than the eleventh century; but much of what can be seen was built by the brother of Saladin, the Ayyubid Sultan al-Adil, who reigned from 1200 until 1218, while the handsome arch of the great gallery on the west front is a later Mameluke refinement. The most impressive views are from the south, with the two large polygonal angle towers, of which only the central section of that to the east survives. The staircase of the south-west tower and the circular chamber in its eastern counterpart are equally satisfying. Despite recent restoration to the south-west tower, the citadel is notable for the quality of the Ayyubid bossed masonry. The north-eastern angle tower is also striking: the cavernous barrel-vaulted galleries of the upper level at the centre of the complex respect the plan of the lower storey, now invisible. But the visitor may wish that there were rather fewer noisy children in need of diversion.

Much of the modern village lies in an arc to the west of the citadel. The heart of the city has been spared development and in recent years an extensive programme of excavation has been undertaken on the northern flank of the hill. At the foot of this is the major monument of Harran, the extraordinary Great Mosque, presumably begun by Marwan II when the place became his capital. The complex was extensively reconstructed in the 1170s for Nur ad-Din and, in 1191–92, by Saladin's governor of Upper Mesopotamia, al-Kamil.

The spectacular tall minaret is a survivor of the original build. Its dominance is emphasized by the disappearance of so much of the rest of the structure. Enough of the foundations and footings

The Great Mosque, fallen decorated blocks.

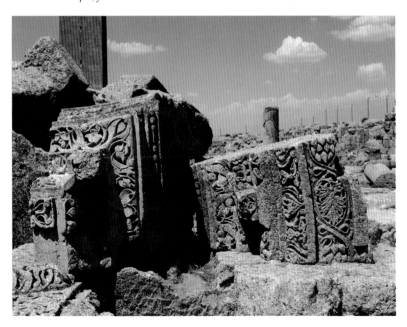

survive, however, to give a sense of the scale of the courtyard with its central pool. The arcaded prayer hall, of which only the odd pier stands, was built under Nur ad-Din. Al-Kamil was responsible for the well-preserved eastern wall of the prayer hall, and the beautiful doorway to the north of it. At the moment the mosque is fenced off, but this does not diminish the visual impact of what remains.

Harran was sacked by the Mongols, led by Hulagu, in 1260 and was evacuated in 1271. The citadel was maintained by the Mamelukes, but by the seventeenth century the place had dwindled in importance. In the 1820s Harran was only used for shelter during the rains. But relatively modern as these are, the traditional beehive houses have an immemorial air. This cannot be said of the pastiches of these built recently as a hotel. Even in a dozen years one is aware of change: wider roads, more motors. And on a recent visit there was no sign of the farmer who, in 1992, needed a lift and somehow managed to balance his plough on the back seat of the modest car I had hired.

50

SUMATAR

❖

THE road east from Harran rises gradually among low hills. After perhaps ten kilometres the road curls to the right round a ridge, to pass the spectacular quarry of Bazala Mağaralari, source of much of the masonry at Harran. Only when one has walked up through the outer workings is the industrial scale of the workings fully apparent. Cuttings in the rock reveal much about the methods of the quarrymen. The silence of the place is broken only by the wind and by the distant rumble of a passing car.

The road continues, to cross a gentle plain, in the centre of which, some 26 kilometres / 16 miles from Harran, is the mellow ruin – in a golden stone that may well have come from the quarries – of a caravanserai, the Han el-Barür, built in 1229 by Husameddin ed-Din, grandson of the Salkutid, Izz ed-Din, on what was no doubt a key route. The pointed gate on the north, with a fine cross-vault, opens to a long courtyard, flanked by the requisite buildings, of which those at the further end are substantially intact. The name of the han, 'caravanserai of the well', suggests why the site was chosen. There are hints of other buildings and reservoirs.

Eight kilometres / 5 miles further on, the road passes the remains of Şuayp Şehir, a cascade of post-Roman houses on the flank of a low hill. The most ambitious of the houses, Byzantine but with many of the appurtenances of late classical elegance, is on the northern slope. The place was little more than a large village. Its Christian inhabitants remained there for some three centuries

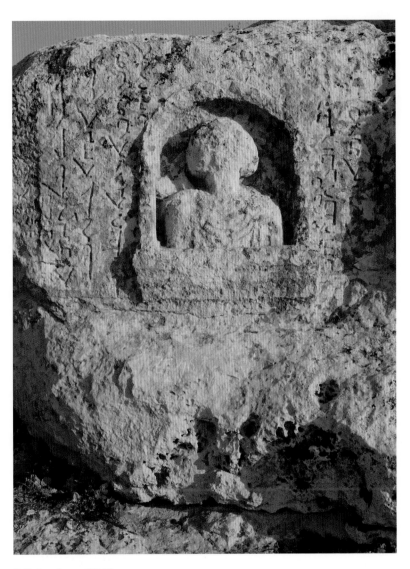

Relief, perhaps of Tiridates.

after the Arab conquest; subsequently the place was abandoned.

The road continues north for the turn to Sumatar, which is unquestionably one of the most atmospheric religious sites in Turkey. The side road passes a large tomb and between the Citadel Mound (on the left) and one of the series of low hills that surround the oval area flanked by the farms of the modern village. Sumatar was in the territory of the kingdom of Edessa, but was a centre for the worship of Sin, the moon god whose cult was established at Harran in the second millennium BC and endured there under Assyrian, Babylonian and Roman rule.

The main shrine at Sumatar was on the hill immediately to the south of the Citadel Mound. This was dedicated in AD 165 by a Tiridates, who is otherwise unknown. Two reliefs, a bust portrait (perhaps of Tiridates), and a full-length in a shell niche are carved into the low stratum of rock that crests the hill, and there are numerous Syriac inscriptions. The horizon is punctuated by the hills surrounding the site, and it is not difficult to understand something of the meaning these must have had to worshippers of the moon and the planets. Four lie in an arc to the south. More or less directly to the west, beyond a lower hillock with a mausoleum, is one with the lower courses of a circular structure of some distinction. There are other mausolea, mostly very ruined, possibly deliberately, on five of the six hills that encircle the village to the north, on the lower slopes of which a number of excavations and tombs can be seen. A rock-cut farm complex is below the northernmost hill. Near the centre of the valley, cut back into its western side, is a substantial excavated chamber with, on its back and side walls, second-century whole-length portrait reliefs, in a very primitive taste, of Tiridates's son Rinai and other local worthies, and, flanking the central niche on the west wall, representations apparently of Sin himself, crowned by a crescent. There is some evidence that the worship of Sin at Harran endured at least until the eleventh century, but it is difficult to believe that this survived at Sumatar into the Byzantine era.

51
RUM KALE

❖

T. E. LAWRENCE, who wrote so eloquently about it, might not immediately recognize Rum Kale, so known for the reddish colour of the rock on which it stands and from which it was largely constructed. The fortress itself survives. But the flooding of the Euphrates valley has transformed its context. The lower half of the cliffs on which the fortress stands, as well as the low ground below these, has been submerged. The position was well chosen, a steep promontory where the Merzuman flowed into the former gorge of the Euphrates. Origi-nally part of the principality of Edessa, Rum Kale was from 1148 the seat of the Armenian patriarchate and became a key Christian outpost in an area that had been taken by Muslim rulers.

In 1292 the castle fell to the Mamelukes, for whom it was also a key frontier post, which explains why they girdled the top of the carefully scarped cliffs with an impressive horseshoe of walls, of which the northern section is particularly ingenious with one gallery supported by another. The rock was cut away at the bases of many of the towers and the narrow southern end of the site was defended in the time-honoured manner of the Near East by a deep rock-cut ditch. The main entrance was from the valley of the Merzuman to the west, defended

Rum Kale from the north-west.

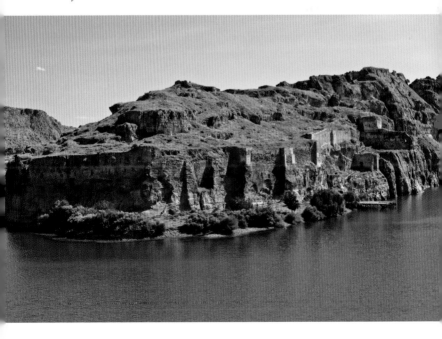

by a small outer gatehouse and a more impressive inner gatehouse of ingenious form with splendid bossed masonry. There is a smaller postern though a tower on the east, to which steps now lead. The area within the walls, which rises to a ridge of rock, was occupied by the upper town. A number of buildings can be identified, including a church, evidently dating from the Armenian period, near which there is a large levelled area, and further north the remains of a palace, which seems to have replaced a second church in the late eighteenth century.

Inevitably the fortifications are most impressive from outside, and thus best seen now by boat. There are regular cruises from Halfeti to the south, on the opposite bank of the swollen river, but it is more satisfactory to come from the west and hire one of the small boats at the successor of Kasaba, the ancient settlement on the opposite bank of the Merzuman. Kasaba was also a place of some size, and numerous structures cut into the cliff can be explored. Kasaba itself has been flooded, as has the lower town that formerly hung at the foot of the cliffs of Rum Kale, but of which very little remained.

Rum Kale served as a prison in early Ottoman times, but gradually dwindled in importance, perhaps because of declining traffic. The Armenians were apparently still able to use the church. Local rulers, including a Kurd, enjoyed a degree of autonomy in the eighteenth century. Subsequently Ottoman rule was reasserted. In 1832, when Muhammed Ali, the usurper of Egypt, sought to conquer Syria, the place was bombarded by and fell to his general, Ibrahim Pasha. Although Rum Kale was recovered by the Ottomans after eight years, it lost its administrative role in 1870. Later visitors saw a vast and largely abandoned fortress that still bore the scars of Ibrahim's artillery. The flooding of the Euphrates has now changed its setting, and yet one could argue that in some ways, for most sightseers, any loss is balanced by the pleasure of seeing the sculpted cliffs and the walls that crown these reflected in the water.

52

THREE MAUSOLEA AND A ROMAN BRIDGE

❖

THE evidence of the past is omnipresent in Anatolia; and one of the pleasures of sightseeing in Turkey is to observe the patterns of this in what is inevitably a living landscape. To reach Kasaba for Rum Kale from Gaziantep it is necessary to cut through the undulating land to the west of the Euphrates, turning off the road to Adiyaman at Yavuzeli. At Kuzayatagi a side road on the left heads northwards for a group of three villages, each with a substantial mausoleum that remind us that the Romans, who made Zeugma to the south on the river a key transport hub, founded or took over numerous other settlements in the area.

Start with Hasanóglu. The solid base of the mausoleum was surmounted by a pyramid, now fallen, supported on angle piers with fluted Corinthian pilasters that were echoed by smaller ones flanking the arched central openings. Shaken by time, the restrained elegance of the mausoleum is only enhanced by the power lines that now festoon it. By contrast, the larger and more complete mausoleum at nearby Hisar has been rather officiously tidied up, the pyramidal roof reconstructed. Far more appealing is the smaller mausoleum at Elifköy a few miles to the north, which has the advantage of being on the fringe of the modern village whose inhabitants seem slightly surprised by the arrival of a stray visitor. Above the base, which has a door to the tomb chamber on the south side, angle piers with pairs of Corinthian pilasters on their outer sides support a concave pyramid surmounted by a large Corin-

thian capital, now shaken out of alignment.

The mausolea all lay close to the key Roman road to Commagene. A few miles north of Elikòy this crossed the Karasu ('Blackwater'), a lesser tributary of the Euphrates which when swollen by the spring floods was a formidable obstacle, by a bridge. Early bridges are among the glories of Turkey. This is a relatively modest example and of the four arches only one and part of another survive. The extant arch is of the Severan period, but the bridge was apparently restored under the Mamelukes. The large blocks of the lower courses of the piers have inevitably been eroded, but part of the upper masonry has fared better, mel-

The mausoleum at Elifköy.

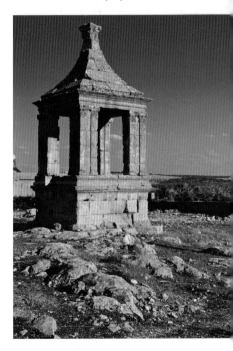

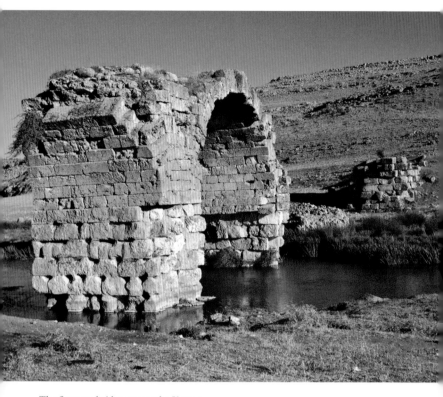

The Severan bridge across the Karasü.

lowed to a golden brown. Broken as it is, the bridge has a timeworn elegance. Sheep graze on the slope to the south and the lengthening shadows of a late afternoon give it a beauty denied to many of its more ambitious counterparts.

A road to the west runs to Araban north-east of Yavuzeli. To the north of the town a tell rises dramatically from the plain, as if to remind us that the Romans and the builders of Rum Kale were no more than interlopers in its territory.

53
GAZIANTEP

❖

RADIATING from its citadel on an ancient tell, Gaziantep, the ancient Ayntab, was a place of some consequence in the Crusader county of Edessa. It grew under the Ayyubids and the Mamelukes, and continued to prosper under Ottoman rule. The oval fortress, with a curtain wall reinforced by numerous towers, is substantially of the Mameluke period. The open area to the south is flanked on the east by a substantial han and by the Tahtali mosque, rebuilt in 1578 for Osman Paşa, governor of Maras. West of the citadel is the unassuming Şirvani Cami, and below it, to the north, are a hamam and another mosque near the line of the river Sacur, now partly covered over. Gaziantep's numerous mosques are widely scattered. Most are of Ottoman date and have affinities with the architecture of Aleppo. To the south-west on an outlying hill, behind the high-rise buildings lining the main streets and beyond the Ataturk Monument, is an area with numerous eighteenth- and nineteenth-century houses, built for the Armenian merchants. They paid for a substantial cathedral, to which the Catholics in about 1890 responded with their now gun-shot, battered church on Atatürk Bulvari.

It is not, however, for its monuments that Gaziantep draws the tourist of today. The city has been a beneficiary of the Birecik dam on the Euphrates, which led to the flooding of most of the major Roman city of Zeugma. The site, on the right bank of the great river, had been inhabited long before the Seleucids recognized its strategic importance as what would now be termed a transport hub, where the route that followed the river crossed the main road to the east, and which thus linked their capitals of Antioch and Seleucia on the Tigris. The Romans stationed a legion at Zeugma, and although this was sacked by Shapur in 256 it remained a place of some consequence until the eleventh century.

Until it was under threat, Zeugma was a dusty place which had little of interest to the casual sightseer: eroded walls on the acropolis hill and efficiently robbed tombs of little visual interest. Few could have guessed that the excavators would find mosaics of exceptional distinction. The number and importance of these fully justified the construction of the impressive Zeugma Mosaic Museum in the northern part of Gaziantep.

Archaeological Museum, Roman mosaic, from Zeugma.

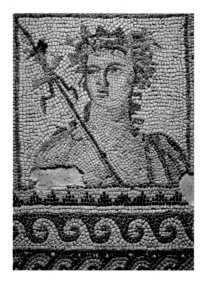

The mosaics are mostly of the second and third centuries. Starting from the west end of the huge main hall, the visitor sees a sequence of mosaics from a number of houses, many of which have been partly reconstructed. The tone is set by a fine representation of *Oceanus and Tethys* from the House of Oceanus (the house names are due to the archaeologists). From the Euphrates Villa there are murals of rather moderate quality and a good mosaic of a reclining river god. The Poseidon Villa, to judge from its mosaics, was of particular splendour: that of Neptune surrounded by fish is outstanding; while a *Birth of Venus* is, most exceptionally, signed by its creator, Zosimus of Samosata. Some of the mosaics have distinguished borders: thus a *Cupid and Psyche* is surrounded by one of acanthus scrolling round a bearded head and fruit of every kind. The most sophisticated in composition is perhaps the *Dionysius and Ariadne* from the House of Diogenes. But it is often in the smaller compartments with bust-length figures that the technique is most effective. Set apart, in a darkened room on the upper floor, is an unusually expressive, albeit fragmentary, head of Terpsichore, open-eyed and with windblown hair. Despite the theatrical display she brings her lost world to momentary life.

54

YESEMEK

QUARRIES are among the most atmospheric survivors of antiquity. Yesemek, on the eastern flank of the rift valley between the mountains of the Amanus and the Kürd Dağ, is a quarry of a highly unusual type. The availability of workable blocks of basalt on a readily accessible and gently sloping site meant that Yesemek became a sculpture workshop on an almost industrial scale. Activity may have begun late in the second millennium BC during the Hittite period, and lasted until the eighth century BC, when the area was part of the neo-Hittite kingdom of Sam'al.

Above the modern village, the visitor crosses a footbridge to an enclosure with recent terraces on which sculptures rescued from outlying areas of the site are arranged. These include examples of the main types: lions, of which the majority are shown from the front only; highly stylized sphinxes; and paired mountain gods, some separated by solar discs. The forms are roughly blocked out, although in many cases details are indicated. But clearly the sculptures would have been completed only after these had reached their destination. Further up, the hillside is strewn with boulders. Among these are more lion heads and sphinxes, with a few paired deities, often set at unexpected angles. There are two much larger recumbent lions intended to flank gateways and sections of a relief of a chariot being used for a hunt.

The low December morning sun creeps round, and catches the mask of a sphinx or the stylized features of a lion. The sounds of cattle being herded

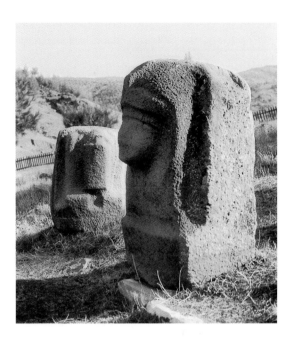

*A sphinx, a less finished
one behind.*

through the village below and the bells of the flocks being driven out to pasture remind one that farming must always have been the mainstay of the local economy, but yet that it must in early times have been sufficiently vigorous to support the sculptors of Yesemek. These worked within settled conventions; they set no store by originality, as indicated by the repetitive forms of so many of the unfinished blocks that litter the hillside at Yemesek. The Hittites and their successors had very different priorities; but, one wonders, what political or religious cataclysm caused demand for the sculptures of Yesemek to fail while so many were still unfinished?

Most visitors to Yesemek arrive or leave by the road from Islahiye, which passes within 2 kilometres / 1.2 miles of a major Hittite site in the rift valley, Tilmen Hüyük, on a low tell protected at either side by the river Karaso and a subsidiary channel. Well sited for defence, Tilmen Hüyük controlled what must have long been a productive plain at the northern end of the valley. Italian excavations have exposed successive layers of construction. But for the amateur the most exciting complex on the tell is the so-called palace at the southern side. This is believed to have been built in three stages between the eighteenth and the thirteenth centuries BC. The palace was largely constructed in mud brick, but the extant masonry of the footings is of excellent quality: there is a handsome gate at the west end; and, in the northern section of the palace, a fine suite of rooms is linked by impressive door jambs with drilled holes for the upper attachments that have long since been lost.

55

BAGRAS AND CURSAT

BAGRAS, in some ways the most impressive Crusader castle in Turkey, was built to control the strategic Belen Pass, the 'Syrian Gates', and thus was crucial to the defence of Antioch. Perched on a rock above a precipice, it must before the advent of artillery have seemed impregnable. And the Templars who held the place from 1153 took steps to ensure that it was, comprehensively subsuming an earlier fortress. Saladin, who conquered Bagras in 1188, demolished the vulnerable south-eastern defences on hearing three years later of the approach of the Second Crusade. In the wake of this, Bagras was seized by King Leon II of Armenian Cilicia. The castle was partly rebuilt before Leon was forced to return it to the Templars, who also restored it. They retained Bagras until the Mameluke conquest of Antioch in 1268. The place still had a certain importance in early Ottoman times. The caravanserai below the village was only abandoned in the early twentieth century: the modern road passes its disintegrating husk.

To reach Bagras, it used to be necessary to walk up from the village that takes the place of the former town – a steep ascent overhung by the castle. But a new road now sweeps round from the south. From this approach, it is much easier to understand the layers of the complex. The original entrance was on the east. From this was reached the second level, built on to the natural rock and defended by a spectacular outer gallery, of the kind familiar from other Crusader castles. A series of buildings

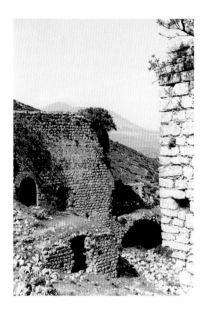

Bagras, the Great Hall of the Templars from the Chapel.

open off the irregular central courtyard. From the upper level of this is reached the Great Hall, the design of which so perfectly expresses the dignified austerity of Templar architecture. The main door, the windows – originally barred – and the internal niches are all of the most satisfying simplicity. And the ambition of the space is self-evident. Opposite is the chapel, rebuilt by Leon II, which has lost its east end and is less rigorous in detail. Behind this is the southern tower, again of Templar build, with windows of a redder and more finely cut stone than the walls.

From the outer walls – or the roof of the hall – one can see precisely why the position of Bagras was chosen, both for defence and for aggression. Sounds rise from the village below: the muezzin, occasional traffic. Before leaving, follow the track to the west, which gradually descends to a tapestry of fields, and turn to see how perfectly the Templar defences exploit the outcrop, which in turn dictated their scale. That so much of Bagras can still be understood is the more remarkable in that little has been done to the place since Mameluke times and it has, thus far, been spared the attentions of the restorer. The setting, however, is not unscathed, as there is a windfarm on the hill to the north.

Bagras was only one of the fortresses that protected Antioch. Half-way to the city, on a terrace crowning a low hill to the west of the modern road, the tower of Alahan was well placed to monitor unauthorized movement. Beyond Antioch, nestling in a beautiful wooded valley, is the episcopal castle of Cursat, now Koz Kalesi, which had been fortified during the earlier Arab occupation. The position was well chosen, protected on its long northern and slender eastern flanks by the steep wall of a valley and to the west by a less precipitous slope. On the south side the rock was partly quarried away to create a moat. The small early towers seem insignificant beside the Crusaders' most obvious contributions: the great curved south-west tower, of honey-coloured horizontally banded masonry rising above its paler footing carved from the natural rock, and the partly fallen tower, of equally meticulous masonry, to the east of this. The main entrance at the north-west corner is reached by a ramp – the gate now designed to keep sheep in rather than tourists out. But, as the local boys well know, steps up the side of the corner tower lead to an opening to the corridor that runs round three sides of the structure; the vault is handled with a vigorous

economy. There follows a dark ramp – the steps worn away – from which a metal construction makes it possible to scramble up into the castle. One arm of the corridor of the second great tower is readily accessible, and what remains of the major room can, with some difficulty, be surveyed. Further round there is an apparently reasonably well-preserved cistern complex, compromised by fallen masonry, and an unusually long vaulted room lit by arrowslits. The one advantage of being escorted by a swarm of boys is the effect of their swinging burning branches to help you, and themselves, avoid the piles of fallen masonry in the dark. The scale of such a storeroom as much as the ingenuity of its defences helps to explain why Cursat was able to hold out against the Mamelukes until 1275, seven years after the fall of Antioch.

Cursat, from the south-west.

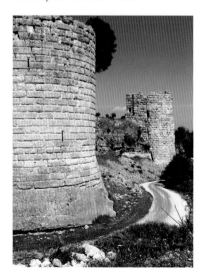

56

ANTAKYA

✿

REFOUNDED in about 300 BC by Seleucus I Nicator and named after his father, Antioch was for some fifteen hundred years a major entrepôt between east and west. From 64 BC the city was the capital of Roman Syria, and it flourished under the long Pax Romana, outshone only by Rome itself and by Alexandria. Disasters struck in the sixth century AD, with a severe earthquake and a Persian invasion. Justinian restored and refortified the city, but it passed to Persian and Arab conquerors, and was not recovered for Byzantium until 969. The Seljuks invested Antioch in 1084. For the rapacious Franks in the army of Bohemond who captured Antioch after a determined siege in 1098, she must have seemed an extraordinary prize, a great walled city stretching from the east bank of the Orontes right up the slopes of Mounts Silpius and Staurin. The Crusader principality in its turn fell to the Mamelukes in 1268, and Antioch entered a long period of decline, which was not arrested by the Ottoman conquest of 1516.

Classical Antioch comes to life in the new Archaeological Museum in the north of the town. This is justly famous for the mosaics found by Princeton University in a series of campaigns in the 1930s. Some of these came from within the ancient city, but the majority are from the nearby suburb of Daphne, now Harbiye. Taken together these offer an extraordinary idea of the luxury of Roman provincial life. Some, like that of the *Seasons*, or the Hunt from Yahto, are on the most ambitious scale. The *Iphige-*

nia from a house on Mount Staurin, datable to around AD 200, is notably effective in the way that light defines the figures. The so-called 'buffet mosaic' shows Ganymede surrounded by a border with the successive courses of a substantial feast; an equally fine *Narcissus* came from the same villa. The merchants of Antioch knew the importance of the sea. Oceanus was clearly a popular subject: the mosaic showing the god and Thetis with representatives of the months is particularly good, but equally interesting to modern taste is the black fisherman, intended to ward off the evil eye. More unexpected is the so-called *Boat of the Psyches*, with Eros and two girls with butterfly wings. The finest of the classical sculptures is a relatively recent arrival, a marvellously preserved sarcophagus of the Sidemara type, of about AD 250. The figures on the sides are of great refinement and the almost wafer-thin carving of the decorative elements is of an extreme precision. The unfinished head of the effigy of the woman on the lid – that of her husband is broken off – reminds us that in the workshop near Afyon which specialized in sarcophagi of the kind it was expected that the portraits of the defunct would be supplied locally. There is also a Roman copy of the *Crouching Venus*. Works of other periods include neo-Hittite sculptures from Tel Tayinat (eighth century BC).

Further evidence of early Antioch can be seen on the lower cliffs of Mount Staurin, including necropolises and the much-eroded Charonion, a 4.5-metre/ 15-foot-high bust of a goddess, datable to the late Seleucid period. This is most easily reached from the entrance to the complex that now surrounds the enlarged cave church, which from an early date was associated with St Peter, who is known to have visited Antioch. In the church, there are fragments of a simple Byzantine mosaic floor with a cross motif. The visitor can decide whether the façade is of the thirteenth century, as one writer has suggested, or was built in 1863 at the instance of Pope Pius IX and with the financial support of the Emperor Napoleon III, as is more plausibly stated on the spot.

For the energetic sightseer, a walk up the valley to the south of the church, which divides Mount Staurin from Mount Silpius, is the most rewarding experience of Antioch. From the wadi

bed there are two options: the first and longer is to take a rough footpath above the highest houses on the left bank; the second to make up the bank on the right by obscure paths to the ancient road which runs along the foot of the cliff face and is in places cut into this. The road turns a corner through a cutting wide enough for wheeled traffic. Ahead is the spectacular viaduct-dam across the gorge. The lower section is of stone with courses of brick and a great arch of brick, probably of the early fifth century. The decision to dam the stream may have been taken under Justinian. The upper part of the masonry is no later than the

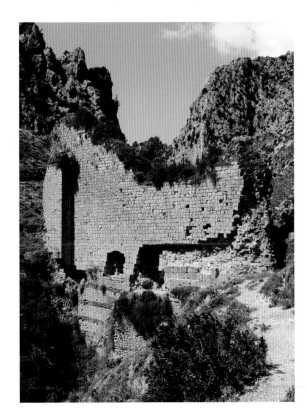

The Byzantine viaduct-dam.

early sixth century; the two arched openings served as sluices and a narrow walkway, still in use, enabled the dam to be crossed at this level. To the east, the Byzantine wall can be seen clinging to the flank of Mount Staurin, at the top of which there is a small tower.

The main path keeps to the right of the dam, mounting a dry streambed on the right where the valley turns to the east. The long stretch of wall that crests the northern ridge of Mount Silpius comes into view. A gate is soon seen, high on the right. It is easy enough to reach this, but thorn bushes make the precipitous climb up the wall anything but pleasant. The easier option is to continue up the rough path to a point at which the gate is out of sight and then, where the path itself seems to peter out, to cut upwards to the right. After a minute or two, a straight stretch of wall is seen. Make for the highest point of this, marked where it turns to the east by a substantial tower, which is the northernmost point of the Byzantine citadel. Take care with the scree.

After the drama of the climb, the citadel may come as something of a disappointment. The position was well chosen. The cliffs to the north-west – now on your right – were impregnable; set back, thus to the left, is a stretch of the original city wall. After their recovery of Antioch in 969, the Byzantines, under Nicephorus Phocas, threw out a wall enclosing a roughly triangular space to defend the high ground to the east. Visually more interesting is the later wall ahead, with seven rounded bastions at a right angle to the precipice. From the west one looks down to the modern city, stretching now far beyond its historic limits; even in December pinks are in flower. The walk onwards, partly through a pinewood, is not arduous, but, one tower apart, the wall has been systematically robbed. The citadel is seen to best advantage in afternoon light and those who don't care for scrambling would do best to drive, following the signs to the Kalesi off the Altınözü road, and then walk northwards through the trees.

Antioch has a Christian present. The imposing nineteenth-century Greek Orthodox church is almost in sight of the surprisingly ambitious Protestant establishment; and both are within 90 metres/100 yards of the most congenial of the city's hotels, the Antik Beyazit. Much is now made of St Peter for the benefit of the tourist, but at Antioch in Byzantine times St Simeon the Younger counted for far more. In 551 he established himself as a stylite in a monastery inspired by that of his earlier namesake at Qalaat Semaan near Aleppo. He remained there until his death in 592, buffeted no doubt by the winds that now power the turbines of the windfarm that surrounds the site on the summit of the Samandağ. The partly rock-cut complex was originally reached through a hall on the west, which opened on to the octagonal court surrounding the column. The monastery became a major centre of pilgrimage, so that two additional churches had to be built at either side of it to the east of the column. The approach is memorable, and so are the views from the monastery, with Mount Cassius and the coast to the south-west and in the east the Orontes valley with, in the distance, Antioch, now hazed by pollution, at the foot of Mount Silpius. The light is at its most perfect in the evening and a visit to the monastery is a happy sequel to a day at Seleucia Pieria.

57
SELEUCIA PIERIA

SELEUCIA PIERIA was founded by Seleucus I Nicator as the port of Antioch. The position he chose could in many respects hardly be bettered. The upper town cascaded down a southern outlier of the Musa Dağ, commanding views over the lower town round the harbour, with the fertile coastal plain north of the mouth of the Orontes beyond and the wonderful silhouette of Mount Cassius. Nowhere can this prospect be better enjoyed than from what remains – part of the podium and a few fluted column drums – of the early Doric temple. Seleucia was surrounded by an extensive defensive wall, sections of which are well preserved. The importance of the port is indicated by the scale of the mole. Part of this survives at full height, and the cuttings for metal clamps can be seen in exposed blocks of the lower courses. And, as is demonstrated by the many tombs, some of vast scale, cut into the cliffs between the upper and the lower towns, and in the extraordinary complex known as Beşikli Mağara, Seleucia's richer inhabitants had extravagant tastes.

But by the first century AD, it was clear that Seleucia's very *raison d'être* was threatened. The stream that flowed down through the town was progressively silting up the harbour. The problem must have been severe. For it inspired one of the major engineering feats of antiquity. A channel large enough to take the full force of the winter floodwaters was tunnelled through the hill north of the lower town and cut into the bedrock below this to divert the water well away from the harbour. Only

when the channel was completed could the original course of the stream be blocked with a dam. As the proud inscription 'DIVVS VESPASIANVS / ET DIVVS TITVS / F C' implies, the project was begun under the Emperor Vespasian (AD 69–79) and his co-Emperor Titus.

The visitor today arrives at the rather scruffy resort of Çevlik to take a road on the right that reaches the channel just above the point where this debouches into a large excavated area behind the modern village. Those who do not like scrambling can follow a path, but it is more satisfying, at least in the dry summer months, to walk up the channel,

The Roman deflection-tunnel from the west.

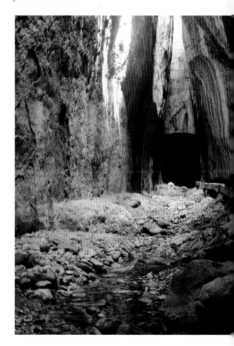

which gradually rises. There is a damaged bridge, of rock left uncut when the channel was excavated. Further on, to the right, is a section where the rock was cut away in post-Byzantine times, apparently in a deliberate attempt to damage the harbour. The going gets rougher, the excavated walls higher, as the contour rises. Then the channel is crossed by the elegant arch of an aqueduct. Beside this there is a flight of steps, well preserved at the top where they have been less exposed to floodwater. There follows a stretch with yet higher flanking walls and then the first, brief, section of tunnel: this seems not to have been cut to surface level because of the robust quality of the rock which emerges on the hillside above, but is no higher than the ensuing open section, some 46 metres/150 feet high. Here the gap between the sides narrows so that they almost meet above.

The final section, of some 137 metres/ 150 yards, which bends to the left, is tunnelled through the higher part of the ridge, emerging in the cliff face. Beyond, on the left, is the Emperors' inscription. Ahead are small fields, the productivity of which must still owe much to the silt of two millennia which has built up against the great Roman dam that diverted the stream into the tunnel. One's admiration for the vision and willpower that saw the project through is tempered by thoughts for the luckless prisoners from Judea who were put to work on it.

58

KARATEPE

❖

THE remains of Karatepe, set in a pinewood in a nature park east of the Cilician plain, introduce us to an unfamiliar neo-Hittite world. But we can profitably go back in time more gradually: the approach road passes the charming Roman site of Hierapolis Castabala, with a colonnaded street, fringed in spring by wild flowers, leading towards a tree-shadowed theatre that in turn rises above the eroded brick husk of a bath. The site is overhung by a rocky acropolis, protected on its further side by a rock-cut ditch that served also as a road, crowned now by a modest Armenian fortress. Like this, the eighth-century BC palace-fortress of Karatepe must have been intended to control the eastern march of Cilicia. But its hill that once stood high above a deep valley rises now from the artificial lake that has swallowed the somewhat earlier fortress of Domuztepe, itself refortified in Roman times, and a small Crusader castle that was part of the defences of the short-lived county of Edessa.

Although the site had been occupied earlier, Karatepe was the creation of King Asitawata, ruler of a minor kingdom that had emerged in the aftermath of the decline of the Hittite empire, who himself was a vassal of the Cilician king. The confidence implied by the king's inscriptions was misplaced. Within a century, his kingdom was swept away by the Assyrians. And Karatepe was abandoned. It was not discovered until 1947.

The visit begins with the museum, outside which are two lions salvaged from Domuztepe: among the exhibits are some eroded reliefs from Domuztepe – one of which was reused in the Roman period – and numerous small finds from Karatepe. A path leads uphill to the restored walls, the lower courses of parts of which survive. The west, or palace, gate is remarkable. Quite correctly the vertical orthostats that line the walls of the entrance ramp and the chamber within, carved with figures and animals shown in profile in low relief and with inscriptions, have been left in place, protected by a visually un-intrusive structure. The original visitor will have been left in no doubt of Asitawata's power. On the left of the outer section the king is shown at a table: servants attend him and visitors proffer gifts. Priests and officials are shown in other reliefs. More appealing are scenes of less elevated life: two people fishing in a small boat; a man with a paddle; birds and animals. Oddly mesmerizing, if unreadable to the uninitiated, are the elegant inscriptions in the Luwian script of the Hittites. Within the gate is a colossal statue of a king on a pedestal carved with lions.

A path leads across the now thickly wooded centre of Karatepe down to the east, or lower, gate, which also is decorated with reliefs. The reliefs of the chamber include one of a boat with reefed sails and oarsmen – a reminder of the importance of the maritime trade – and another of an ox being sacrificed, as well as hunting scenes. At the top of the ramp, the door is flanked by a pair of sphinxes. On either side there are further reliefs, the subjects of which are as oddly juxtaposed as any at Karatepe. Thus, on the left, the sphinx is followed by a block with a king and a deer; by a startling full-face winged sun-god; by a standing woman nursing her child; by a hunting scene; by a block with two lions trapping

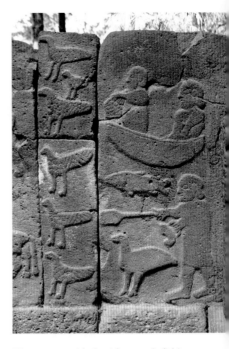

The west gate, block with a couple fishing from a boat, a man with a paddle, birds and a fish.

a man and vultures above; by one of a bear being hunted; by an inscribed orthostat; by a fearsome god, again in full-face which the sculptor clearly found challenging in low relief, naked and with an implausibly long penis; and finally by a statue of a lion, to which there is a pair on the opposite, south, wall. We should not suppose that the arrangement was accidental. Outside the gate, where the ground falls away, the walls were placed to take full advantage of the slope. The views that these commanded are blocked by tangled woodland, so that even the lake is invisible. In spring fiercely blue irises grow beside the path back to the museum.

59
ANAVARZA

❖

JAGGED hills erupt from the Cilician plain, none more dramatically than that below which the town of Anazarbus lay. The place came to prominence in the first century BC and, although the local ruler, Tarcondimotus, had renamed it in honour of Augustus in 19 BC, it was only in the following century that Rome took control. By AD 207 Anazarbus ranked with Tarsus as a metropolis, and under the Emperor Theodosius (408–50) it was the main city of the province of Cilicia Secunda. In the eighth century Arabs wrenched control from the Byzantines, who regained it, only to lose it to the Armenian Prince Thoros I, whose capital the city became in 1100. The Byzantines later retook Anazarbus, but it was recovered by Thoros II. In 1293 King Hetum and his nephew were murdered there – despite their alliance with the Mongols – by a Mongol convert to Islam; and in 1374 Anazarbus was with Sis one of the last Armenian fortresses to fall to the Mamelukes, whose work of destruction is ironically responsible for the survival of so much of the early city.

Most visitors approach from the south by the Ceyhan road, and then turn eastwards towards the cluster of hills that enfold the town to the east and the south. The ridge ahead bristles with fortifications. The road meets the line of the late Roman walls by a reasonably well-preserved gate. The walls encircle a level area, roughly oval, that extends to the bottom of the cliff to the east. Within this are a number of buildings: a crumbling bath complex of brick and the shattered carcass of a large basilica nearby, occa-sional walls and aligned column drums. In winter the soil is a dark brown, but in the spring sheep and cattle graze among the lush nettles. Always one is aware of the looming presence of the cliff. In this, north of the walls, some 27 metres/30 yards up, is a cavern in which there was a pre-Roman shrine to Zeus, Hera and Ares. The substantial Roman aqueduct strides off majestically to the north, the extant arches hanging with stalactites after two millennia's exposure of their porous stone: only six arches are intact, but the stumps of others can be followed for some miles across the plain. At the southern end of the city a substantial section of the main colonnaded street has recently been cleared. This leads to the imposing triumphal arch, of fine ashlar and tufa on a concrete core, thought to be of the period of Septimius Severus. Further south, outside the wall, is the stadium. On the north side this may have been no more than a wooden structure, but at the back it was cut in two places into the hillside: the benches here are well preserved, and above these there are holes in the rock face for the wooden supports of the awnings. Remarkably, the central spina is in place. On the slope behind the stadium are some of Anazarbus's many tombs. Beyond the western end of the stadium, placed in a curve of the hillside, are the surviving sections of the amphitheatre.

To the east of the stadium the line of the southern hill falls away: at the lowest point, in late Roman or Byzantine times, it was quarried through, both to cut off access to the acropolis hill and to create a convenient road to the east. There is a

The Roman town overhung by the Armenian fortress.

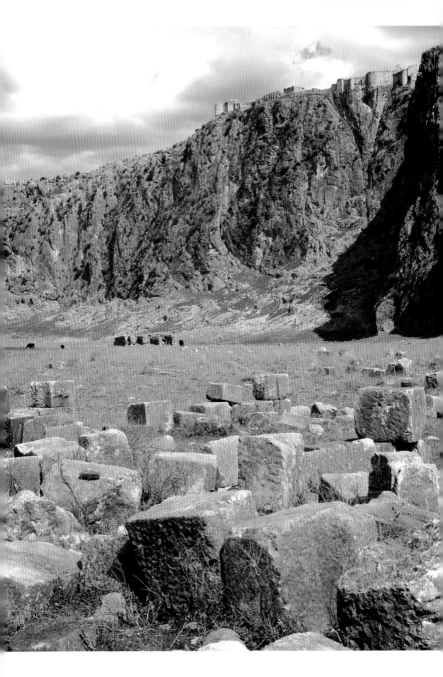

cross with an associated inscription on the south wall of the rock, and in the slopes of the wide valley beyond are yet more tombs. Returning to the city, take a path rising on the right to the substantial wreckage of the theatre. Behind this are tombs. On one there is a crudely executed relief: one gymnast supports another doing a handstand, while two others wrestle, the pair separated by their trainer. This is to the south-east of the theatre, in the lower group of tombs.

Behind the theatre, an ancient rock-cut path, with steps that vary from less than one metre to over two metres in width, climbs up towards the prodigious fortifications that are the most memorable feature of Anavarza. The position lent itself to defence. To the west, over the town, the cliffs fall vertiginously; to the east the drop, although less dramatic, gave an almost equal advantage. Only from the south, despite the rising rock-strewn ground, was attack in overwhelming force feasible. A great wall built of spoil from the Roman and Byzantine town was thrown across the flank of the hill, apparently in the eighth century during Haroun al-Raschid's Arab occupation. The rock-cut steps lead to the gate in this.

By the time the Armenians retook Anazarbus, ideas about fortifications had developed. Their solution was to rebuild the section of the wall east of the gate, with four circular towers, the largest at the south-eastern corner. The masonry is bossed; there is a well-preserved battlement walk and the rooms inside the towers are of fine quality. On one occasion, as I came down a flight of steps, a shepherd appeared. We shared my chocolate and he explained that he was a student. He was surprisingly well informed about the place, and certainly cared a great deal more about it than the self-styled 'paratroop commander' who had overtaken me on a previous visit.

The great Armenian wall – which is particularly impressive when seen from the south – is continued, albeit less spectacularly, on the east side of the hill, and there is a garderobe ('whay jay', WC, as my self-appointed guide explained). Near the south-east corner of the enceinte is the Church of the Armenian Kings. Part of an inscription survives on the eastern wall and there are scattered blocks with sections of the text nearby. In the apse there are worn fragments of murals, including the wing of an angel (or, as the student-shepherd would have it, a 'burrd').

The ground tapers as it rises. At the top, beyond a rock-cut ditch that must once have been crossed by a drawbridge, is a majestic tower faced with reused marble blocks. An inscription records that this was built in 1188 by Leon II. There are three storeys, the topmost a barrel-vaulted gallery that can be seen from below. A door in the side wall to the left admits to the impressive vaulted entrance hall: on the ceiling are two blocks marked with arrows, for which there is no obvious explanation.

Across a second rock-hewn moat is the second enceinte, enclosing a smaller area than the first, which slopes more emphatically to the west. There is much of interest: a postern that has a portcullis to the east; a long passage with two carved capitals, the finer of stylized flowers; a small chapel; and, on the west, a series of subterranean stores and cisterns. Most memorable of all is a room of modest size with a window, the base of which is almost level with the floor. The rock seems to project and one has the sense of hanging above the abandoned city, and reading it like a map on which the stumps of columns mark the intersections of the streets. One sees too the lines of both the aqueducts, Roman and Byzantine, stretching away across the level ground.

The highest point of the fortress is marked by another substantial tower. But this is not the end. For the wall continues along the crest of the ridge, turning as the rock dictated, descending to rise again, with further towers, before running down to the narrow watershed with the hill to the north and struggling once again upwards. Only the most agile should endeavour to follow it.

Anavarza used to be remote. Derek Hill, who had camped there, was rather shocked when I admitted to visiting it from a comfortable hotel in Yumurtalik, which, as Ayas, was the port that contributed so much to the Armenian exchequer. Today, most visitors are Turks. And part of the charm of the place is that it remains an unselfconscious village. An elderly man walks through the triumphal arch followed by his eight sheep; a woman lights a fire by the roadside; children are curious but not insistent; and the only echo of the turbulence of the past is the sudden eruption of a cockfight in a farmyard.

60

YILAN KALESI

❖

THE ARMENIANS of Cilicia did not forget the lessons of the loss of their native territory to the Seljuks. Their castles reveal how determined they were to protect the productive and strategically important land they had seized. Anavarza was a case apart, a capital where the survival of Roman and Byzantine buildings – and materials – allowed a degree of show of which there were fewer signs elsewhere.

Yilan Kalesi ('Castle of the Snake'), probably built under Leon II in the late twelfth century, exemplifies Armenian defensive building. It denied access to the Cilician heartland from the coastal plain. The ridge of rock on which the castle stands rises above the west bank of the river Ceyhan, the classical Pyramus, at a point where it snakes round to pass between this outcrop and a larger group of hills to the south, before flowing southwards to the great Roman bridge repaired by Justinian at Misis. A modern side road rises to a saddle and from here there is a steep path to the castle.

There are three lines of defence. The path reaches a gate in a wall with round towers of characteristic roughly bossed masonry which bars the way between two cliff faces. Yet steeper is the route to the second gate, with a portcullis, flanked by more imposing towers. A final scramble leads upwards to the main gate, flanked by a large round tower and another projecting from a massive block with the handsome rectangular entrance. The main enclosure is slung between the summit on which it stands and another of similar height to the east. On the south

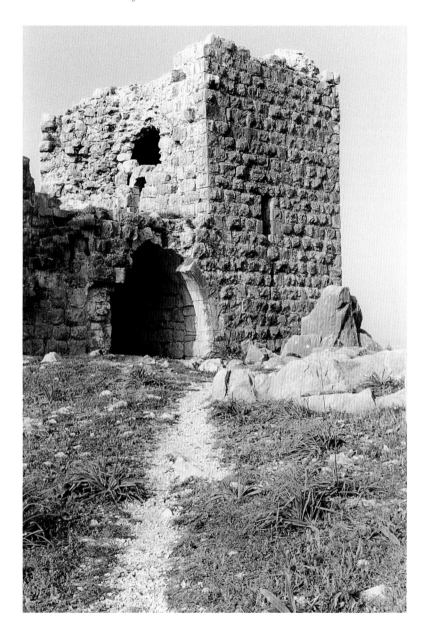

Yilan Kalesi: the keep.

the enclosure is protected by cliffs, to the north by a powerful wall that follows the contour of the rock. Within there are a massive vaulted cistern, to which steps descend, and storerooms. On the south side there is a small chapel. The finest surviving room is in the furthest tower, the keep. This is barrel-vaulted with a handsome door – once presumably accessible from a wooden stair – with beautifully arched openings for the arrow-slits and a garderobe served by a diagonal chute. On my first visit, a herdsboy showed me the way, in a helpful and uninterfering manner. He paused at one tower to clamour to his flock below; by the time he had shown me how to climb into the keep, his animals were beginning to charge through the main gate into the upper enclosure.

Some Armenian castles are equally accessible: for example Agzit, beyond Kadirli, once Flaviopolis, where a Byzantine church survives as a mosque. Others are more demanding. Tumlu, in sight of both Anavarza and Yilan Kalesi, is best reached by a postern high above a gully. Least accessible of all perhaps is Ak Kalesi, which commanded the pass from Kidirli to Andiron and thus a route to Seljuk territory. I lost my way clambering among the rocks, rewarded by cyclamen and primroses but not by the violets that grow so plentifully at Agzit. Appropriately, the grandest Armenian fortress of Cilicia is at Kazan, formerly Sis, which, like Anavarza, was conquered from the Byzantines by Thoros II. The castle he found, rising in three enclosures on its spine of rock, was strengthened by the Armenians, who, when their principality was elevated as the kingdom of Lesser Armenia in 1199, chose Sis as their capital. The great chamber in the main tower still gives some sense of its regal past.

61
ADANA
❖

THE INCLUSION of Adana in this survey may surprise: for it surprises me, as my own first impression was not encouraging. The town has grown exponentially, and yet somehow enough evidence of the past survives to offer that sense of continuity with the present that I find so rewarding.

Adana came to prominence when the Romans occupied Cilicia in the first century BC and became a significant staging post and subsequently a stronghold on the route through the Cilician Gates, between central Anatolia and Syria. Moreover, the city controlled the approach to the Cilician plain, Smooth Cilicia, from Rough, or Rugged, Cilicia to the west, where the Taurus mountains descend abruptly to the coast. The great Roman bridge across the river Sarus – now the Ceyhan, the Taş Köprü, 984 feet/300 metres in length – was a major engineering achievement. Apparently built by the 'mechanicus' Auxentius in the late fourth century AD, it was reconstructed under the Emperor Justinian by the Caliph Memoun and subsequently, so that not all the openings retain their Roman form. Now only reflected by the dam-tamed waters of the river, the bridge has recently been restored and still seems somehow to defy the towering Hilton Hotel on the eastern bank.

With the fall of Armenian Cilicia, Adana passed to the Mamelukes. The Ulu Cami, between the centre of the modern town and the great bridge, was begun in 1507 by Emir Halil of the Ramazanoğlu family, but only completed in 1541 by his grandson, Mustafa.

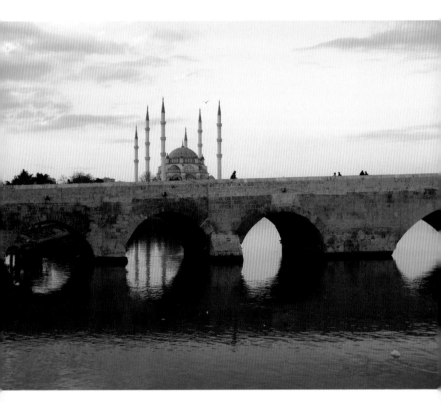

Adana: the Roman bridge with the Sabançi Mosque.

This is a singularly beautiful complex. There are two elegant polygonal minarets. The gate on the west, with wonderful stalactite decoration and two suspended pendants, opens to a corridor, of which the dome of the first section reflects the form of the very unusual stalactite-like outer structure. The portal on the east front is also finely decorated. The marble-paved courtyard has a triple arcade on the long northern side and a double one to the west.

The façade of the mosque is on the south, with three doors to the prayer hall. In this one is immediately struck by an unexpected chromatic richness. The mihrab is partly of marble, but the central section and the spectacular lunette above are set with magnificent tiles from Iznik. How efficiently orders for such commissions could be met at long distance is shown by the way in which the pattern fits the outer frame of the lunette and by the selection of smaller flowers for the narrow sections where this tapers. There is a clear hierarchy in the tiles that cover the lower sections of the walls of the mosque and which are consistently framed by bands of more strongly coloured tiles. Those on the south wall complement the decoration of the mihrab; those of the lateral walls are more restrained; while tiles from Kütahya with less expensive colours serve for the eastern part of the entrance wall, and for the room to the west, from which a small cemetery may be seen. The prayer hall has other treasures: an early wooden gallery and the marble mimber. To the left of the prayer hall, a window opens to the domed türbe, with more matching Kütahya tiles; the three tombs are also tiled. It is indeed the tiles that make the mosque so memorable and encourage one to linger, puzzling the guardian as he rolls out carpets in the courtyard and scrapes away the pigeon droppings.

South of the mosque are a number of associated buildings, including an elegant medrese of 1540 and the kulliye begun in 1493, which with a later türbe are clustered around a small park. Across this, west of the engaging clock tower put up in 1882 by an Ottoman official, is the entrance to another Ramazan foundation, the Çarsi Hamami, built by Halil's son, Piri. This well-restored and maintained building is still in use. Further west, beyond what remains of the original souks, is the Yağ Camii ('Butter Mosque'), set in a charming courtyard: the arched prayer hall, with a stone mimber, rests on Roman column drums and was built on to an apsed church of two bays divided by triple-pilaster piers, which now serves as a lateral extension of the mosque.

62
VAHKA

❖

DRAMATIC as the Armenian castles of Smooth Cilicia are on their spines of rock, none perhaps is as spectacularly placed as Vahka (Fekke Kale). North of Kozan the valley of the Göksu rises between chains of hills towards a pass crossing to one of the great historic routes across central Anatolia. The valley was of obvious strategic importance as the Byzantines recognized, founding their castle on an easily defensible outcrop high above, and to the west of, the river a few kilometres north of Fekke.

The position meant that little could move in the valley without being observed. For it was as a command post that Vahka was useful to its successive occupants. The fortress was seized from the Byzantines in about 1190 by Constantine, successor of Rupen, the founder of the Armenian principality in Cilicia. Vahka was held by his heir, Thoros I (1100–29), whose brother Leon I (1129–37) lost it to the Emperor John II Comnenos after the fall of Anavarza in 1137. In 1139 the castle fell to the Dashimend Mohammed ibn Ghazi, only to be recovered in about 1148 by Thoros II (d. 1168), who had escaped from captivity in Constantinople. Apparently reconstructed under Leon II, it would remain the key northern bastion of Rupenid Cilicia until this fell to the Mamelukes in the late fourteenth century.

The fortress is silhouetted against the sky. A narrow road climbs steeply between groups of farmsteads, and twists upwards. The walls, built in a stone that is paler than the grey cliff from which these rise, are strengthened with

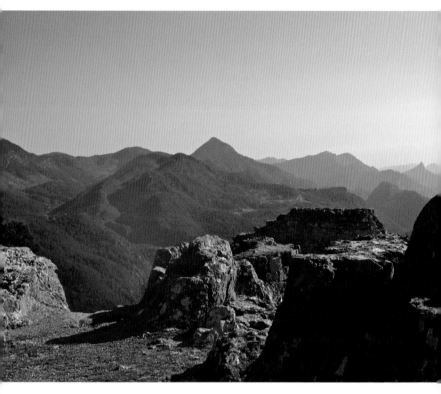

Vahka: view southwards with ridges descending to the Cilician plain.

rounded towers. The western section is for the most part well preserved, although the face of one of the rounded towers has begun to fall away. A large isolated square tower near the centre has quoins of a pinkish stone, clearly intended in part for visual effect. Much of the masonry is bossed, differences in application implying successive phases of construction.

It is an easy walk to the partly rock-cut ramp that leads up to the lower gatehouse at the south-eastern angle. From this, a wide stairway rises to the irregular enclosure. There is a substantial cistern cut into the rock, and the remains of a barrel-vaulted storeroom. More striking visually is a beautifully functional square pier of impeccable smooth masonry that splays upwards to fuse with a partly fallen vault. What survives of the internal arrangements of the towers that dominate the approach is, by contrast, not particularly impressive. But the views are prodigious, not least in the late afternoon when a tonic light suffuses the jagged ranges that fall away southwards towards the Cilician plain.

63
ŞAR: COMANA

❖

OF THE many Roman cities in Turkey none perhaps seems more remote than Comana, locked in a valley of the Anti-Taurus south-east of Kayseri and well placed for the ancient routes southwards for the Cilician plain and for Maras, to which in part it owed its prosperity.

Comana Cappadociae lay on either side of the Siriz, a tributary of the Ceyhan. It became a substantial Roman town, and by the end of the second century was the seat of a bishopric, which survived until the thirteenth century. Modern Şar is less accessible than its predecessor. From the road from Kozan to Pinarbasi, turn northwards for the small town of Tufanbeyli and there to the right, before going left on the Ayvat road. At the head of the valley fork right for Elemnali; go up through a village and follow the road downwards. The first conspicuous monument of Comana is a most handsome Roman mausoleum that was adapted as a church in the fifth century. The pedimented façade is substantially intact, and the outline of the apse of the church has been revealed in a recent excavation.

Less ambitious tombs are cut into the rock to the left of the road as this descends to the centre of the former city. Many of the modern houses, the oldest of which were built by Armenian settlers in the nineteenth century, are partly built of spoil; and it seems almost miraculous that the elegant carved door case (the Ala Kapi or 'dappled gate') of a temple was spared, partly because this also was re-used as a church, in the sixth century. A tumble of blocks from the portico deco-

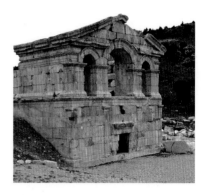

The Roman mausoleum adapted as a church.

rated with acanthus lie below the door.

The Byzantines built a new church below the temple, by the junction of the road behind this near the river: part of the lower section survives. On the south side of the river, hemmed in by farm buildings, is what remains of another, relatively substantial, church. Further east, above the river, is the theatre. Much of the cavea has been filled in, but some of the upper rows of seats at either side are visible, as are two arches that led to the internal corridors. A substantial Armenian house, with a veranda on both floors, takes the place of the stage building. Behind the theatre is the brick husk of a bath building; and high in the encircling cliffs above are more rock-cut tombs: others can be seen to the north of the river.

The visitor to Şar is still something of a rarity and will not pass unnoticed. Nor will he forget the place although the remains of Comana are modest when compared with those of other classical cities in Turkey. Their wild setting and the charm of the village houses indeed leave indelible impressions.

64

KAYSERI

❖

NORTH of Mount Erciyes, the Erciya Daği, and at the intersection of ancient routes, Kayseri is the natural metropolis of Anatolia. As Mazarca, it was the capital of the Cappadocian kingdom, which Antony awarded to Archelaus and which on his death in AD 17 became the Roman province of Cappadocia; the town was renamed Caesarea in honour of Tiberius. Caesarea in time became a major Christian centre, and prospered. By the fifth century Anatolia was less stable, and as a result the citadel was constructed under Justinian (527–65). Arab incursions followed, but despite Armenian reinforcement, the city fell to the Seljuks under Kilaç Arslan II, who nominated it his secondary capital. The Seljuks were displaced by the Mongols in 1243. In 1335 the Mongol governor of Kayseri, Eretna, took the city, and his family, the Eretnids, held a substantial area of central Anatolia until 1380. The Ottoman Beyazit I conquered Kayseri in 1397, but later it was ruled by the Karamanids and the Mamelukes before Selim I recovered it for his line in 1517.

The city has grown exponentially in recent years, and now boasts a tram system of which the city fathers of Edinburgh might be envious. None the less the citadel remains the dominant building of central Kayseri. Justinian's fortress was recast by the Seljuks – although what is clearly the inner face of a Byzantine gateway survives in the stretch of town wall to the north. The so-called Yoqua Burc ('Fat Tower') was constructed in 1212 for Izzettin Keykavus I. The two main entrances are protected by

barbicans and the complex now serves as a market.

Opposite the citadel, and thus outside the original city, is the most appealing and earliest religious complex of Seljuk Kayseri, the Hunat Hatun Külliyesi founded by the Sultana Mahpori Hunat Hatun, widow of Sultan Alaeddin Keykubad I, in 1239. The mosque, with a much-restored main doorway, contains a notable mihrab and an exceptional mimber, with finely carved detail. The Sultana's türbe, which is raised on a stalactite base, is placed to the left of the entrance, effectively cutting into a corner of the otherwise symmetrical plan. The türbe is richly carved in the dark stone used for so many of the monuments of Kayseri, relieved only by the white marble colonettes that divide each of the six windows. The simple, but very satisfying, interior is reached through what is now a metalwork shop in the corner of the associated medrese. The latter has a fine, and partly original, entrance, rounded angle projections and down spouts in the form of beasts, and, in many details, recalls the great Seljuk caravanserais. The final element of the complex is the hamam, still in use, and proudly maintained by the proprietor, whose family have owned it for seventy-five years.

Two other Seljuk foundations are east of the citadel, both dwarfed by the Hilton Hotel and its multi-storey neighbours. The Sahibiye Medresesi of 1268, built for Keyküsrev III's vizier, Sahip Ata Fahrettin Ali, with a beautiful entrance, is now a bazaar. So is one of the two sections of the Çifte Medrese, founded by Sultan Giyasettin Keyhüsrev I and his sister, Gevher Nesibe, who died in 1204 and is buried in the other and larger establishment. This was intended as the

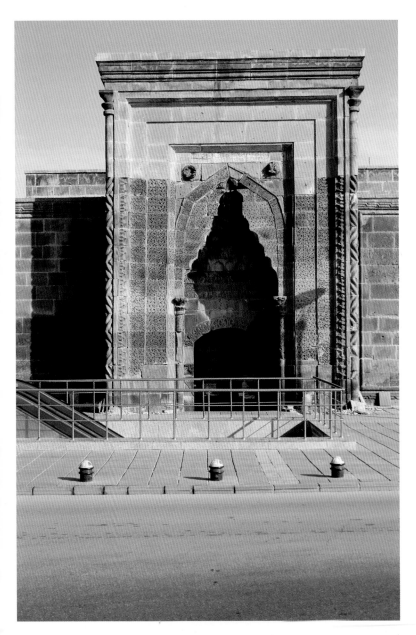

The Sahibiye Medresesi, with the escalators to the new underpass.

equivalent of a teaching hospital; much restored, it is now appropriately a museum of medical history. Nearer the citadel is the finest Ottoman contribution to the town, the Kurşunlu mosque of 1585. This has plausibly been attributed to no less an architect than Sinan: the portico is elegantly handled and the stained glass of the upper windows is unusually good.

Across the Atatürk Park from the mosque is the much-restored Çifte Medrese, the combined hospital and medical school founded in 1206. This now houses the exemplary Seljuk Museum, with some fine ceramics, including a group of tiles with representations of figures and animals from the Hunat Hatun hamam. Two very fine Seljuk mosques are to the west of the centre. The Lala Camii with its rows of arcades is admirably simple in design: while the Gülük Camii, with a splendid entrance at its north-western corner, is equally satisfying and the mimber of turquoise tiles must be the single most beautiful work of art in the city.

Kayseri has long been an entrepôt. Stretching from the citadel are the souks, including the domed Bedesten of 1497, now used by carpet exporters; the Vezir Hani of 1723, with one main and two subsidiary courtyards; and the enormous bazaar of 1859 that no doubt really does house 500 shops. Nearby is the equally large Ulu Cami, begun in 1136 but subsequently altered for Giyasettin Keyhüsrev I. The supporting arcades incorporate numerous Roman and Byzantine capitals, including one of the 'flying acanthus' type. Much of the heart of the town has been redeveloped, so the eighteenth- and nineteenth-century Gürgüpoğlu House is a precious survival: this makes an excellent setting for the Ethnography Museum, which unexpectedly includes a group of Seljuk tiles with representations of figures and animals from the Hunat Hatun hamam.

The Seljuks of Kayseri had a particular taste for erecting türbes. Inevitably these have been encroached upon by the modern city. Following the walls south-east from the citadel, one comes first to the Alaca Kümbeti of 1280, stranded on a traffic island. Further out, beyond the simple han mosque of 1136 and the associated kümbet of 1188, is the richly decorated Döner Kümbeti, erected in 1267 for Princess Shah Cihan Hatun. To the left of this a road leads to the Kayseri Museum, which houses many of the finds from nearby Kültepe. The Bronze Age pottery is particularly remarkable, ranging from an exquisite beaker with a swan handle to terracotta hip baths with handles at the sides. The classical era is represented by a relatively unusual brass sarcophagus from Mazarca.

65
SULTAN HANI

AMONG the greatest monuments of
Anatolia are the hans, or caravanserais,
which the Seljuks built in the thirteenth
century to serve the caravans that used
the long-established road system. For the
Seljuks well understood that trade – and
the custom duties this brought – was the
life-blood of their economy.

Sultan Hani, 50 kilometres/31 miles
from Kayseri on the road to Sivas, is a
splendid example dating from 1230–6.
Even in our age of the car the great hans
impress from a distance. Sultan Hani,
which covers an area of 3,813 square
metres/34,265 square feet, certainly does
so, with its massive walls reinforced by
relatively small projections. The entrance
is from the north, a vaulted gateway
with stalactite decoration that opens to
the courtyard, with at its heart a small,
raised mescit, the prayer hall of which is
reached by steep flights of steps. On the
right side and flanking the doorway
were rooms that provided what was necessary for the traveller: a kitchen, a place
to eat and inevitably a hamam. A large
door opposite the entrance leads to a
magnificent hall, with five aisles of equal
width, extending for seven bays and
crowned by a central dome. This was
used for stabling camels and in the
winter. Dark yet intensely impressive, it
reminds one of the great tithe barns of
medieval England, which, however, lack
the austere discipline of the Seljuk structure. Sultan Hani was well restored in
1950, and more work has been done
recently.

Not far to the south-west is the similar
and slightly later Karatay Hani (1236–

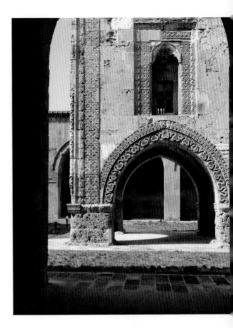

The Mescit.

46), finished under Giyasettin Keyhüsrev
II. This is comparable in plan, and the
masonry is particularly fine: as in the
contemporary Hunat Hatun Külliyesi at
Kayseri, a hint of fantasy was allowed in
the carving of the water spouts, designed
to direct rain and melting snow from the
walls, and here human as well as animal
forms are used. Surrounded by a scattered village in a shallow valley that in
the summer glows with golden crops,
Karatay Hani used to lie like a stranded
monster, for the line of the Roman road
east from Kayseri had been abandoned.
More recently the planners have recognized the advantage of the ancient route
and so, sadly, tarmac now sweeps insis-
tently past Karatay.

The road westwards from Kayseri to
their capital, Konya, was clearly of par-

ticular importance to the Seljuks. But for the sightseer, the stretch of this from Nevşehir to Aksaray is particularly satisfying. Just west of a ridge from which Mount Erciyes, above Kayseri, can still be seen, is Alay Hani, with a fine gateway and the ruin of a relatively small courtyard caravanserai, now alas too ruthlessly restored. Next comes Tepesidelik Hani, with a shattered domed hall, of three tall and two lower sections. Neither prepares one for what follows, Ağzi Kara Hani. Here, perhaps because of the lie of the ground, the pattern of Sultan Hani is subtly changed. The great gateway opens on to a familiar court with a central domed mescit. But the covered hall is on the left of this. While the courtyard was built for Alaeddin Keykubad I in 1231, the hall was added by the Sultan's successor, Hoca Mesut, in 1239. The beauty of the han is enhanced by the setting, on the edge of a modest village. On the rising ground behind the han are old farm buildings, where guard dogs, happily chained, make it clear that they do not share their owners' unfailing sense of hospitality. Beyond Aksaray is the justly celebrated Sultan Hani of 1229, majestic in scale, which gave its name to the town that has grown around it.

66
NIĞDE AND ESKI GÜMÜŞ
❖

LIKE other Turkish cities, Niğde has grown in recent decades and now covers a substantial area north and west of the citadel ridge. Tin may have brought early settlers, but whatever settlement there may have been must have been secondary to Tyana some twelve kilometres to the south, which in Roman and Byzantine times prospered as a key stage on the major route through the Cilician Gates to the south. The Seljuks were in occupation in the eleventh century, and Niğde is first mentioned in a document of 1188. By 1333, when Ibn Battuta found it largely in ruins, the place had suffered as a result of the Mongol invasions, but it subsequently revived under the Karamanids, with whose defeat in 1467 it would be incorporated in the Ottoman empire.

The citadel is at the northern end of the ridge. Partly constructed under Alaeddin Keykubad, it is dominated by the formidable octagonal tower built soon after the Ottoman occupation. Just behind this is the charming small porticoed Rahmaniye mosque of 1747. Further south is the Alaeddin Camii, with a beautiful entrance to the east and three domes supported on sturdy piers, built in 1223 for Alaeddin Keykubad. Opposite this is a fountain of 1421. Below the ridge to the west is the large seventeenth-century Bedesten, and to the south of this the Sungur Bey mosque of 1335. The portals on the north and east façades are elaborately decorated: the interior was altered after a serious fire that destroyed the original wooden columns. The bey's mausoleum is at the south-east corner. Further south is the Ak medrese, a Karamanid foundation of 1409. There are a number of later mosques in the commercial centre of the modern town, to the north-west of which is a trio of fourteenth-century türbe. The most refined is the richly decorated kumbet of Hüdavent Hatun, daughter of Sultan Rukneddin, now at the centre of a small park: this was built in 1312.

Some six kilometres north-east of Nigde, in the village of Gümüşler, is the remarkable monastery known as Eski Gümüş. A low cliff descending from the east is honeycombed with excavations. A few hundred yards uphill an entrance in the cliff face leads though a passage to an excavated courtyard, roughly square and some fifteen yards deep. The sides of the courtyard are punctured with openings to the rooms required for a monastic community of some size. Opposite the entrance a cutting opens to a narthex, which was never completed, from which the church is reached. Rock-cut, this is planned as a cross within a square, the central dome supported by four columnar piers; part of the patterned painted decoration survives.

What makes the church so remarkable is the calibre of the eleventh-century murals which, almost miraculously, have not been vandalized, although time has not been kind to the plaster on which these were painted, and many sections of roughly scored rock upon which this would have been applied are now visible. The central apse is decorated in three tiers, with the Pantocrator above. In that on the left the Virgin stands, her surviving hand outstretched, with saints. Above the arch in the north (left) wall is a fine scene of the *Nativity*, below, a narrower compartment of the *Presentation*: within the arch, and thus viewable at

close quarters, are finely individualized representations of the Baptist and Saint Stephen. To the left, partly screened by a pier, is the exceptionally impressive *Angel of the Annunciation*.

Accessible by a metal stair, there is a room above the narthex. Most remarkably the walls of this were painted with scenes from Aesop in an undulating landscape. It is now difficult to appreciate the main mural as a whole, as even with a torch much of the detail is impenetrable, but such sections as that of the wolf pursuing a lamb can be made out. The style is noticeably less refined than that of the murals in the church. But the scheme is an unique survival.

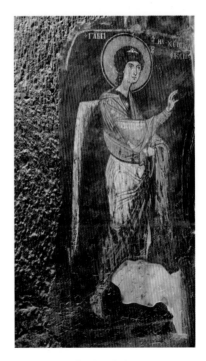

Eski Gümüş, the Angel of the Annunciation, mural.

67
GÖREME

THE CHURCHES of Cappadocia are collectively among the wonders of Turkey. Nowhere else can the religious aspirations and commitment of the Byzantine world be experienced in quite the same way – for the celebrated monasteries of Mount Athos never served wider communities as the churches of Cappadocia did. By the seventh century the Byzantine hold on central Anatolia was already threatened by Arab incursions. That Cappadocia became a Christian redoubt is partly explained by the character of the terrain, an extraordinary landscape created as the tufa deposits of Mount Erciyes and other now extinct volcanoes were eroded in a land where rain can be dramatic and wind remorseless. Valleys provided shelter and elsewhere the relatively easily worked volcanic stone facilitated the excavation of the 'underground cities' that in time of need offered security to those who lived in more exposed areas.

Ürgüp is arguably the best centre from which to explore the sites of Christian Cappadocia, and the excavated cliffs that dominate the town show how extensive a population was accommodated in early times. Four kilometres/2.5 miles north-west, a road descends to the smaller village of Göreme, through a dramatic landscape passing eroded cones that erupt at either side of the valley: the entrance to the Open Air Museum is on the left. Here a well-marked circuit guides the visitor to a sequence of churches concentrated in a surprisingly small area. The majority are relatively simple, decorated during the

iconoclastic period with red lines that pick out capitals and other architectural elements, and in some cases replicate pointing – for which of course there was no call in rock-cut structures.

Three churches are of particular artistic interest. The tunnel-approached Elmali Kilise ('Apple Church') is muralled in a palette of slate grey, deep red and ochre with white. The modelling of the forms is particularly effective – as is seen, for example, in the heads of Christ and the Archangels in many of the nine low domes. The murals are intelligently integrated so that, for example, the *Crucifixion* on the right wall is carried up to relate to the angels in the dome above. Higher up the hillside is the better-preserved Karanlik Kilise ('Dark Church'), set above a terrace with associated buildings as others of the churches are. The decoration is remarkable for the beautiful harmonies of grey and brown and ochre so evident in the narthex and for the diverting detail of many of the compositions in the body of the church, not least the *Entry to Jerusalem* of the first section of the central barrel vault. Here the colour is more intense than in the closely related murals in the Elmali Kilise. Particularly memorable are the *Last Supper*, in which a huge fish is set out on platter, and the splendid arched *Nativity*, in which a ray from the representation of the Child being washed links the scene with the *Calling of the Magi* in the vault above. The third church with significant murals is the Çarikli ('Sandals') Kilise; here green also is used extensively. The scenes of the *Nativity* and the *Journey of the Magi* are placed in the same way as in the Dark Church, but here the setting of the latter is particularly appropriate. One of the shepherds is at the top of a pink cone as slender as any of those in the valley, while the Magi's horses are on a less steep hillock. All three schemes are datable to the late twelfth or early thirteenth centuries.

The most ambitious of the Göreme churches is the Tokali Kilise ('Buckle Church') on the opposite side of the road. The first section, which represents the original church, has murals of about 910–20. This leads to the great transverse nave, with three apses behind screen walls and arcades at the sides, five blind on the right and six – five opening to a subsidiary chapel – on the left. The tenth-century murals are commensurately ambitious in scale, and the use of a blue ground adds to their sense of richness. The extant sections of the decoration of the vault are impressive and were evidently influential: thus the *Ascension* would be followed by the painter of the atrium of the Dark Church. The *Annunciation*, in which the blue of the Virgin's robe is deeper in hue than that of the backgrounds, is appropriately monumental. Particularly engaging also are the *Nativity* and the *Adoration of the Magi*.

Two fine churches can be reached from a turn to the left before entering the village of Göreme, at the centre of which there is a cone with the ruined temple front of a Roman tomb. To the north lies the charming rock-cut village of Çavuşin, with high on a cliff the impressive ruin of the substantial fifth-century Church of St John the Baptist. From the village a minor road leads to paths through the Güllüdere valley which is of spectacular beauty. There are a number of churches of which the most remarkable, high up and in a detached cone, is the Haçli church with some impressive murals and associated monastic structures. On the cliff north of the village is the Güveercinlik Kilise ('Dovecote' or

'Pidgeon Church') with reasonably well preserved murals painted after the Emperor Nicephorus Phocas visited the area in 964–5. Further on, a turn to the right is marked to Paşabağı, with a church dedicated to St Simon Stylites below an oratory reached by a vertical cutting with footholds, and Zelve, where a monastic settlement spread over three narrow valleys, two of which are linked by a tunnel. The chapels are for the most part decorated only with crosses, but the place has immense charm, particularly in winter when there are few tourists.

The extensively rock-cut village of Ortahisar, roughly between Göreme and

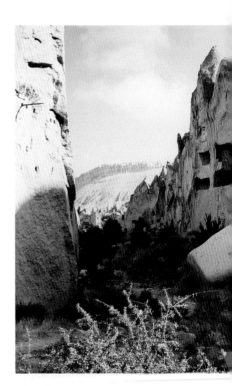

The valley at Zelve.

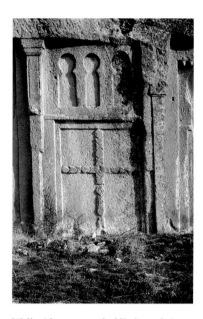

Wall with a cross and a blind arcade in the Hallaç monastery.

Ürgüp, is dominated by a dramatic rock. Those who are frustrated by being unable to climb this – for security reasons – may instead go a couple of miles to the west and explore the so-called Kale at Üçhisar, which is crowned by Byzantine tombs and is a wonderful vantage point. The churches of Ortahisar are not easily found, but one, the Hallaç Hospital monastery, can be reached from a side road on the way to Ürgüp. Set round a terrace in the rock, the complex is remarkable for the decorated façades – both in relief and pigment. The relatively modest front of the main church on the east cliff does not prepare one for the soaring domed interior, supported originally by four columns: here too red paint is used to articulate detail. On the north side there is a handsome barrel-

vaulted church, and at the north-west corner a partly collapsed domed structure with columns at the corners. Most unusually, the form of an outstretched man was left uncut in the angle of one of the arches.

Pancarlik, perhaps the most magically placed of all the churches of Cappadocia, is reached from a turn some 3 kilometres/1.9 miles south of Ürgüp on the road to Mustafapaşa. This side road passes the church of Sarica , only discovered in 1996 and recently restored, below which, in isolated cones, are two fine, but much damaged, domed churches, the smaller of which has a series of eight niches in the rock-cut drum. Pankarlik is 1 kilometre/0.6 miles westwards, on a promontory overhanging the valley that runs to Ortahisar. The murals are relatively well preserved but only accessible when the custodian is about. The views over the eroded landscape to the north, and to the cone of Erciyes to the east, are extraordinary. And there is an associated monastery in a buttress of the gully to the south.

South of Mustafapaşa, itself with substantial rock-cut buildings, is the village of Cemil with a late Greek church. Further on, not far from the road, and cut within three outcrops, is the Keşlik Kilise monastery, with three churches and refectories. Beyond, some 30 kilometres/18.6 miles from Ürgüp, is the village of Soğanli, where two valleys meet. Recent roads pass near the lower churches, of which the early tenth-century Barbara Kilise in the left-hand valley, with good murals of the period, and the Yilanli Kilise ('Snake Church') in the right-hand valley are perhaps the most interesting. But the more remarkable churches are high above this, on the opposite flank. Both the Kubbeli

('Domed') Kilise and the smaller Sakli ('Hidden') Kilise have domes which were also hewn externally. The two valleys remain wonderfully unspoiled, their churches, however remarkable, dwarfed by the great cliffs above.

The 'underground cities' of Cappadocia are phenomena that have an understandable fascination for some visitors. Burrowed into the soft volcanic tufa, these are inevitably similar with their tiers of passages and rooms, with cupboards and cooking facilities and holes for lamps, not to mention the ventilation shafts and ducts that were necessary when large numbers were concentrated in spaces so constricted. The finest is arguably that at Derinkuyu, some 25 kilometres/15.5 miles west of Soğanli. This is 55 metres/180 feet and eight storeys deep, and there is a substantial cruciform church at the penultimate level. Kaymarkli, 9 kilometres/5.6 miles to the north, has a similar, but as yet not fully excavated, 'underground city'. Such places are not for those who suffer from claustrophobia, but are eloquent of the fear in which the early Christian communities of Cappadocia lived.

It is not for such excavations that I return to Cappadocia, nor merely for the churches, most fascinating as these are. All landscapes are of their nature ancient. But because of the pattern of erosion we are particularly aware of this antiquity in the valleys round Göreme and Ürgüp. These are fragile. And it is for this reason that it is vital not only that such projects as that to restore the old town of Ürgüp are supported, but also that future development, whether of housing or tourist facilities, is most rigorously controlled.

68
IHLARA

THE ROAD to Ihlara from Aksaray crosses a rolling plain dominated from the south-west by the imperious cone of Hasan Daği. The first hint of what is in store comes on the approach to Selime, a massive outcrop above the Melendiz Dere, which runs plentifully in the summer – and in mid-winter is a surging river. The lower flanks of this are honeycombed with the rock-cut structures of what was evidently a substantial town. The site entrance leads to a path which winds upwards to the large aisled cathedral, with smoke-damaged murals, and a number of associated structures of commensurate scale. Some 6 kilometres/4 miles further south is the turn, on the left, to the village of Belisirma, the Byzantine Peristrema, where the river emerges from a spectacular valley with its dramatic cliffs. The ambitious Ala Kilise ('White Church'), is just above the village on the left. The rock-hewn façade is magnificent, but unfortunately the very accessibility of the place means that the murals of the domed interior have suffered grievously.

The subsidiary northern entrance to the Open Air Museum is on the west bank of the river, opposite the village, which with its pansiyons would be the best base for a full circuit of the valley's churches. Two fine churches are just above the ticket office. The more ambitious, the Direkli ('Columned') Kilise, with a nave flanked by two aisles, was excavated in the reign of Basil II (976–1025). The murals echo the taste of metropolitan Byzantium, as do those of the Bahattin Samanliği Kilise not far to

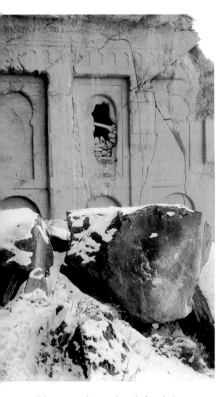

Ihlara: a rock-cut church façade in snow.

ture. Inevitably the rock-cut churches and the many other excavated buildings follow the lower line of the cliffs, but flights of wooden steps mean that it is no longer necessary to scramble up through fallen rock. One is never far from the sound of rushing water, as the river continues to carve its way. Walking upstream, one comes, in reverse order, to the barriers of rock that forced the streambed to writhe and turn.

Before the first bend of the river is the path to the Church of St George, with frescoes including one of the founder, Basileios, an emir in the service of the Seljuk Sultan of Konya, and his wife Tamara, flanking the saint; outside the church, much of which has fallen away, is a niche with the saint on his white horse slaying a serpentine two-headed dragon. Much further on are two churches with murals, the Sümbülü ('Hyacinth') Kilise and the Ağaç Alti Kilise ('Church under the Tree'). Nearby a bridge crosses to the east bank, just south of the Yilanli ('Snake') Kilise with its harrowing depictions of the torments of hell, in which snakes submit four women to select punishments: the execution is crude but effective.

Back on the west bank and near the next right-hand bend in the river is the Pürendi Seki ('Terrace') Kilise, with a characteristic cycle of scenes of the life of Christ, from the *Annunciation* to the *Deposition*. Not far beyond is the Kokar ('Fragrant') Kilise, with a yet finer sequence, starting logically to the left of the entrance with the *Annunciation*: in the *Crucifixion* Christ is shown robed while the two thieves are naked. Below the scenes are relatively well-preserved *trompe l'oeils* of hangings decorated with flowers. Further south across the river, which can be forded without difficulty, is

the left, which include a sequence of scenes from the New Testament. These too have suffered, and indeed the visitor should be warned that none of the mural cycles in the valley is as well preserved as the most celebrated schemes at Göreme and Eski Gümüş. The charm of the churches between Belisirma and the village of Ihlara, some 8 kilometres/5 miles upstream, is in their setting.

In the summer the canyon is protected from the full brunt of the heat. In the winter, with frozen snow, it has a different magic. But finding the key churches then becomes something of an adven-

the Eğri Tas ('Slanting Stones') Kilise, part of which has fallen away. The flat vault is decorated with biblical scenes round the cross. Beyond this, at a bend where the cliff circles to the east before continuing to the south, is the unexpectedly monumental Karanlik Kale ('Dark Fort'), a monastery which, in architectural terms, is certainly the most ambitious of the rock churches of Ihlara.

The valley is a place of enchantment: the towering cliffs catching the sunlight; the river, never silent; the poplars and pistachio trees; the occasional field. There is only one false note, the restaurant by the main entrance to the Open Air Museum, which stands out like an eyesore. The modern flight of steps below this reaches the valley near the southern cluster of churches. Take this at the cost of losing something of the excitement of the valley. But do so if there is snow or ice: in these conditions the road up from the Belisirma entrance defeated my hired car and it would have been impossible to get away if the sun had not partly melted the ice above the village on the opposite side of the valley.

69
KONYA

❖

FIRST inhabited over four millennia ago, Konya was a significant city long before the advent of Alexander the Great, whom the indefatigable fourteenth-century Tangerine traveller Ibn Battuta supposed to have founded it. Alexander's Seleucid successors were ousted by the Attalids of Pergamum, but of their Iconium and its Roman and Byzantine successors nothing of consequence survives. The Seljuks first raided the city in 1069, and a century later captured it. Konya became the capital of their sultanate of Rum, only to fall, in 1242, to the Mongols, who were succeeded by the Karamanids – whose emirate was based on Karaman, some 116 kilometres/72 miles to the south; they, in turn, were defeated by the Ottomans in 1467.

Konya's position near the western end of a vast plain and at the hub of a series of ancient routes made her a valuable prize. And, as the great series of Seljuk caravanserais on the road from the east demonstrates, trade was an important source of the city's wealth. Even today, as pylons and factories stretch northwards across the steppe, the Sadeddin Hani, north-east of the town, refuses to be over-awed. And despite a massive increase in population and the almost complete obliteration of domestic buildings that antedate the age of concrete, Konya still bears the imprint of her Seljuk past.

At the centre of the city is the oval Alaeddin Park on the tell of the prehistoric town. This is crowned by the Alaeddin Camii, begun about 1150 and completed some seventy years later. The

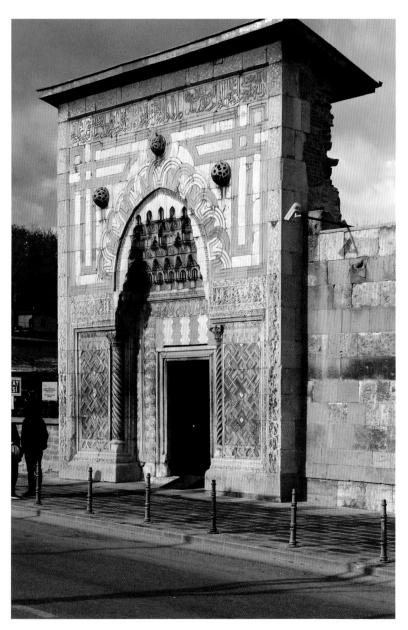

Konya: the Büyük Karatay Medresesi.

north façade, with much appropriated material and decoration, is splendid. The entrance leads to the main prayer hall, built for Sultan Alaeddin Keykubad I (1219–36), with a veritable plantation of forty-two ancient columns capped by classical or Byzantine capitals. Beyond is the domed central section, completed by Sultan Kilic Arslan II (1156–88), but begun by his father, Mesud I (1116–56), to which Izzettin Keykavus I (1210–19) added the western prayer hall. The carved wooden mimber, of about 1155, is of exceptional distinction. Adjoining the mosque to the north is the Alaeddin Köşkü, a tower apparently used for residential purposes by the later Seljuk sultans.

Below this, across a busy road, is the Büyük Karatay Medresesi founded by Celaleddin Karatay, who served his Seljuk masters and was chosen as regent in face of the Mongol onslaught. The doorway is a masterpiece of controlled decoration, with interlaced motifs and marble enrichments, dominated by a Kufic inscription. The impressive main room is crowned by a majestic dome decorated with blue and gold tiles and supported on pendentives with the names of the earliest four caliphs. The medrese now serves as a museum of tiles, including the remarkable group with representation of both humans and animals excavated at Kubadobad, Alaeddin Keykubad I's palace by the lake of Beyşehir.

Opposite the Alaeddin Park on the west is the Ince Minare Medresesi, the eponymous slender minaret of which, decorated with blue and red tiles, is now less slender than it was, as this has been reduced in height by over half. The gateway is memorable for the energy of the detail. The builder was Emir Sahip Ata

Fahrettin Ali, who employed an architect called Keluk. The complex is used as a museum of sculpture and contains an inventive series of reliefs of animals, including an elephant and imaginary creatures, made for Alaeddin Keykubad I, apparently in 1221. A number of fine Seljuk carved doors are exhibited in a side room. Sahip Ata also turned to Keluk for his foundation, consisting of a mescit, an elaborate tomb and a hamam, which is still in use. Finished in 1258, this is some 250 metres/275 yards south-east of the Alaeddin Park on the Sahip Ata Caddesi. The main portal is striking, and rather unusually incorporates in its base two classical sarcophagi, one decorated with human masks. Immediately to the west of this complex is the Archaeological Museum, which documents the development of the area before the advent of the Seljuks. Pride of place goes to one of the great masterpieces of Roman sculpture from Anatolia, a sarcophagus of Sidamara type found in 1958, which is in exceptional condition. On the sides, in deep relief, are the twelve Labours of Hercules, while at one end is an evidently realistic and palpably sympathetic portrayal of the man for whom the tomb was intended.

The main artery of the modern town runs east from the Alaeddin Park. Ahead is the large Selimiye mosque, built under Selim I the Sot (1566–74). With its main dome answered by those of the portico, this exemplifies the style of Sinan. Beyond is the most celebrated monument of Konya, the Mevlana Tekke, the shrine of the thirteenth-century mystic Jalal ad-Din ar-Rumi, generally known as Mevlana. His father was invited to Konya by Alaeddin Keykubad I in 1228: and Mevlana died here in 1273. The extant structures, clustering round the green-tiled conical dome of the türbe of 1397, were built in the early Ottoman period. The complex is entered through the garden at the back. Tourists – who will be outnumbered by pilgrims – walk round to enter the building from the west to reach the mausoleum. Beside this is the circular semahane in which the Mevlana's followers, the dervishes, danced. More remarkable than the building are the treasures displayed within it. The carpets include a miraculous Persian example, with flowers sprouting from curling stems in the central field. There are also some fine illuminated manuscripts, including a magnificent Quran of 1452. Yet pride of place must go to the April Bowl, adorned with damascened tondi of horsemen and seated potentates flanked by attendants, set in a wonderfully elaborate decorative field. Presented to the tekke by the Mongol Sultan Ebu Said Bahadir Han in 1333, this was intended as the receptacle for rain that fell in the spring, which was used for medicinal purposes.

Many of the more interesting sites in reach of Konya are to the south: Karaman, Binbir Kilise (no. 72) and Isauria (no. 71), not to mention Çatalhüyük, where the lowest level of the tell is of about 6,500 BC, but there is little to interest those who are not moved by impacted strata of mud bricks. Anyone motoring to the west towards Isparta should pause, however briefly, at Kadir Hani. The caravanserai is beside the main road. Its builders evidently relished their power over the monuments of their predecessors. Roman and Byzantine blocks were ruthlessly reused, crosses set on their sides and inscriptions deliberately inverted.

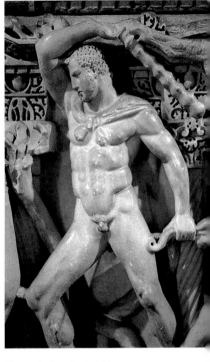

Konya Archaeological Museum: Sidemara-type sarcophagus, Hercules (detail).

70
BEYŞEHIR AND EFLATUN PINAR

IN THE sweltering summers, the hills to the west must always have appealed to the inhabitants of Konya, and it is hardly surprising that Sultan Alaeddin Keykubad I built his great summer palace of Kubadobad beside Lake Beyşehir.

Almost exactly halfway from Konya to Beyşehir, a substantial Seljuk building is seen on a rise in an amphitheatre of hills. Below this is a handsome Seljuk caravanserai of rather unusual plan. As this is relatively narrow – the covered area was only three bays wide by six deep – the courtyard was not large enough to contain the mescit; it was therefore placed, with open arches below on three sides, to the left of the entrance, and bal-anced by a building with single rooms on two floors. Interest is given to the façade by the use of blocks of contrasting colour, but the charm of the place is that it remains in open country.

Beyşehir too was a Seljuk foundation. The founder was Emir Eşref, whose son, Eşrefoğlu Seyfeddin Süleyman, was in the service of Sultan Giyasettin Keyhüsrev II (1264–83). He built the mosque that bears his name. Resting on forty-one wooden columns, mostly octagonal, this is a remarkable survival with its painted capitals and beams, mihrab tiled in turquoise, blue and black, and a worthy mimber. Beside the mosque, and visible through a window from this, is the founder's türbe in which he was buried in 1302. The interior of the dome is a marvel of turquoise and black tilework. Seyfeddin Süleyman also founded the medrese behind the mosque: this has a fine portal and is now undergoing an alarmingly thorough internal reconstruc-

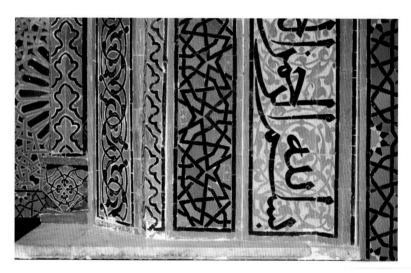

Beyşehir, Eşrefoğlu Mosque: tiled decoration of minber (detail).

tion. Higher up is the Bedesten, originally completed in 1299 but restored under Süleyman the Magnificent, also recently attended to, and on the far side of this there is a yet earlier bath complex. Near by are a number of old houses, which have also been put in order.

Fortunately the modern town has grown up on the opposite bank of the river that enters the lake at Beyşehir and so the mosque and the related buildings have not been encroached upon, although the castle of the Eşrefoğlu has left no trace.

Beyşehir was the successor of a Byzantine city and possibly of a Roman town. But the area had of course been inhabited long before. Some 20 kilometres / 12.4 miles north of the town is what some claim to be the most magical of extant Hittite constructions, the Eflatun Pinar ('Violet Spring'). The Hittites had a deep reverence for water and here a perpetual spring emerges with gushing force. Recent excavation has only enhanced the appeal of the site, in rolling country a few kilometres east of the lake. The turn is discreetly marked on the main Isparta road, but there is no hint that one should cut sharply left after 5 kilometres / 3 miles. The road comes down to a dip with a few trees.

To the right, across a large rectangular cistern, into which water from the spring behind was channelled, is a remarkable structure with, at the top, in deep relief, the winged sun, supported below and at the sides by two tiers of figures with raised arms, under which are five figures with crossed hands. There are holes in the stomachs of the latter, through which the water flowed. It was at one time thought that the whole was a later assemblage, but this can hardly be the case, and the south side with bossed

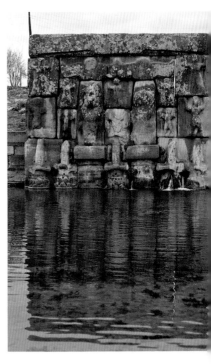

Eflatun Pinar, the Hittite fountain.

blocks is clearly of a piece. On the opposite, west, side of the pool there was a balancing structure of which much less survives. Behind this is an extraordinary sculpture of three sizeable bulls, hewn from a single block, but now set on a concrete base. Despite the proximity of a decaying house and its larger modern successor, the visitor to Elflatun Pinar knows that he or she is a trespasser in a world that it is now impossible to fully comprehend, but is at least left in no doubt as to how special the place must have seemed in Hittite eyes. One can, however, only regret the recent 'landscape works' which are unworthy of the place.

71
ISAURIA

❖

ISAURIA, now known as Sengibar Kalesi, is not on an obvious tourist trail. Few guidebooks trouble with it, and my two maps put it in different places; an official in the tourist office at Konya, who claimed to have been there, plumped for the wrong location. And but for the seductive illustrations in *Classical Anatolia: The Glory of Hellenism* by that veteran of cosmopolitan Florence, Harry Brewster, I might not have persevered. The Roman city of Isauria was the capital of the province of the same name, wilder and poorer than Pisidia to the west and less strategically placed than Cilicia to the south-east. It was the most important town on the road linking Konya with Anemurium on the coast. The setting, some 100 kilometres / 62 miles south-west of Konya, must always have been bleak; and only a power as disciplined as Rome would have built and sustained a city in so austere a terrain. Spring, as I found, comes late to Isauria.

From Konya, take the road for Karaman and fork right at İçeriçumra, pausing after 25 kilometres / 15.5 miles or so to see the fine early bridge at Dineksaray. At a crossroads some 93 kilometres / 58 miles from Konya, turn right – west – towards Bozkir. Before the village of Ulupinar, the road skirts the northern flank of the hill on which Isauria lies. To the west this crosses a side valley, from which tracks lead upwards. From a distance the impressive north-western tower of the city walls is clearly visible. But it cannot be seen from the bottom of the slope. After a time, scattered shards brought down by the winter rain cheer one on. The ancient route from the west leads up past a necropolis, with sophisticated tombs cut into outcrops of rock, to the west gate of the city. A rougher ascent leads to the north-western tower which, at roughly 12 metres / 40 feet, stands to almost full height. The polygonal masonry is excellent. Beyond there is another reasonably well-preserved tower. From both towers the views northwards across lower ground to snow-capped hills are commanding. I walked on across the high point of the city, with a scattering of confused walls, and down to the well-preserved Arch of Hadrian, austere in its simplicity. Nearby is the platform of a small temple. The arch is on the cardo, the main street of the ancient city, near the junction with a cross street that ran to the west gate.

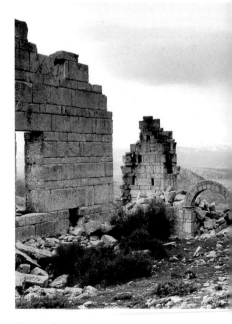

The south gate.

The cardo runs downhill, past vestigial traces of the agora and a stoa. In the outcrop to the east there is a sizeable quarry. The great south gate – the approach from Anemurium – is unquestionably the most memorable of the buildings of Isauria. The ancient engineers took every advantage of the steeply rising ground. Make down, on what must be the alignment of the Roman road, passing a number of all-too-efficiently robbed tombs, and then turn back, to gain some sense of the impression the gate must originally have made.

The western section of the city walls can be followed, with towers placed to exploit the cliffs that offered a natural protection to the site. Criss-crossing what was once a busy town, it slowly struck me that, the occasional bird apart, there is no sign whatever of life: no animals, no herdsmen – no human distractions from the incredible snow-studded hills on the horizon. On the way down I lingered in the western necropolis, coming upon more tombs and mounting two or three rock-cut flights of steps, leading to – nothing.

72
BINBIR KILISE

❖

KARAMAN was an important place in Seljuk times, astride the main road from Konya to the sea at Silifke. Its Karamanid rulers controlled a substantial territory and the town still boasts a quorum of monuments: a castle; the Mevlani mosque which echoes its counterpart at Konya; the spectacular façade of the Hatoumi Medresesi, with interlacing designs, delicate niches within the jambs and, above the door, darker blocks alternating with the pale stone, which do not prepare one for its present function, as a restaurant; and the fine sixteenth-century hamam nearby. But the truth is that Karaman's magic has been eroded.

Much more appealing are the ruins of a large group of early churches high on the eastern flank of the Kara Dağ massif, some 40 kilometres / 25 miles away. Despite the Turkish name, Binbir Kilise, there are not a thousand and one churches; but the area was clearly an important Christian centre from the fifth until the tenth centuries, although it has no recorded history. Little has been written about it since the publication of *The Thousand and One Churches* by Sir William Ramsay and Gertrude Bell in 1909. The road lifts itself from the plain, crosses a low pass and comes down to the village of Madenşehir, before climbing again towards the small settlement of Dequile, set in a narrow basin, flanked by protecting ridges of exposed rock.

At Dequile there are still a dozen or so churches, one of which appears to have been pressed into service as a mosque. Parts of others are now used as storerooms. The structures were simple

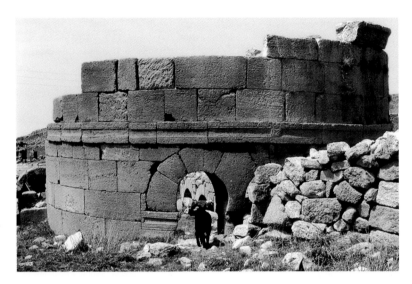

Binbir Kilisi: church at Dequile.

enough. Some have arcaded aisles, their lintels carved with crosses, and double windows in the apses, several of which are relatively well preserved. Above hangs the snow-crested Kara Dağ, near the summit of which there are further churches. The moden village itself has charm, with its scattering of turf-roofed stone houses, many evidently built of appropriated material; a small boy herds goats while an old woman calls.

Some of the more appealing ruins are outside the village: two solitary door posts, yellow with lichen, on an outcrop with an excavated platform; and an empty tomb below a rock that overlooks the approach. Particularly lovely is a church with a small narthex and an arcaded flank, buried now to the level of the arches. The silence is broken by sounds of clashing tortoiseshells and although there is as yet no sign of leaf in a well-maintained orchard, the pale pink blossom is already bursting.

Madenşehir is less atmospheric. I parked by an unpretending mosque and cut past the village, making for the very substantial apse that can be seen from the road. The huge scale is unexpected. The masonry is excellent, but the apse has no window. Arches survive that supported the two subsidiary apses, now gone. Two trunks of the façade of the church still stand. Nearby is a cistern with steps between stunted trees. Curiosity – and the will to avoid an unfriendly dog – made me take another path back. This passes a fine Roman tomb encroached upon by old houses. Re-used blocks can be seen in many buildings. I came across a sarcophagus put to service as a trough; and then a second.

The finest of the churches is to the south of the village. The approach is through a narthex with two outer doors, and one opening to the nave. Although the southern side of this has fallen in, all

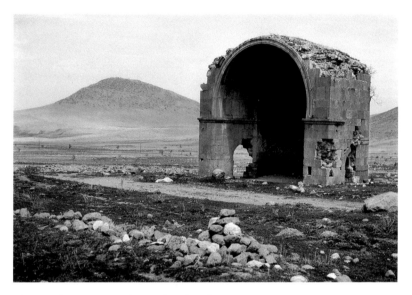

The apse of the large church east of Madenşehir.

ten arches of the left side are intact to roof level, as is the apse, which again is windowless, no doubt for sound structural reasons. The size of the church, and of its larger counterpart east of the village, testifies to the aspiration of the Christian community that flourished in this isolated setting. One can only be grateful that the nomadic habits of their Muslim successors have meant that the masonry of Binbir Kilise has, in part at least, escaped recycling.

73
IVRIZ

❖

AMONG the most haunting monuments left by the Hittites are their rock reliefs. Widely scattered across their former territory, these proclaim at once the power and the piety of their empire. Four well-known reliefs may, with some determination, be seen in the wild valleys south of Mount Erciyes. But these, like the Urartian and Assyrian examples opposite the Ishak Paşa Sarayi and at Eğil, have been eroded by three millennia's exposure. At Ivriz, miraculously, the intentions of both patron and carver can still be sensed.

The Hittites were as alert as their successors to the strategic importance of the Cilician Gates, linking the great plains of central Anatolia to the Mediterranean coast. Ereğli is some 50 kilometres/31 miles west of the northern approach to the defile. Despite its Roman past and place on the Seljuk routes to Karaman and Konya, the modern town is devoid of interest. To the south looms the steep flank of the Taurus mountains, snowbound in winter and gruelling in the summer's heat. Head due south. The railway line marks the boundary of urban expansion. The road, now signposted for Ivriz, becomes a lane, winding among farms and orchards as the Taurus loom larger. The village of Ivriz enjoys a calm, traditional prosperity. At the far end is a pool overhung by trees. This is fed by a perennial spring in the rock – now controlled by a small dam on which the villagers and their fields depend. So did their Hittite predecessors, whose reverence for such water sources is attested elsewhere and not least at Eflatun Pinar. Above the spring, on a rock facing southeast and thus happily protected from the prevailing winds, is the relief carved during the reign of the late Hittite King Warpawalas of Tuwanuwa in the second half of the eighth century BC.

The relief is nearly 6 metres/20 feet high. On the left, in profile to the right, is the god Tarhu. He wears a horned headdress and a robe with a hem that descends to a point, with shoes of a characteristic Hittite type. He clasps a sheaf of corn in his left hand and in the other holds a vine branch with bunches of grapes, proclaiming his role in the Hittite pantheon. Opposite, smaller in scale and placed on a section of uncut rock, is the king, his head with a proper deference at a lower level than the god's, his hands raised in obeisance. His richly patterned robe is Assyrian in derivation, but the brooch of his outer garment is of

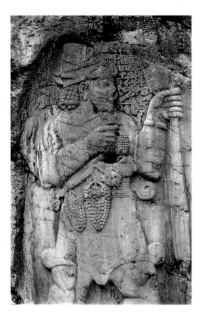

The god Tarhu, detail of Hittite relief.

Phrygian type. Behind the god is the inscription identifying the king, whose name is also known from a contemporary Assyrian text.

The outcrop is at the foot of a boulder-strewn slope. A steep walk leads across to a higher valley in which there is a second carving, identical in design but without any inscription. Near by are the scant remains of much later brick buildings. Allow time, as the village children may not know the route, and try to go in the morning when the sun clarifies the detail of the more accessible of the two reliefs.

74

KANLIDIVANE AND ÖKÜZLÜ

MODERN development along the main coastal road in Cilicia has taken its toll of classical sites. The street of columns at Pompeiopolis, the Turkish Viranşehir, is now overlooked by apartment blocks. West of Limonlü, across the the river known in antiquity as the Lamus, approached from a side road to a resort, the impressive rump of a late Roman palace known as Akkale, built apparently for one Illus, still stands in isolation set back above the shore.

Some 3 kilometres/1.9 miles east of Ayas, a road climbs north for 4 kilometres/2.4 miles to Kanlidivane, previously Kanytelis or Neapolis. The place must have seemed as extraordinary in its heyday as it does now. The odd sarcophagus and a built tomb on the hillside hardly prepare one for what is to come: a Hellenistic tower of polygonal masonry, inscriptions on the eighth and tenth blocks at the south-western corner of which announce that this was dedicated to Zeus of Olba by the priest Teucros; and a substantial Byzantine church on the rim of a deep, almost-circular chasm. Near these are three other Byzantine churches, all of basilica type, a substantial Byzantine cistern and, in varying states of decay, a wide scattering of houses of the period. Higher up is a fine Roman temple tomb.

Steps lead to a ramp that descends into the chasm. Halfway down on the south face of this is a relief with two men and four women: on the right an older man and one of the women are seated; the others stand. They may, or may not,

have belonged to the same Olban priestly family as Teucros. Further down, at the north-western face of the rock, is a second relief, of a warrior in a Roman tunic. The cliff is undercut most dramatically on the north side, below the church. Under this and a little to the left, wide steps cut diagonally into the rock mount in two flights to a natural cave which has been extended. This must have had some specific function, but as piles of sheep droppings show has now been put to more casual use.

The church above the chasm is the most ambitious of those at Kanlidivane. An inscription on the finely detailed door in the narthex identifies the builder as Papylos. Arcades flanked the nave, but now only the piers abutting on the apse survive, with beautifully stylized capitals. The other churches are simpler, but their very number suggests the scale and prosperity of the place in what must have been its prolonged Byzantine phase. The road continues northwards, passing close to the temple tomb. Three rather magical sites are within relatively easy reach: Öküzlü, Emirzeli and Cantörien.

Öküzlü is to the south of the modern village of the name, approached by a track from the west. This leads first to a ruined mansion, with arched ribs that still defy gravity. Further on is an ambitious church, the east end of which is substantially intact. Four of the seven sections of the arcade above this remain in place. Acanthus capitals apart, decoration is restrained. To the south the lower courses of another church serve as a cow byre. Beyond this an ancient paved road leads downhill before rising to a further

Opposite: Kanlidivane: the church of Papylos above the chasm.

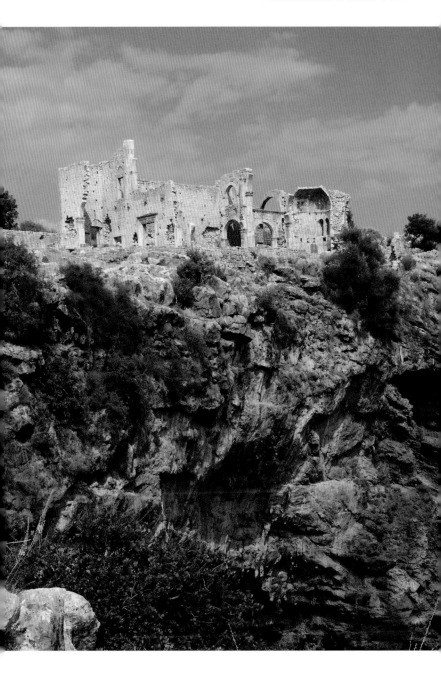

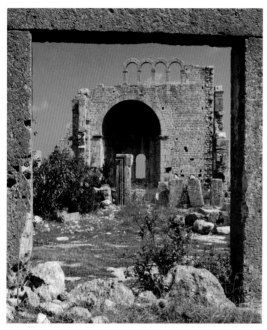

The church at Öküzlü.

church, the surviving section of which stands precariously despite an early endeavour to strengthen this by narrowing the original window of two lights. Emirzeli, further west, is a more tangled site in rougher country. Near the road there is a characteristic Byzantine church, its elegant lateral arcade with capitals the decoration of which is merely incised. Other churches and Byzantine buildings cluster on the slope. Opposite, crowning a spine of rock, is an impressive Hellenistic fortress, with walls of fine polygonal masonry, and at its northern tip a substantial tower, with a prominent relief of a phallus.

The most direct route back to the coast leading to Ayas passes another notable Hellenistic fortress, Cantörien on a narrow ridge overlooking a valley to the west. Much of the polygonal masonry is more or less intact, as is that of a contemporary Temple of Hermes, with a relief of his caduceus to the right of the opening above the door behind the now fallen portico in antis. The Byzantines left their trace here too, with a church enriched with acanthus capitals and other buildings.

From Cantörien it takes about half an hour to descend to Ayas, the ancient port of Elaeusa, which was rebranded as Sebaste – the Greek form of his name – in honour of Augustus. Battered sarcophagi line the road as this reaches the modern houses. A little further on the Via Appia of Sebaste stretches eastwards: there are several fine and well-preserved temple tombs. The Roman town below has fared less well, although recent excavation by Italian archaeologists has brought much to light.

75
ADAMKAYALAR, CENNET-CEHENNEM AND PASLI

THE modern resort of Kizkalesi, admirable base for the sightseer as it is, and the busy coastal road inevitably influence a first impression of the remains of ancient Corycos, however striking the *coup d'oeil* of the Island (or Maiden's) Castle, built for the Byzantine admiral Eustathios in 1151, and its counterpart, the formidable Land Castle, largely constructed by the Armenians in the thirteenth century. The latter incorporates on its western front the sea gate of the Roman town: an ancient pier stretches from the corner of the fortress and to the east other remains of the port can be traced. Further on is a huge cistern originally fed by an aqueduct from the River Lamus, several built sections of which

can be seen near the road from Limonlü. Across the main road from the Land Castle is part of the necropolis, with a number of reliefs. A processional route leads eastwards to a remarkable sequence of Byzantine churches that deserve to be better known.

Two unusually fascinating sites are in easy reach of Kizkalesi; Adamkayalar and Cennet-Cehennem. Adamkayalar is reached from the turn by the post office at Kizkalesi. The road climbs and after a couple of miles there is a fine Hellenistic tower of regular blocks on the right. Further on, a track to the left leads, in 2 kilometres/1.2 miles, to Adamkayaler. This crosses a rock-strewn hillside and is well signed. Near a polygonal building, of similar construction to the tower at Kanlidivane, arrows point down a narrow streambed, which descends to a bend in the deep canyon cut by the apparently insignificant river that reaches the sea at Corycus. There are ancient steps in the rock, carefully placed to minimize expo-

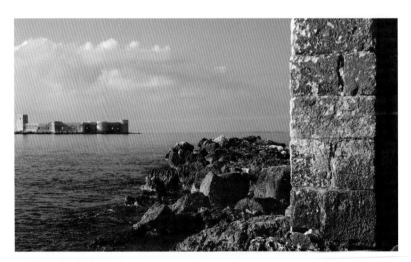

The Island Castle seen from the mole of the Land Castle.

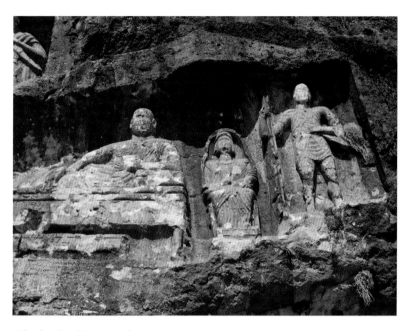

Adamkayalar: Roman tombs.

sure to occasional flash flooding in what is generally a dry terrain. The path drops steeply and then cuts to the right, at the foot of the cliff face.

The necropolis is not large. In all there are thirteen reliefs: several of soldiers in Roman dress, very similar to the warrior at Kanlidivane; a seated woman; a particularly well-preserved man reclining on a sarcophagus; and a group with a man and a child flanking a figure of another. Associated with the reliefs are holes for posts and other excavations in the rock. To the right, footholds facilitate access to a shelf higher up with more post holes and a small wall at the western extremity. The place must always have been sequestered. Even the birdsong is muted. But as I made my way upwards, a dark bird of prey circles into view, his cry like the creaking of rusty hinges: 'yer wach nar wach nar'. Then, back on the hillside, a herdsman instructs his goats: 'ay ch ch ch', 'phre phre wey', 'phre phre she she'. He is dressed in black, unconsciously matching the sleek coats of most of his sheep; but his utterances lack the melody of the bells of his goats.

Adamkayalar is uniquely atmospheric partly because it is relatively inaccessible. The same cannot be said of Cennet-Cehennem, the most interesting of the Corycan caves, the chasms otherwise known as Heaven and Hell, which is approached from Narinkuyu, the village west of Kizkalesi. The caves were known in ancient times, as is attested by Strabo, and near the site entrance is the outer wall in polygonal masonry of a Hellenistic Temple of Zeus, the main structure of which was cannibalised for a church in the fourth or fifth century. The chasm lies to the north. Steps descend steeply towards the mouth of a deep cave. At the point where the roof of this afforded protection from rain, an elegant chapel dedicated to the Virgin was built by an individual called Paulus. Although the mural in the small apse has suffered, the building itself, never roofed, is exceptionally well preserved. Beyond the chapel steps lead down to an underground stream, the Aous, which the ancients took for a tributary of the Styx.

The whole area knew prosperity in Hellenistic and Byzantine times. Three kilometres to the north, at Hasanaliler, the road passes a ruined basilica, with an intact apse and south arcade. Further on are two fine Hellenistic towers, at Gökburç and Ovacik, the latter of polygonal masonry with a relief of a dagger above the door. From near Ovacik a road on the left leads to the very extensive partly rock-cut site of Takkadin, itself four kilometres north of Pasli. Two and a half kilometres from the last is the most magnificent of Cilician mausolea, the Mausoleum of the Fearless King (Megzit Kalesi), so named from the substantial phallus on the outer wall of the podium. The porticoed front faces out across the valley. Behind, by a modest farmhouse, is a massive oil press that hints at the industrial scale of ancient agriculture.

Further west, best reached by way of Ovacik and Imamli, are a trio of sites on

Cennet-Cehennem: the church at the entrance to the cavern.

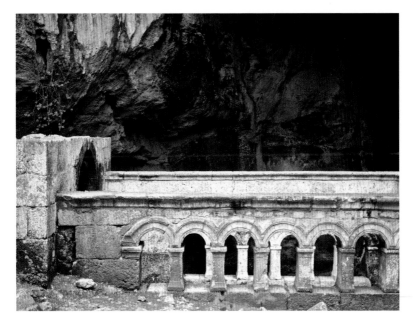

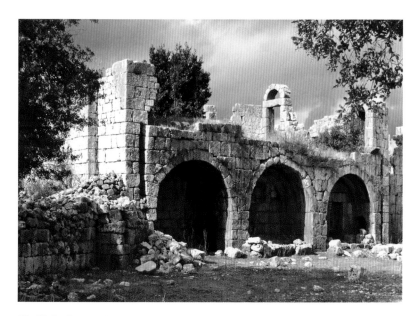

Sinekkale: the mansion.

the way down to the coast road at Karad-edeli. The most memorable is Sinekkale. Turn south in Imamli and then after half a kilometre fork right: after three kilome-tres, by a Hellenistic tower, Kürtesir Kalesi, a path leads to the left. Sinekkale is a substantial country house, lost among fields and scrub. Enough sur-vives for one to get an idea of the scale of some of the rooms. Above the door of a small Hellenistic building nearby is a relief with a dagger and a device with a circle with two protrusions. Continuing southwards, after a kilometre the road intersects the site known is Işikkale, with a Byzantine basilica with Corinthian cap-itals in the arcades, a number of houses and, inevitably, tombs. That the next set-tlement, the more substantial town at Karakabakli, is only a kilometre further on indicates how intensely the area was inhabited in Byzantine times. At the cen-tre is a modest tetrapylon, a clear state-ment of civic ambition. There are two churches and a number of houses, including one of particular charm to the east of the site, with on the first floor a door surmounted by an open lunette and flanked by pairs of small arches divided by columns. Five lesser sites are within reach of the road on the five-kilometre stretch to Karadedeli. For these and so much else in the area Celâl Taşkiran's *Silifke and Environs* is the indispensible guide.

76

OLBA AND DIOCAESAREA

❖

OLBA may not have been founded by the eponymous nephew of Homer's Ajax, as Strabo tells us, but the city was an early foundation. As the towers of the acropolis hill above the village of Ura show it was a place of some importance, largely no doubt on account of its shrine, the great Temple of Zeus, some three miles to the north-west, that dominates the modern village of Uzuncaburç. The hereditary priests, some of whom also bore the name Olba, came to control a substantial area of Rough Cilicia, retaining a degree of independence under Roman rule in the first century AD. The religious centre was renamed Diocaesarea in honour of the Emperor Vespasian (AD 69–79). After the adoption of Christianity as the religion of the Empire, the temple was adapted as a cathedral. But the remoteness of the site, over 1,000 metres/3,800 feet above sea level and some 32 kilometres/20 miles inland from Silifke, contributed to a long decline after the Byzantine period.

Uzuncaburç, the modern village, can be reached from Mut; and there is a lesser road from the coast at Kizkalesi. But the best approach is from Silifke. And this route has the advantage of passing through the village of Demircili, near which are six most handsome temple tombs associated with the Roman town of Imbriogon. One group of three is on a south-sloping terrace overlooking the village to the left of the road; and further on, to the right of this, there is a particularly attractive double-tiered example.

The road gradually rises, climbing out of the valley. Eventually, the eye is caught by a spectacular pyramid-crowned Hellenistic mausoleum, some 16 metres/53 feet high, reached by an easy walk along a ridge. The road turns downwards and then rises again, towards what was the centre of the ancient town, marked by the five splendid limestone columns of an arch which crossed the colonnaded street that was the central artery of the town, and the route by which pilgrims from Corycus would have reached the precinct of the great Temple of Zeus Olbius, 183 metres/200 yards along this on the left. Founded by Seleucus I Nicator early in

Olba: the aqueduct, with a tower of the acropolis behind.

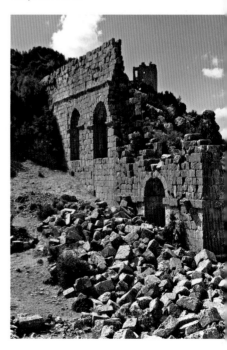

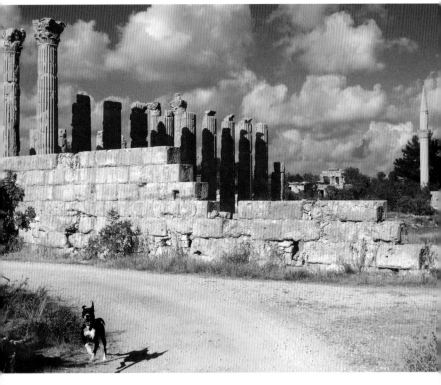

Diocaesarea: the Temple of Zeus Olbius.

the third century BC, this was apparently the earliest Corinthian temple in Asia Minor. Thirty – of the original thirty-two – columns survive to give some sense of the scale and height of the temple. The alterations effected by the Byzantines to create an apse, and the puny arches of the two side doors they added on the lateral colonnades, show how efficiently the building was put to Christian use. But the regular blocks of the cella walls proved an irresistible bait to later inhabitants. A number of sections of a richly carved frieze have been placed near the northern wall of the enclosure and the

soaring fluted columns impress from any angle.

To the west the colonnaded street runs to the Roman Temple of Tyche, goddess of fortune, the cella of which was set behind a screen of six elegant columns. Of these five remain. These are of granite – which does not occur locally – and have elegant Corinthian capitals. This exceptionally elegant building is of the late first century, and bears an inscription identifying the donors, Oppius and his wife Kyria, who must, one supposes, have considered that fortune had favoured them. Turning back down the colonnaded street, another road leads on the left – north – to the well-preserved north-western gate, a triumphal arch built, as an inscription attests, under the Emperor Arcadius (AD 395–408).

The reasonably well-preserved theatre built during the joint rule of Marcus Aurelius and Lucius Verus, and thus between AD 161 and 164, is to the east of the arch across the colonnaded street, turning its back, as it were, to the modern road. The cavea, with seating for 2,500 people, faces south. Nothing of the stage building survives. Further north is a substantial Hellenistic tower, some 22.5 metres/74 feet high, which was repaired in the third century, and no doubt subsequently. Much of the internal structure can still be made out. Near by are the main buildings of the modern village. To the north of these, the line of the old road is flanked by an extensive necropolis.

Olba in her heyday must have been impressive; and the pilgrims who struggled up from the coastal plain to do homage to her priestly rulers must have relished the higher air and stronger winds. Now the way that the past and present co-exist is particularly appealing. Farm vehicles progress up and down the street of columns; and the tourist knows that his or her passing will leave no mark on the immemorial life of the place.

A road to the left in Uzuncaburç descends to Ura. At the centre of the village, backing on to the acropolis, is what remains of the nymphaeum, a necessary public monument of a Roman town, by the much-looted theatre. The nymphaeum was supplied with water by an aqueduct built under Septimius Severus (193–211 AD). This crosses the valley at the opposite end of the acropolis hill. There were arches on two levels, but much of the upper section has fallen: none the less the golden beauty of the stone is unforgettable. Passing the aqueduct the road continues to a junction. Turn left there: nearly a kilometre further on, just above the road, there is a tomb with a somewhat eroded relief of a funerary feast.

Return to the junction and, if you wish to take the Kizkalesi road, turn left. It is perhaps twenty-five minutes to Cambazli, another Hellenistic site the importance of which is implied by six substantial temple tombs that hang above the road. Further on is an astonishingly complete and unexpectedly large basilica prefaced by a narthex that, somewhat unusually, extends beyond the width of the church. The quality of the architectural detail is of a high order. From Cambazli the descent to Kizkalesi takes under an hour.

77

ALAHAN

❖

MODERN Silifke has little appeal. But her great citadel broods over the valley of the Göksu, the ancient Calycadana which with the Iron Gates of Cilicia to the east is the one of the great historic routes from the coast through the Taurus mountains to Konya and the Anatolian heartland. It was in the Göksu that the Emperor Frederick Barbarossa was drowned during the First Crusade in 1090. Roughly following its ancient predecessor's course, the road rises steadily. The valley widens before reaching the unselfconscious town of Mut, founded in the first century by a high priest of Olba, Marcus Aurelius Polemo. The Byzantine citadel was strengthened by the Karamanids in the fourteenth century. Just below this is their Lal Ağa Camii, shadowed by trees, with a beautiful entrance and a fine minaret. Beside this is the Hocendi türbe, with a steep pyramidal roof. From Mut a road cuts to the east through the hills for Olba.

The main road continues its climb northwards. After about 20 kilometres / 12.4 miles, a short spur on the right twists up the flank of the valley for Alahan, one of the most splendidly placed Christian sites in Turkey. Begun in the late fifth century, the monastery was built on a long terrace or shelf, running west to east, backed by the mountainside. To the south and west the ground falls away steeply.

The visitor comes first, at the western end of the terrace, to the late fifth-century Church of the Evangelists. The position was exposed and the building has suffered badly. The main door survives,

with reliefs of the symbols of the Four Evangelists and two rarer subjects, the Archangels Gabriel and Michael triumphant respectively over the cults of Mithras and Cybele, who had been worshipped almost within living memory when the church was built. There were three naves, divided by screens of Corinthian columns.

Next comes the baptistery, its sunken font still preserved. Further on, partly excavated from the cliff behind, are the monastic buildings, including the refectory, a kitchen and storerooms. These are overlooked by the impressive ruins of the great church at the eastern end of the terrace. The façade is preceded by a narthex. The doors opening from this are enriched by narrow panels with wonderfully precise fish and leaf motifs. The church is of basilical form, the higher central section supported on slim Corinthian columns at ground level and on elegantly constructed arcades above. Its beauty is due to the harmony of the elements and the accuracy of the masonry. Time has not stood still. Much of the upper level has fallen away on the less protected southern side, and many blocks rest at precarious angles. But none the less the visitor can understand the builders' intentions and has the sense of being in a caged, if not a captured, space. The energetic will walk round the southern side of the structure to see it from the east; and then clamber up the rock behind to reach the level of the upper storey and look both downwards to the church and outwards through the arcades and the western windows across the plunging valley to distant hills.

Alahan must always have been remote. While Olba was close enough to the coast to endure as the base of a priestly dynasty for centuries, a pilgrim-

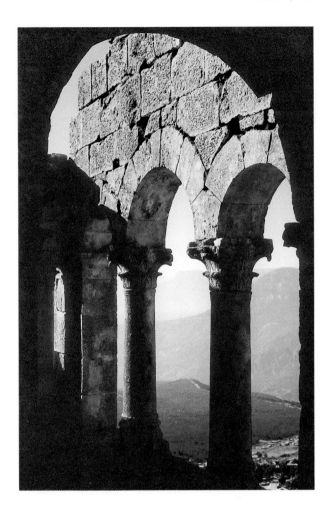

The main church, detail, with the valley of the Göksu.

age to Alahan must have been demanding. And this may in part explain why there is so little trace of later Byzantine work. With the Seljuk conquest, Alahan was passed by, veiled no doubt from view by a natural canopy of trees. Happily the position was too remote for it to make economic sense for the Karamanids to recycle the masonry; and so the ruins of Alahan stood undisturbed until the Goughs began to disentangle and document these in 1961, under the aegis of the British Institute of Archaeology at Ankara.

78

TAKMAR KALESI

❧

THE COAST of Rough Cilicia is well defended by nature. But none the less the importance of the route northwards up the valley of the Göksu, the ancient Calycadana, and the productivity of numerous lesser valleys that descend to the coast meant that medieval rulers devoted much ingenuity to its protection.

At Silifke, the ancient Seleucia ad Calycadnum, Seleucus I Nicator's acropolis was refortified by the Byzantines. The imposing circuit of their wall, with twenty-three towers, is roughly oval. Within the enceinte there are massive storerooms, some of which have been excavated, and cisterns. The site is commanding: great efforts have been made in recent times to renew several towers and a stretch of wall on the south-east side. West of Silifke, the eastern promontory of the bay on which the little town of Boğsak now sits was defended by Liman Kalesi, built apparently by the Seljuks. The ruins are now in a military area.

Four kilometres/2.5 miles beyond Boğsak, a road on the right, not particularly well marked, rises steeply and after 3 kilometres/1.9 miles the remarkable main front of Takmar Kalesi is seen on the left, crowning a hill below the road. The position was one of great strength, as was understood by both the Armenians and the Knights Hospitaler, who seem to have taken over by 1210. To the south-west, where the site abuts on a cliff, defence was hardly necessary. The fall of the ground to the north-west and south-east was so steep that no more than solid walls were called for. Only to the north-east were more sophisticated defences necessary. Here, there are four round towers. These are faced with particularly finely bossed masonry. Many blocks are significantly smaller than those of the one bossed round tower of the Land Castle at Kizkalesi: these still bear, very clearly, signs of the chiselling by which they were pared down; and there are numerous masons' marks, many repeated both on the same and on other towers.

The engineer responsible for the structure was an architect of considerable refinement, aware surely of crusader developments. This alone, and the beauty of the untrammelled setting on the stony hill, would make Takmar a place of particular magic. But it is the view that is most extraordinary. To the east the castle watches the Bay of Boğsak and surveys the coastal plain below Silifke: to the west, Takmar looks down the fertile valley that stretches to the bay behind Cape Cavaliere; while over the lower ridge on the opposite side of this valley the faint outline of Cyprus can be seen.

Much further – about 90 kilometres/56 miles – west is yet another substantial Byzantine fortress, Softa Kalesi. This is seen to particular advantage from the west, where great circular bastions defended the most exposed salient of the hill. The Romans had recognized the strategic value of the site, and the Byzantine castle was reinforced both by the Armenians, as they expanded their Cilician state westwards, and by their Ottoman successors.

Opposite: the towers, with bossed masonry.

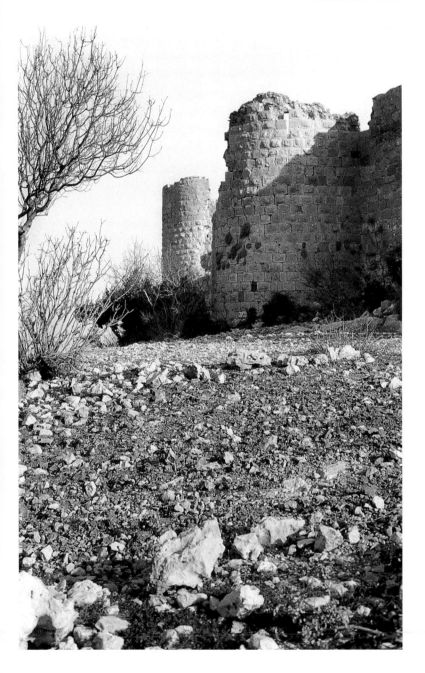

79

ANAMUR

ROUGH Cilicia is worthy of the name. Even now the twisting coastal road is demanding. And, partly because so many hotels have been built on the few areas of level ground near the sea, traffic is heavy. Ten kilometres /6.2 miles beyond Softa Kalesi a wide valley is reached, fertile with the silt deposits of millennia. At its eastern side is the great castle of Anamur: some 7 kilometres/4.3 miles away at the further end of the beach, beyond the modern town, are the extensive ruins of its ancient predecessor.

Anemurium was not a great city. But it prospered in Roman times, on the agriculture of the hinterland and trade with Cyprus. As Captain Beaufort wrote in 1817, buildings that appear from the distance to be the remains of a city prove to be tombs, built of rough limestone hardcore. Further on are churches, three bath complexes, a palestra, the inevitable theatre and the aqueducts on which the town depended. The buildings have lost their marble or stucco facings and therefore are not particularly elegant. Yet the place has a strange fascination as the waves crash below. To the south of the site is the acropolis hill, now very overgrown. As a result it is not easy to follow the walls, the extant sections of which are presumably largely of Byzantine date. But it is worth persevering, not least for the prospect across the town to the necropolis and over the coast to the east.

The castle of Anamur – Mamure Kalesi in Turkish – rises directly from the shore. The place had been fortified in earlier times. Under the Armenians it became the western bulwark of their

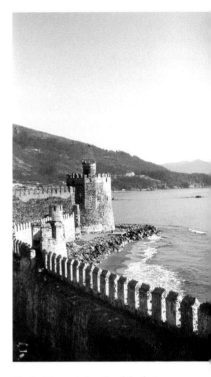

The battlemented walls of the fortress.

Cilician realm, well placed at once to block movement along the coast and incursion from the sea. From 1375 control passed to the Lusignans of Cyprus: they were followed by the Seljuk Karamanids and, in the sixteenth century, by the Ottomans. Successive occupants maintained the fortress even in Ottoman times, which is why it remains one of the most perfectly preserved of medieval fortresses, Turkey's counterpart to Caernarvon or Carcassonne.

The main approach is from the east, across the stream that fed the moat on the landward side. The gatehouse is linked to the tower at the south-east angle on the shore, with a series of passages and rooms on successive levels. The ground within the enceinte is divided into two baileys of unequal size by a substantial wall. In the larger, on the north, there is a sizeable mosque. Storerooms are built into the curtain towers and regular flights of steps mount to the battlements. There is a postern to the moat, where in spring the croaking of frogs blocks out extraneous sounds. The southern bailey ends in a formidable tower. One can clamber down to the shore, where waves break on the jagged rocks that have protected the building from erosion. And more steps – which should be treated with respect – climb to the upper walkway. To the east are the mountains of Rough Cilicia, to the west the bay with the acropolis of Anemurium at its extremity. And at whatever time of day, unless it is overcast, the eye is drawn by the sharp shadows cast by the crenellated walls.

80

ALANYA

❖

THE excitement of the first distant view of the great rock of Alanya and the towering grandeur of the hills behind cannot fail to impress. One would know at a glance that whoever controlled it, Alanya, like Gibraltar or its closer Yemeni counterpart Qana, long held the key to both economic and political power. The Greek city of Coracesium has left only traces of the Hellenistic defensive walls. The Selucids were ousted by pirates – to whom control of the forests inland must have been of particular value. They were routed in a naval battle by Pompey in 67 BC. Later Antony would present the place to Cleopatra, on whose fall it passed to Rome. The Byzantines renamed Coracesium Kalonoros – the beautiful mountain. After the debacle at Manzikert in 1071, the Armenians seized the place, but this westward expansion of the Cicilian kingdom was unsustainable. Kalonoros was exchanged in about 1221 with the Seljuk Sultan, Alaeddin Keykubad I, who renamed it Alaiye, his own city. The splendid fortifications with which the Sultan girdled Alanya reflect not only its significance to the ruler of Konya and central Anatolia as a major port on the Mediterranean, but also his own personal interest in it. Alaeddin Keykubad's successors, however, lost the city to the Karamanids, under whom this remained a major entrepôt, visited by, among others, Ibn Battuta. The Ottoman conquest of 1471 must have marked a phase in Alanya's slow decline, which was to be reversed only in the post-war years. Intensive tourist development, particu-

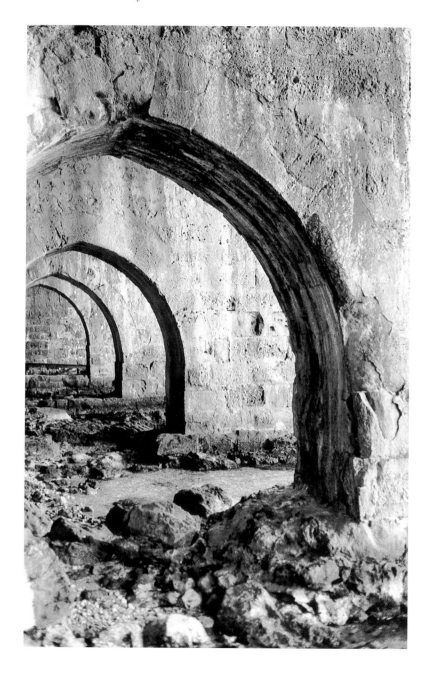

larly in the lower town, has at least ensured that steps are being taken to preserve the Seljuk monuments.

Alanya's importance to the Seljuks is expressed most obviously by the massive scale of the octagonal Kizil Kule (the 'Red Tower') which overlooks it and links the land walls with those along the sea. Built in 1226, this was planned by a celebrated architect, Ebu Ali of Aleppo, and its great citadel was one of the more imposing fortresses of the epoch in western Asia. Each of the five internal storeys is divided into sections corresponding with the eight sides and at the centre there is a cistern large enough to serve for a prolonged siege. A fine stretch of the lower walls of the enceinte follows the shoreline to the south, leading after some two hundred metres to a remarkable survival, the vaulted tersane, or dockyard. It is divided into five equal and linked sections, each over 40 metres/130 feet long and some 7.5 metres/24.6 feet wide, opening to the sea. As in the great hans, one is left in no doubt of the ruthless efficiency of the Seljuk administrative machine. With the constant lapping of the water and the pattern of shade and light, the tersane has an unexpected magic. Beyond this is a second tower, built as an arsenal.

From the Kizil Kule, a road strikes south for an attractive area of the old town, on the steep incline of the promontory. The surviving houses are most remarkable for the way they exploit the difficult terrain. A further road writhes upwards for the great citadel with which the Seljuks crowned the rock. Halfway up there is an impressive double gate, where the road crosses the line of the

Opposite: Alanya, the tersane.

lower town wall. Persian inscriptions established a date of between 1226 and 1231. Nearby is a modest Byzantine church, the Arap Evliyasi, which the Seljuks re-commissioned as a mosque.

Higher up is the Iç Kale ('Inner Castle'), the walls leading to which incorporate a few ashlar courses of Hellenistic date. Connected with this, to the north, is the Ehmedek, where scattered houses take the place of Seljuk predecessors. Alaeddin Keykubad I constructed a mosque nearby, but this was replaced by the Ottoman Süleymaniye Camii. A Seljuk survivor is the Akşebe Türbesi, a tomb that is still much venerated. This is dwarfed by a seventeenth-century neighbour, a han now in use as the Bedesten Hotel. The Iç Kale itself was originally entered from the east. Within is a large area surrounded by buildings, including another Byzantine church. To the west the ground falls sheer to the sea; and from the south-western angle the city wall zigzags down the rock. The museum is in the modern town and houses finds from Alanya itself and other local sites. These include a very respectable Roman bronze of Hercules.

West of Alanya, near the ancient coastal route, are two notable Seljuk caravanserais. Şarafsa Hani, of 1236–46, is beside the motorway, while Alarahan, a few kilometres inland, built for Alaeddin Keykubad I in 1231–3, has been ruthlessly restored and is now used as a bazaar. The plan is highly unusual with a very narrow central court.

Overlooking the han is a towering rock of Alarakale, as criss-crossed with curtain walls as Alanya itself, which briefly marked the western extremity of the Armenian kingdom. A boy offered to act as a guide and as he brandished a torch I did not dissent. We struck up from the river to enter the surviving section of a 'tunnel', or covered ramp, with steps, partly rock-cut, but largely built of rough-cast stone and with regular light sources, some now blocked. The ascent goes up some hundreds of feet to the lower ward of the castle, which has numerous towers. The steps continue to the upper ward. I went on alone, making finally for the keep, entering by a postern. If it is wet at Alarakale, move with care.

81
ASPENDUS
❧

THE Pamphylian plain, a fertile swathe about 90 kilometres / 56 miles from east to west, sandwiched between the mountains of Pisidia and the sea, boasts some of the most impressive sites of classical Asia Minor. Crossing the river Melas, the Manavgat Çayi, the curious can choose between the little-frequented town, now identified as Lybde rather than Seleucia, whose admirably preserved market building is shadowed by pines a few miles inland, and over-exposed Side on the shore. There, the spectacular Roman theatre now presides over the amenities of a holiday village. Nearby in the well-preserved baths is the fine site museum. The elaborate nymphaeum outside the main north gate has been partly reconstructed as has one interior wall of the even more lavish State Agora south-east of the theatre. In the open area between this and the landwalls is the substantial ruin of the episcopal palace, with a small chapel that retains part of its beautiful marble decoration, carved with ivy and other plant motifs.

Aspendus, Side's rival to the west, is said to have been founded by colonists from Argos, and early in the fifth century ranked with her neighbour and rival Side as one of the two main cities of Pamphylia. Contested later in the century by Athens and the Persians, Aspendus fell to Alexander in 333 BC, and was subsequently controlled by the Seleucids; but it is to her prosperous centuries under Roman rule that the great buildings of the city are owed.

Although not far from the modern high road, Aspendus has been spared the indignities suffered by Side. A minor road passes an elegant – and functional – Seljuk bridge over the Eurymedon and skirts a large thermal structure of the brick which the Romans used with such authority, before the great theatre built in the second century AD looms into sight. Partly because it was cut into the flank of the acropolis hill of the Hellenistic city, the theatre is almost miraculously well preserved, rivalled in this respect only by Bosra in not-so-distant Syria.

The entrance is through the substructure of the towering stage building. One emerges in the semi-circular orchestra to be overwhelmed by the rising tiers of the benches – there are forty rows of seats, many with inscriptions that record the names of those who had proprietary claims. These are divided vertically by stairs and horizontally by one passage, the diazoma. It is only as one climbs upwards that the full opulence of the stage building becomes evident: the columns have for the most part been lost, but the richly carved niches and friezes integrated with the wall survive, as does a battered relief of Bacchus in the pediment. Over the two doors at the sides are dedicatory inscriptions of the brothers, Curtius Crispinus and Curtius Auspicatus, who paid for the building.

Inevitably a monument as impressive as the theatre is a magnet for visitors. These come in busloads. But few are given time to wander on the acropolis behind the theatre. Grass paths cut through shrubs and bushes to a number of buildings of interest. Round the open space of the Agora the most substantial, which survives more or less to full height, is the square annexe to the largely destroyed basilica, which no doubt owes its endurance to the four buttresses, partly of bossed masonry, on the side

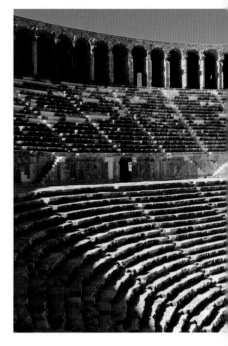

The theatre.

walls. At the foot of the eastern slope, north of the theatre, is the stadium, similar in scale to, but very much less well preserved than, its counterpart at Perge.

The views from the acropolis are tremendous: at either side stretches the Pamphylian plain, with the dramatic protuberance of Sillyum in the west and to the north the untamed silhouette of the mountains. In the middle distance is the second of the unforgettable monuments of Aspendus, the majestic aqueduct, which brought the water on which the city depended from the hills. This may be of the second century AD and its sophistication was doubtless made possible by a recorded gift of two million denarii 'for the introduction of water'

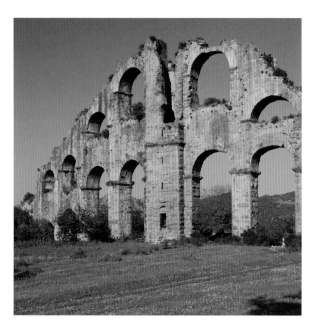

Aspendus: the aqueduct, raised section on the north side of the valley.

from the tactfully named Tiberius Claudius Italicus. The aqueduct crosses a wide marshy valley on a series of arches, rising at either side to towers some 30 metres/100 feet high before turning to run into the flank of the hill and disappear from view. Seen from the acropolis, the aqueduct is a thing of great beauty, but it is as a work of engineering that it commands our respect. The function of the towers, or more specifically of the open basins at the tops of these, was to allow air to escape from the piped channel and thus to improve the flow of the water. For the Romans learnt to make water rise under gravitational pressure, and had, as this building proves, the structural mastery to achieve this on an ambitious scale.

It is a rough scramble down from the acropolis to the aqueduct. So those with limited time may choose to follow the road north from the car park by the theatre and then make by a track to the left for the southernmost section. Chickens roost under the piers and in the spring a bank of lupins catches the eye. The energetic used to be able to clamber to the doorway some 2.5 metres/8 feet from the base of the corner pier, but this has now been blocked with sturdy bars. The door leads to a stair that turns within the pier and eventually emerges at the upper level. The stretch of the aqueduct on the far side of the valley is almost equally well preserved: happily the staircase within the central pier is still accessible, so one can still look down to the low houses that cluster below and survey the ebb and flow of village life. There are numerous other aqueducts in Asia Minor: many are considerably longer, but none is so impressive.

82
SELGE

SELGE, high in the hills of ancient Pisidia, is said to have been founded by the legendary Calchas and subsequently taken over by colonists from Sparta. Circumstance and trade encouraged links less with other Pisidian cities than with those of Pamphylia to the south, and by the fifth century Selge's silver coinage was, in Professor Bean's words, 'virtually indistinguishable' from that of Aspendus. The Selgians welcomed Alexander in 333 BC, and emerged victorious from a siege of 220 BC, which was described in considerable detail by the Hellenistic historian Polybius. Allocated by Mark Antony to Amyntas's client kingdom of Galatia, Selge was subsequently incorporated in the Roman Empire. Her coinage was discontinued in the third century AD, and despite the productivity of her cultivatable land Selge lapsed into obscurity, her name echoed in that of the modern village, Zerk.

To the citizens of Aspendus Selge must always have seemed remote, hidden in the jagged hills that massed on their northern horizon. It still does. And after several visits one is only the more aware of this. The modern road follows the river Eurymedon, passing the village of Beşkonak. Gradually the hills close in. The road reaches a well-preserved single-span Roman bridge – with, until very recently, no hint of a parapet. Beyond this is another, equally elegant Roman bridge, above of a deep pool with water that remains cool even on the hottest summer's day. Nearby the modern road twists upwards, writhing round

the line of its Roman predecessor, up which I walked once when the first bridge was closed to traffic. Much of the original paving survives, mounting through woodland to the flank of a steep ridge. A subsidiary valley comes into view below, with the occasional timber-framed house. By road it is some 10 kilometres/6.2 miles to the modern village of Zerk, and even now Freya Stark's account in *Alexander's Path* of her arrival in 1956 does not seem exaggerated. The road winds up, past larger fields, to a scattering of houses on a south-facing slope. From the top of this, the city can be seen, the acropolis on the left and to the right, against the hillside, the massive

Roman bridge across a tributary of the Eurymedon.

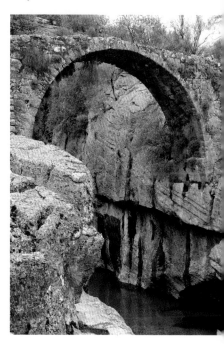

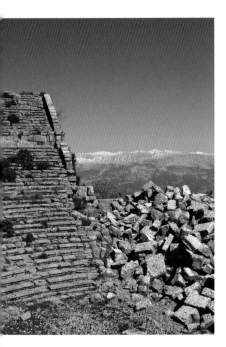

Selge: the theatre.

theatre. But the joy of Selge is that it is not a sanitized site: there are more timber houses on the level area ahead, and others flank the road that curls round to skirt the acropolis hill.

The austere Greek theatre is the great monument of Selge. The cavea survives in reasonable condition, because the builders took full advantage of the hillside. The stone is a pale grey. Even when one has not walked, it is a place in which to linger. The later Roman stage building has collapsed into a jumble with which no contemporary sculptor could compete, thus liberating the view. To the south-east the ground falls away to the tremendous valley carved by the river; even late in the spring there is still snow on the crests of the hills. To the west, between houses and small fields, is what survives of the stadium. Above this are the tumbled ruins of several buildings, including at least one temple, on a ridge overlooking an elegant monument that is now surrounded by a small fields, violently green with young corn in the spring. At the high point of the acropolis to the south is what remains of a substantial Byzantine church.

Selge's position was well chosen. No enemy could take it by surprise, even from the north. The city wall was originally over 3 kilometres / 1.9 miles long; and much of the line survives. Within this the curious may chance on the occasional carved block, on scatterings of shards or the hint of lesser buildings: in places the bedrock is exposed, because no opportunity for grazing has been wasted. The best-preserved section of the walls, with a gate and a substantial tower, is to the west.

The villagers of Zerk are now spared the abject poverty described by Freya Stark and by Professor Bean. Despite improvements to the road, they are too sane to depend on the tourist trade, although some of the women offer traditional knitted goods. No one who goes to Selge, or has time to follow the ancient road downwards, will fail to respond to the immemorial magic of the place.

83

SILLYUM

IN ANTIQUITY Sillyum was outshone by greater neighbours, Aspendus
and Perge, from both of which it is in
sight. And today it remains the least visited of the three. Like Perge, the city may
have claimed to have been founded by
the seer Mopsus. But it is not mentioned
before the fourth century BC and only
began to issue coins a century later. Yet
unlike any other city in the area except
Termessus, Sillyum was strong enough
to successfully defy Alexander in 333 BC.

*Steps to buildings near the edge of the
acropolis.*

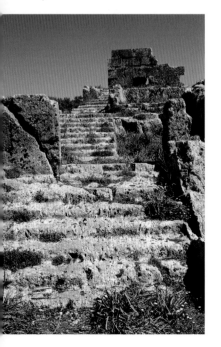

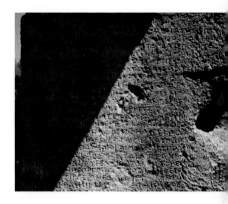

*Inscription on a door-jamb on the
acropolis.*

The site is easily made out, a roughly
oval flat-topped outcrop some 91
metres / 300 feet high that erupts abruptly from the plain. An insignificant
settlement is in its foot. The land is still
fertile. Little enough remains of the
lower town, which spreads to the south-
west of the acropolis hill: some walls of a
palace; a fine Hellenistic tower, four-
square; a stretch of the town wall. But
above these are the very substantial
remains of the prodigious buttressed
Hellenistic ramp that led up to the acropolis, which elsewhere was very effectively protected by cliffs and only
accessible by narrow paths. The ramp,
which was intended for wheeled traffic
and bears the marks of this, was built
against the hillside, and doubles back,
before turning again to climb to the
upper level. Any assailant would have
been vulnerable to counter-attack from
above, and at the top the final approach
was properly guarded.

The most distinguished building on
the acropolis is near the Byzantine
fortress at the south-western extremity.
This is not particularly large, but, on one

of the jambs of the main door, bears an inscription of thirty-seven lines which is of Hellenistic date: this is the most substantial known text in the Pamphylian language, which depended on Greek and used Greek lettering. Nearby is a larger hall, some 55 metres/180 feet long with ten windows of varying size on the west wall: the holes for the fastenings and bolts of the third from the southern end are unusually elaborate.

There is little to see at the centre of the acropolis, now thickly overgrown with scrub. So it is best to follow the circuit of the cliff, although care must be taken. On the south side, much of the theatre literally fell away as a result of an earthquake in 1969. And further on there are alarming fissures in the rock, sections of which seem bound to sheer off in their turn. This is unfortunate, as many domestic buildings were cut into the rim of the cliff. Excavations of the kind are common enough elsewhere in Turkey, but here the rooms with their differing levels and cavities for storage mean that one feels unusually close to the lives of the earlier Greek settlers. They too must have known the waving asphodels we see, but doubtless took for granted the vast sweep of the prospect at their feet.

I first walked to Sillyum on a Friday morning in the spring, hearing the call of the muezzins to the faithful working in their almost too violently green fields. Many places are at their most magical in the morning. But Sillyum I love best in the afternoon, as the shadows lengthen to the east and the ramp is thrown into sharper relief.

84

ADADA

THE classical cities of Pisidia have a potent magic, partly because their rugged settings in the Taurus are for the most part unsullied by modern development. Adada exemplifies this to perfection. It is now relatively easily reached by a well-marked road from south of Eğirdir, itself a happy base for sightseeing with its Byzantine castle, a restored Seljuk mosque facing a former medrese partly built with material from a caravansarai two miles to the south, of which only the rubble core is left. The road passes to the west of Aksu, where a Roman bridge crosses the fledgling Eurymedon to a shrine below a sacred cavern. The turn to Adada is on the left after 50 kilometres/30 miles, just north of the successor village of Sağrac and 5 kilometers/3 miles short of Sütçuler.

First mentioned as an ally of Termessus in the second century BC, Adada was, as its monuments attest, very prosperous in the early Imperial period: in the Byzantine era its bishop was second to that of Antiochia in the area, but by the ninth century Adada had ceased to be of significance. The road curls upwards and then crosses what was the centre of the city. Park by the helpful map, for Adada is not fully covered in most guidebooks. Ahead to the right of the road is the Temple of Trajan, who visited Pisidia in AD 114: the north wall survives to cornice height. Across the road are two equally fine temples. That of the Emperors was built by Theodorus, son of Nikomakhorus: the cella is substantially intact, and, most unusually, the blocks of the south front were left with the quarry-

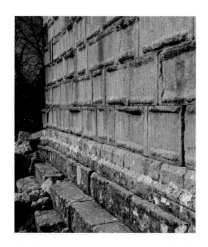

The Temple of the Emperors, lateral wall with untrimmed blocks.

men's protruding edges and not pared down as would have been intended. The Temple of the Emperors and Zeus-Serapis is also relatively well-preserved, the portico tumbled below the cella. Behind this and to the north, cut into the flank of the encircling ridge, is the theatre of which only the lower section survives.

Re-cross the road and head downwards, through the former heart of the city, strewn with stones and fragments of bricks and tiles. Descend to the streambed between the high hill to the east and the acropolis of the city on the right. The going is quite rough. In places ancient walls line the stream and fragments of buildings are visible among the dense trees. Follow the stream to reach – on its west side – a marvellous section of Roman road that curls for a considerable distance towards the valley. The blocks, some as wide as nine feet, are laid sideways and in the steeper sections there are low steps. Eventually the road peters

out, and it is time to return uphill, dazed by the sunlight that bounces off the pale paving stones.

Where the paved road ends, those with stout shoes and thorn-proof clothes should cut uphill for a substantial early wall, with steps on its further side, behind which is the less well-constructed carcass of the substantial Byzantine church. Head on uphill, but with due care, for the summit of the ridge, which is defended by low walls and commands a superb panorama of the site. A better path runs down to what was the civic centre of Adada, the splendid paved agora, on the east of which a wide flight of steps mounts to the city's central shrine, of which little now survives.

Adada was discovered in 1888 by, among others, the great late Victorian archaeologist Sir William Ramsay, and happily remains very much as he found it. No one who loves ruins in wild places with a rich native flora – cyclamen, violets and grape hyacinths in March – will think the excursion wasted.

The Roman road below Adada.

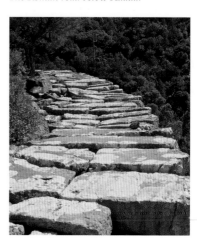

85
ANTIOCHEIA IN PISIDIA

PISIDIAN Antioch was founded by Antiochus I Soter (280–61 BC), son of Seleucus I Nicator. Seleucid rule ended with the Roman victory at Magnesia in 188 BC. The city was to enjoy a long period of prosperity under the Romans, who ceded it to the King of Galatia in 39 BC, but under Augustus in 25 BC elevated it as a colonia. Saint Paul visited the city in about 48 AD. Subsequently the seat of a bishopric, Antiocheia was badly affected by Arab incursions during the seventh and eighth centuries and after the Byzantine defeat at Manzikert fell to Oğuz Turks, after whose leader the nearby town of Yalvaç was named.

Inevitably much is made of Saint Paul's visit. There is a small informative museum with finds from the site in the town, including a small marble dog and some good reliefs. Antiochia was spread over the low hill above this. The site entrance is just below the city wall, which was largely rebuilt in Byzantine times. Numerous decorated blocks are marshalled near the ancient road which leads up to the second-century west gate with three arches that was the ceremonial entrance to the city.

Its paved roads are the most memorable features of Antiocheia, and inevitably one imagines Saint Paul walking up and down these. The gate opens to a paved piazza. Ahead is the junction with the Decumanus Maximus that rises gradually, passing the Hellenistic theatre which was restored in 311–13, to inter-sect with the Cardo Maximus. The section of this to the left has been excavated. The first junction is with a street to the right that opens to the Square of Tiberius. From this steps mount to the fragmentary propylon of the major imperial monument of the city, the Temple of Augustus: little but the podium survives, standing forward from the cliff, which has been cut to form a semi-circular wall, against which tiered colonnades, respectively Corinthian and Ionic, were placed. The temple probably took the place of that of the local deity, Men-Askaénos, whose eunuch high priest presided over arcane rituals, which must have outraged the early Christians. Their most prominent church was on the far side of the cardo: foundations and fragments of walls indicate its size. The cardo ends with the so-called Road Square, behind which was a handsome nymphaeum, of which relatively little survives. West of this, within the city wall, is the fragmentary north church, below which was a bath complex.

The charm of Antiocheia is its position. The surrounding hills, snow-clad until well into the spring, seem in sunlight to answer the white paving stones of the ancient streets. Snaking along a low ridge running to the north is a particularly beautiful Roman aqueduct, several sections of which are largely intact. The masonry expresses the ruthless efficiency of Rome, whose administrators would not have approved of the way wild cherries and other trees have encroached upon the structure, despite the beauty of their white-and-pink blossom in due season.

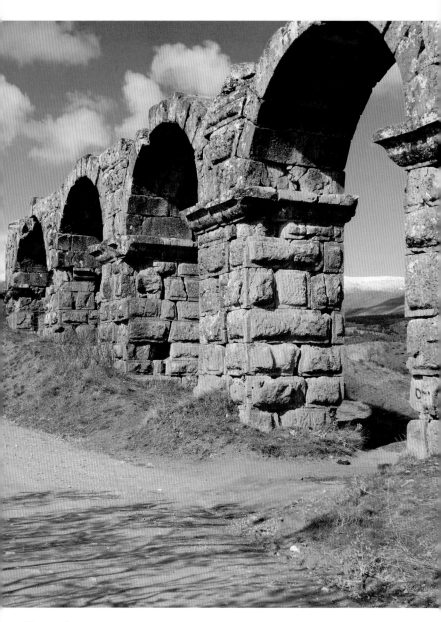

The aqueduct.

86

SAGALASSUS

PISIDIA remains a wild territory. The modern successor to the ancient road through the Döşeme Gorge sweeps ruthlessly through the hills and several remarkable sites are now thus within easy reach of the coast.

After a pass, a turn to the left leads to Ariassus, where a fine triumphal arch still spans the cardo that runs up the trough of a narrow valley past ruined civic buildings to a group of tombs at the crest. The main road descends to a wide valley, with to the right the Susuz Hani of about 1246, unusual for the reliefs of the entrance, and a little further on, 3 kilometres/1.9 miles to the west, the picturesquely ruinous Incir Hani, built in 1238 under the Sultan Giyasettin Keyhüsrev II. Here the door to the covered section is finely carved.

Beyond Buçak a road to the right leads to Sagalassus, which is at some 1,500 metres/4,900 feet the highest of the cities of ancient Pisidia. Well protected by nature, Sagalassus only surrendered to Alexander after a spirited defence in 333 BC. The city's agricultural wealth is indicated by the tribute in both silver and grain that she paid to Rome in 189 BC. Later, when Rome took permanent control of Asia Minor, Sagalassus retained her regional pre-eminence, and in time became the seat of a bishop. Her subsequent decline was, however, inexorable. The road circles down to a broad valley, where women work in the fields. From the village of Ağlasun – the name, as so often, preserves that of its predecessor – a side road leads northwards, diverging from its steeper ancient precursor to

climb round to the site entrance, on the level of the centre of the city that rose in successive terraces below the precipitous flank of Akdağ.

There is much to see. Follow the path to the northern wall of the substantial bath complex. This abuts on the paved lower agora, which has now been cleared. To the north, against the retaining wall of the terrace above, was the nymphaeum of Hadrian, while at a lower level on the west was the Ionic temple of Apollo Clarios, subsequently adapted as a church. It is worth following the cardo downhill to the southern extremity of the city, where the ground falls away. Returning, one is aware both of the constraints the steeply terraced site imposed on the plan of Sagalassus and of the visual opportunities the patrons and architects of the public buildings could exploit. Moreover, one gains some sense of the impression the place must have made on those who struggled up the steep road to reach the town.

Splendid as the lower agora is, this hardly prepares us for the drama of the larger upper agora, where the visitor is confronted by the lower section of the spectacular nymphaeum of Antonius Pius. This is as richly textured as, say, the famous library at Ephesus. But here the controlled rhythm of the eleven bays, alternately projecting and recessed, contrasts with the towering cliff behind. Water flows again as was intended. In front of the nymphaeum are part of a monument to Tyche and four columns that commemorate the family who paid for the agora to be laid out. To the west of this is a sequence of public buildings: the fine odeum, a Doric temple and the heroon, the last enriched by copies of the reliefs which, with other sculptures from Sagalassus – including the recently dis-

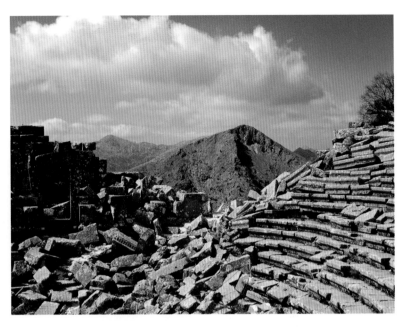

The theatre, with the fallen stage building.

covered statue of Hadrian – and from Cremna are in the Archaeological Museum at Burdur.

The dead were nobly commemorated at Sagalassus. There is a scatter of sarcophagi, some decorated with Medusa masks and other motifs, on the slope to the west of the Temple of Apollo. Groups of pigeonhole tombs are cut into the lower cliffs above the town and below these a series of substantial mausolea line the track that curls to the west. Some way to the east of the nymphaeum is the source of its water, the charming Hellenistic well house. Beyond and a little above this is what was until the recent excavations the most spectacular ruin at Sagalassus, the great Roman theatre in a fold of the hillside north-east of the city.

This dates from the second century AD. Virtually all the seats remain in place, but the stage building has been reduced by time to a prodigious tumble of blocks, piled as these fell. The original positions of many of these can be worked out with some precision. One can only hope that these will not be coaxed back into place.

When Freya Stark visited Sagalassus in 1956 she was surprised to meet a couple who had motored from Switzerland. Twice I have had the place to myself, and more recently two officers and their driver came up for a brief *coup d'oeil*. But it certainly deserves a larger audience, as the petrol company AYGAZ, which contributed to the reconstruction of the nymphaeum of Antonius Pius, must understand.

87

CREMNA AND MYLAS

❖

FROM Sagalassos the sloping hill of Cremna is in clear view to the south. This is best approached from Buçak, the route south-eastwards to Korcailler, which was evidently important in early Ottoman times, as two covered cisterns attest. In antiquity Cremna must have controlled the way: a small road climbs up to the left through the successor village of Çamlik. In the late Hellenistic period, Cremna was one of the most important of Pisidian cities, issuing coins in the first century BC. Siezed by King Amyntas of Galatia, it was recovered for Rome, becoming a colony under Augustus. Roman rule was disrupted by an adventurer, Lydius, about AD 270, and only recovered after a prolonged siege.

It is not difficult to understand why the city was thought to be impregnable. It stands on a high sloping plateau, protected except on the west – where evidence of the Roman siege works was found – by cliffs of varying height. Park by the site entrance (there is no guard) and walk upwards to the right, keeping to the flank below the upper face of the cliff, much of which was cut away in antiquity. A path more or less follows what must have been an ancient way, rising up to a subsidiary gateway, two ribs arching which are in place. Some way below, on a high natural terrace, there are small fields, verdant in spring, from which the ground plunges to a deep valley: beyond the Taurus fall away towards the coast.

Continue upwards to the bath building, the most substantial structure in the city. To the north of this, on a stepped

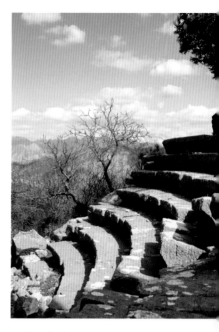

Mylas: the theatre.

podium, is a much-eroded temple, carved elements of which lie sprawled below. The other civic amenities of Roman Cremna were nearby: the imprint of the theatre is cut into the hilltop above the bath; and the jumbled chaos of the inevitable colonnaded street crosses the plateau below. The visitor can wander at will, picking his way across the site or walking round the crust of the plateau.

Cremna was a substantial place. This cannot really be said of its neighbour to the south, sometimes identified as Mylas, which is reached by returning to the Korcailler road and taking a marked turn to the east. From this a path fringed by scrub leads upwards to a ridge. A damaged sarcophagus is the first sign of the ancient town. Further on there is a vandalized shrine, cut into the rock. There are more sarcophagi and, below to the left, a large and relatively well-preserved Hellenistic building. The path keeps to the ridge, running in places along the remains of a defensive wall rising up to the summit of the hill. Against the north side of this is what survives of a particularly beautiful and beautifully placed small Hellenistic theatre, partly rock-cut. Much of a substantial structure stands below this. There is a glorious confusion of other ruins lower down and on a shelf that stretches eastwards from under the summit. From this eyrie the inhabitants could see downwards over the valley of the Aksu to the rock of Sillyon above the Pamphylian plain.

88

ANTALYA AND PERGE

FEW Turkish cities have changed so dramatically in recent decades as Antalya. A foundation as its ancient name, Attaleia, implies of King Attalus II of Pergamum (160–39 BC), this remained the major port of western Pamphylia for the duration of the Roman era, prospering under Byzantium and, from 1206, under the Seljuks.

The visitor now has to penetrate long canyons of modern development to reach the ancient town, Kaleci. This still preserves sections of its early walls and much of the fabric of the eighteenth- and nineteenth-century Ottoman town, put rather successfully to tourist use. The well-restored Arch of Hadrian, who visited Attaleia in AD 130, is a structure of consummate elegance, as the original sections of the vaults of the arches show. It is flanked by two finely bossed towers, one of which was restored in the tenth century. Equally impressive is the massive mausoleum that hangs above the coast and exemplifies the full muscularity of Roman taste. Near the centre of the town is the carcass of a fifth-century church, itself replacing a Roman temple, which was adapted as a mosque by a son of Beyazit II, the Kesik Minare Camii. To the west of the town, below the former walls, is the signal monument of Seljuk Antalya, the beautiful fluted minaret of brick built in 1230 under Sultan Alaeddin Keykubad. Beside this is the mosque, resting on Roman columns, many with fine Corinthian capitals: the complex also includes a tekke and a hamam.

Kaleci is the best base for visitors to the sites of Pamphilia and eastern Lycia:

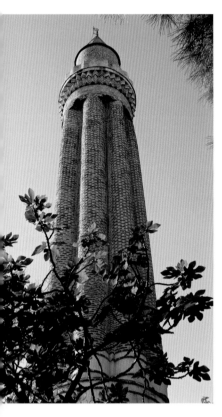

Antalya: the minaret.

and the impressive Archaeological Museum, some three kilometres to the west on what was the fringe of the conurbation, offers the best introduction to many of these. The cumulative impact of the finds from prehistoric sites, notably the Kerain cave, is impressive. But inevitably it is the classical holdings that dominate: the fourth-century BC stela from Elmali; Hellenistic reliefs from the heroon of Pericles at Limyra; notable Roman sarcophagi; and the vast quantity of Roman sculpture from Perge, arranged in several rooms. Perge's wealth is

attested not least by the sequence of marbles from the theatre and from the south baths. With the exception of the portraits, most of the statues are copies of Greek originals, including that after Lysippos's *Hercules*, of which the museum at Boston was irresponsible enough to buy the smuggled upper half and then was rather slow to return it. Much of the sculpture is conventional enough, but a spirited *Marsyas* has a dynamism to which the young Bernini would have responded. The *clou* of the Byzantine collection is part of the illegally excavated Corydalla Treasure, the remainder of which will no doubt eventually return from Dunbarton Oaks. There are also some good local carpets.

The visitor to the museum will wish to visit Perge, some twelve miles to the east. The site, a flat-topped hill south of a stream, inevitably attracted early settlers. The city claimed to have been founded after the Trojan War and sprawled over the lower ground south of the hill, long before any attempt to impose a Hippodamian plan, as the main streets had to respect existing structures, long since lost. The visitor approaches from the south. Cut into the ridge to the west is the well-preserved theatre, long closed. Below this is the fine stadium. The circuit of the city proper begins with the late City Gate. Ahead is the Hellenistic Gate with a curved court on its inner side, a gift of the city's most determined benefactress, Plancia Magna. Ahead is the Colonnaded Street, with to the right the Agora, most of the columns of the stoas of which have been re-erected, and, set back on the left, the very substantial South Baths, source of so much of the sculpture at Antalya.

The street draws one on. A small church was inserted into this, just before

89

THE VIA SESEUTE

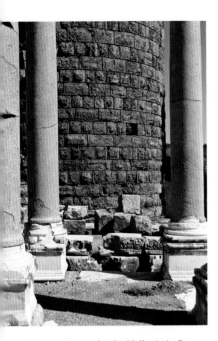

Perge: columns by the Hellenistic Gate.

SEVERAL major ancient roads intersected at Antalya, notably that which ran
northwards, linking the western end of
the Pamphylian plain with the rugged
territory of Pisidia. A few miles west of
this route is Evdir Hani, one of the earliest Seljuk caravanserais in the area, built
in 1217 under Sultan Izzettin Keykavus I
and reflecting Syrian models. Further
north, just before the modern highway
starts its long climb from the plain, is
Kirkgöz Hani, built in the reign of
Giyasettin Keyhüsrev II (1236–46). This
is impressive in scale, but much less
refined in detail than its earlier neighbour. The next caravanserai on the route,
Incir Hani, was some 40 kilometres / 25
miles to the north. The great caravans
that climbed upwards from Kirkgöz
Hani faced a long day.

The modern road rises through the
Çubak Gorge. Its ancient predecessor
took a more easterly route, climbing to
reach the narrow Doşeme Gorge. Turn
right near Kirkgöz Hani on a side road
that makes for a cluster of ruins at the
edge of the plain. A late fort, four-square,
and a bath house are the survivors of the
settlement, some of whose inhabitants
were buried in the necropolises which
fringe the cliffs that brood over the site.
Between these rises a narrow valley,
which was referred to by Polybius as
the climax, or ladder, long before the
Romans constructed their road, the Via
Seseute. This was intended for wheeled
traffic, unlike its better-preserved Byzantine successor, in which there are steps
on the steeper inclines. The sides of the
later road are of wide blocks, while

the junction with the main cross road. To
the left this runs past the splendid colonnade flanking the North Baths to the
North-west Gate. Ahead, below the
acropolis, is the nymphaeum. Those with
time should follow the path behind this
up to the acropolis, from which the plan
of the city is best appreciated. Sheep now
graze. There are fragmentary walls and
rock cuttings within the crust of the protecting cliffs. In spring mating frogs in
the stream below drown out other
sounds. The hills loom to the north: to
the east, rising from the plain, is the outcrop of Sillyum.

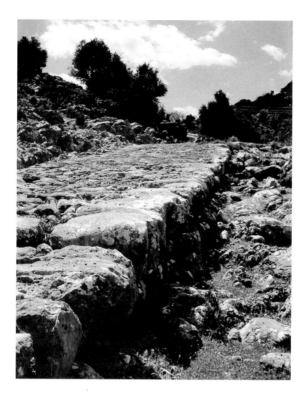

The Via Seseute.

smaller stones were laid between these. There are more scattered sarcophagi as the ascent begins, mostly smashed. Higher up the road there are sharp bends. A solitary woman passes, making downhill, and goats graze on the flanks of the valley.

After rather less than the 5 kilometres/3 miles implied by the otherwise dependable *Blue Guide*, one reaches a well-preserved Hellenistic watchtower. Beyond this is another settlement, with a gate that controlled the road, domestic buildings, small churches and more sarcophagi – one of which, as a man laden with wood pointed out to me, is decorated with a relief of a putto. The road descends to the north, raised a little above the ground, and curves to come to an abrupt end where the valley opens out. I cast about for a continuation, but then a man, whose dogs had raised the alarm, offered me tea. I sat back, bootless, against his embroidered mats and waited while he went through the customary rigmarole. Conversation was problematic, but luckily I had a small box of dried figs, which he accepted as an acknowledgement of his hospitality. The descent was a delight. And I remembered gratefully Freya Stark's *Alexander's Path*, which had prompted me to visit this magical and untrammelled artery of the ancient world.

90

TERMESSUS

❖

'A MOST untidy place!' Such was the opinion of Termessus of that cult figure among plant-hunters, the late Primrose Warburg, who went there in search of rare colchicums. Termessus is untidy. Its untidiness is indeed not the least of its attractions. But there are others: for of all the classical sites of Asia Minor, few equal Termessus in the beauty of its monuments, and only Heracleia perhaps contends in the drama of its setting. The city was founded at an early date, not by Greek colonists but by Pisidians, and its inhabitants, the Solymi, are first mentioned in Homer's account in the Iliad of the trials undergone by Bellerophon. In 333 BC, Alexander forced his way through the territory of the Termessians, but wisely abstained from attacking their city. The independent spirit of this is attested by evidence of a later war with the Lycian League. By about 70 BC the city was allied with Rome, but until the third century AD it retained its theoretical autonomy, as its coinage proudly attests. Under the Byzantines Termessus was the seat of a bishop, but gradually its importance declined and the site had long been abandoned when Spratt and Forbes described it in their *Travels in Lycia* of 1847.

The position was well chosen, over 1,000 metres/3,280 feet above sea level on a shelf below Mount Solymus, the Güllük Dağ, well placed to control the main westerly route to the Pamphylian plain. As an early wall across the valley to the north shows, the Termessians exacted dues from passing traffic. A subsidiary road climbs up a wooded valley to the south, ending among trees just below the lower fortifications.

Try to go soon after dawn. The main path, well marked, leads steeply upwards, skirting the gently sloping area on which many of the lesser domestic buildings of the city stood. To the south the great cliff of Mount Solymus hangs over the place. The path passes the large gymnasium. Although shaken by earthquakes, the building has not lost its beauty: the disciplined masonry is of a high order, with elegant niches and doorcases and, high up, a cornice with lion masks. A rough path runs to the south, passing further buildings, and then a scattering of tombs below the theatre, but the more conventional way to this is to return to the main path, past a stretch of the upper city wall, above which, at a diagonal, is the shattered street of columns with numerous inscribed bases. When straying from the path, watch out for the numerous cisterns that were vital to the city's life and now endanger the unwary.

The theatre is not huge, and has lost a few of the upper rows of its benches. But what remains is spectacular enough. The stage building is reasonably well preserved. Beyond this towers the sheer west face of Mount Solymus. To the left lay the city, stretching downhill; and on the right the ground plunges to a yet deeper valley, beyond which the sea is framed by lower hills. In the spring there are cyclamen that seem to dance in the inevitable wind.

Behind the theatre are a number of exceptionally fine smaller buildings, of which the most elegant is perhaps the odeum. Near this are two little temples. Some way beyond, amid tangled shrubs and trees, is the so-called Founder's House, with an inscription on a door

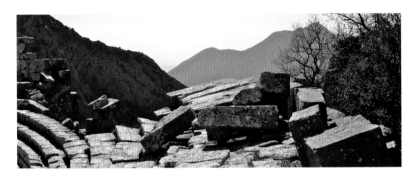

Termessus: the theatre.

stating that this had been built by one Bessos, in which Spratt found – in 1842 – a block with a bird, on two rounded humps 'in the form of half an egg'. Bean records another block with a bird with displayed wings, but was unable to find that described by Spratt, whose sketch of it he reproduced. But the block in question – or the counterpart to it, as the design reverses Spratt's illustration and includes finials at the corners corresponding to those on the fragment Bean saw – survives nearby, partly covered by scrub: I photographed it in 1991, but the undergrowth has once again taken over.

Higher up, the path continues to the south-west. Here is the main acropolis. Characteristic Lycian sarcophagi and groups of tombs erupt from the outcrops. These are the solid monuments of a hardy race, the forms severe, with in most cases the minimum of decoration. The path is well trodden, as there is an observation post on the ridge to the south-west. On the way down, the theatre inevitably draws me back. Whether in the sunlight of September or the spring, in rain or when cloud or mist shrouds part of the prospect, the magic of the place is irresistible. Once I sat to read a canto of *Don Juan*; and only a mas-

terpiece of that order can hold the attention there.

When finally it is time to leave, the world has woken and other tourists invade one's solitude, make across the sloping centre of the town, where trees shadow the chaos of jumbled masonry, for the lower cliffs of the mountain that dominates the site on the north. Here are further tombs. And of these one is as romantic as any vision conjured by Byron. For beside it is a relief of a warrior on a horse. He has been plausibly identified as Alcetas, one of Alexander's former generals, who committed suicide in 319 BC rather than surrender to a victorious rival, Antigonus. The latter, frustrated of his intended triumph, for three days vented his wrath on Alcetas's corpse, but this was later honoured by the Termessians. The hindquarters of the horse have gone and the warrior's head has been battered, but the rest of the relief has been protected by the overhanging rock; and so, if the identification as Alcetas is accepted, this wonderfully observed Hellenistic sculpture is a compelling link with a drama chronicled in grim detail by the Roman historian Diodorus.

91
PHASELIS AND OLYMPUS

FROM Antalya the mountains of Lycia are seen in memorable silhouette. But distance masks the rugged nature of the range, the narrow valleys of which supported some of the most independent communities of ancient Asia Minor. The Lycians were the timber suppliers of the Hellenistic world and they looked naturally to the sea. The sprawl of modern Antalya stretches westwards along the coast to the very margin of the Pamphylian plain. But beyond this things change. Although the modest towns have all grown and accessible beaches have been developed, pinewoods still dominate the territory as these descend from the flanks of Mount Olympus.

We sense the importance of shipping to the Lycians very clearly at Phaselis with its three harbours set among beautiful pinewoods less than a mile from the main road. At Phaselis we are on historic ground. The city claimed to have been founded from Rhodes in 690 BC and its commercial importance a century later is shown by the fact that it was the only city in the area to be associated in the foundation of the main shrine in the Greek city of Naucratis on the Delta of the Nile. Phaselis clearly did not suffer under Persian rule. It was here that Alexander paused early in 333 BC on his heroic progress eastwards. His successors in Egypt and Syria in turn controlled Phaselis, which the Romans granted to Rhodes in 190 BC: the Rhodians in their turn lost control, and Phaselis, like Olympos, fell to Cilician pirates, who were in 78 BC expelled by Rome.

The approach road ends beside the remains of that almost inevitable amenity of an ancient city, the aqueduct, just inland from the north and central harbours. The ancient visitor would probably have arrived by sea, perhaps at the large southern harbour which is overlooked by the fortifications on the formidable, but now very overgrown, acropolis. Ancient blocks can be seen. The visitor would have entered the city through the now much reduced Gate of Hadrian, who visited Phaselis in AD 129, and proceeded along the central street that turns between the agora and the theatre, some way up the slope to the east. He would have had the choice of two bath complexes, both relatively modest. But he would not have breathed in the scent of the pines as we do, or had the sensation of walking on cushions of pine-needles.

Phaselis: pier of the inner harbour.

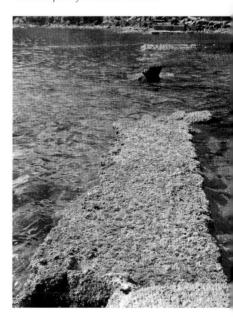

Phaselis has the charm of its associations. But none of the civic buildings is as intriguing as what survives of the small central harbour. Much of the quays on both sides of this remain in place and at the east end extensions of these projected to towers of which the bases survive, leaving a narrow entrance which when necessary could have been blocked by chains. Fallen blocks lie scattered under the lapping water. The quay on the south side of the north harbour is also partly preserved.

Although it is Phaselis that stands below Mount Olympus, that name was taken by its southern neighbour. This can be reached by a new road to the visitor centre or by the turn before this to the village of Cirali, from where it is a short walk south along a beautiful pebble beach to the ruins of Olympus. The first sight is of Byzantine fortifications that seem to defy gravity on the acropolis hill. Beyond, a river emerges from a deep valley. Ancient Olympus lay on both sides of the river, which runs dry in the summer but was crossed by a bridge of which part of a pier survives. It used to be an impenetrable and confusing site. But the archaeologists have transformed this, and well-marked paths lead to the main points of interest. The Baths of Vespasian and the theatre are on the south bank. Opposite, below the acropolis, is what survives of the substantial episcopal palace and a large, very ruined, church. This is near the *clou* of the place, the impeccable main doorway of what must have been a Hellenistic temple of unusual sophistication. This seems the more remarkable for being surrounded by so much less refined Byzantine masonry that has called for recent repointing.

92

ANDRIACE

❖

WHILE Phaselis may originally have been a Pamphylian city, both it and Olympus adhered to the Lycian League codified in 167 BC. The coastal road continues to the Lycian heartland, descending to the growing town of Kamluca, near which are the pine-shaded ruins of Rhodiapolis, a Rhodian foundation as the name implies. Near the relatively modest theatre are fragments of the long inscription recording the numerous benefactions made by its plutocrat Opramoas from his now-shattered tomb. He made donations in numerous other Lycian cities, but there is no trace of his temples to Fortuna and Nemesis at Rhodiapolis itself. West of Kamluca is Limyra, where changed land levels now mean that the sea has retreated from the ancient port, set at the base of the hills. The theatre is beside a modern side road. There are tombs nearby, one of particular distinction. More cluster in the slopes above, which rise steeply to the acropolis on an isolated protrusion that breaks forward from the massif. At the very top there is a small fifth-century BC fortress, as impeccable in construction as any military structure of the period. Limyra was watered by a minor stream. To the west is the Akcay, the ancient Arycandus: some 12 miles/21 kilometres up the valley is Arycanda with a delicate theatre, well-preserved baths and an elegant temple high on steep west-facing terraces, which must always have demanded careful maintainance.

The next major valley is that of the Demre Cay, the classical Myrus, from which Saint Nicholas's Myra takes its

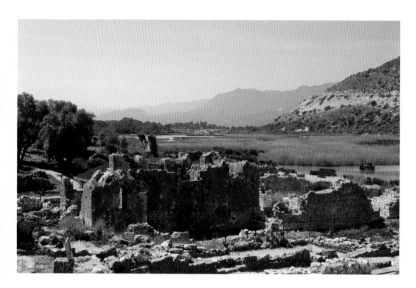

View of Andriace.

name. The modern town of Kale has inevitably grown and greenhouses cover much of the more productive ground. Much is made of the church from which the bones of Saint Nicholas were borne off to Bari in 1087. Visually rather more memorable are the two clusters of tombs carved into the cliff face in the fourth century BC, and the most handsome and admirable preserved theatre where, in 1987, the guard took my copy of Bean's *Lycian Turkey* and showed me a photograph of himself in youth.

Myra is firmly on the tourist trail, but until recently less attention was paid to her former port of Andriace, some 3 kilometres / 1.9 miles away. Andriace is near the eastern tip of a deep sound and the yachtsmen who anchor there today know well why the hard-headed mariners of the ancient world exploited its facilities. The land slopes gently towards a protective ridge. The great granary

used to stand alone. But excavations have now added to the interest of the site. Two churches and the harbour gate have been consolidated and some of the wharves and storerooms can be seen.

To the English, the Emperor Hadrian's name is inevitably associated with the wall that he willed into existence to define the northern frontier of Roman Britain. Hadrian was a supremely energetic man, ever alert to the interests, both military and administrative, of his empire. And the granary at Andriace testifies to the ruthless efficiency of his regime and, of course, to the equally ruthless vigour with which the narrow fertile areas of the hinterland were cultivated under Roman rule.

Like the similar building at Patara, the port of the Xanthus valley to the west, the granary still stands to roof level. The ashlar masonry is of excellent quality, and despite invasive scrub and trees it

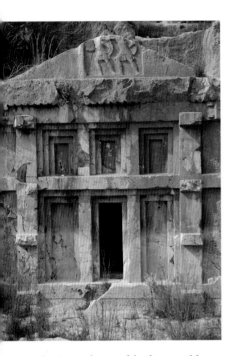

Lycian tomb west of the theatre at Myra.

quite simply to durability. Their achievement will only disappoint those who like their ruins to look ruinous. But this has a sobering message for our age: for, as we now know, the Romans' efficient agricultural exploitation of Asia Minor came at the enduring cost of serious erosion.

A Byzantine inscription near the second door from the west records the preparation of new weights and measures for both Myra and the city of Arneae, and thus offers a fascinating insight into the Lycian economy. Arneae, with its splendid fortifications and a trio of beautiful tombs, stands on a terraced promontory high above the inland Kasaba plain, which it controlled. The ruins can be reached by a turn on the left off the route east from Kasaba as it climbs out of the valley. In antiquity, as now, the plain was immensely productive. It was drained by the River Myrus, which reaches the sea at Myra and was also the source of the city's water. At the head of the narrow valley, south of the village of Dirgenler, steps of the ancient road along this survive. On the opposite bank of the ravine, crowning a triangular outcrop, is the castle of Dereagzi, where the Byzantines reconstructed a Lycian fortress. The strategic importance of the site is also indicated by the size of the nearby ninth- or tenth-century church, which Spratt understandably assumed to be a cathedral. The crops of the Arneans made a vital contribution to the export trade of Andriace, and the Kasaba plain remained a mainstay of Lycia's prosperity under Byzantine rule.

used to be easy to progress through the sequence of storerooms in the building. The granary has now been roofed to serve as a museum and the functional timber portico replaced. It represents Roman architecture at its most functional: the doors are of the simplest, and no thought whatever was given to decorative effect. It is the very sturdiness of Hadrianic Rome that impresses. While the Lycian tomb cutters sought to imitate the elaborate details of earlier wooden structures, Hadrian's contractors aspired

93
CYANEAE

❖

WEST of Andriace the road reaches another small coastal plain, and then climbs westward to yet wilder country, passing the small tomb-strewn acropolis of Sura. Pause there and then walk down to the deep valley below, where a handsome temple, the cella walls as sharply cut as when they were constructed, presides over a reed bed. A few miles northwest is the track to Trysa: much of its sculpture is now in Vienna. Handsome tombs fan out from the acropolis.

Cyaneae, 15 kilometres/9.3 miles to the west, must have been the metropolis of the area. The road passes below the prominent hill that so obviously lent itself to the defensive needs of the early settlers, about whom nothing specific is known. The more memorable approach is from the small village of Yavu at the foot of the south-eastern slope. A path leads upwards, merging with the ancient track which becomes a processional way, so numerous are the sarcophagi. There are rock-cut steps, and nearby a small relief of horses and other animals. Further on is the walled acropolis, the interior of which is a confused, and in places impenetrable, tangle of collapsed walls and intertwined trees. The highest point is to the south. Below this, high on the southern face of the hill, is a particularly satisfying group of tombs, both built and excavated, in a narrow ravine. One of these has a charming leaf-patterned roof. Sounds rise from the main road and there are stark hills on the opposite side of the valley.

From the western wall of the acropolis, the way leads downwards past a series of substantial tombs, the grey stone of which must have been quarried nearby. The sarcophagi are for the most part of the same pattern and it is their grouping rather than their detail that impresses. Beyond, set into the curve of a lower hill, is the theatre, also built of the remorselessly grey local stone, rough in texture. Much survives. But one senses that the structure has been shaken by successive earthquakes. Many of the rows of seats are slightly out of alignment and the building must always have been exposed – for such was the price of founding a major city in so commanding a position. From the theatre it is a brief walk westwards to the modern road, as it twists upwards to higher ground, passing the turn for Üçağiz, before plunging again to reach the sea at Kaş, the ancient Phellus, where a fine Lycian tomb is squeezed by commercial buildings. The beautiful Hellenistic theatre, however, facing out to the sea, has mercifully not yet been encroached upon by the expanding town.

The theatre.

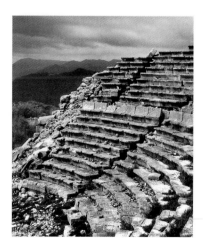

94

ISTLADA AND HOYRAN

❖

THE Sound of Kekova must be the most delectable place in Lycia. And there is nowhere perhaps that the observant amateur can better understand the pattern of settlement in classical Asia Minor. The modern village of Üçağiz is served by a road that joins the main route some 10 kilometres / 6.2 miles west of Cyaneae. With its moorings and modest pansiyons, this is a perfect place from which to explore; but already the small restaurant is full of tax-evading English yachtsmen and the village is in danger of 'development'. Immediately to the east of the village, hugging the shoreline, are the acropolis and necropolises of Teimiussa. And one can either walk on a rough track above the shore or take a boat to Simena, on the promontory diagonally across the bay to the south-east. This was occupied in antiquity, although the existing battlemented castle is medieval. Within the walls there is a small odeum cut into the bedrock, and other excavations of which the most elegant is a house tomb of the so-called house type, inspired by the elevation of a timber structure. The charming houses of the village run down to the little harbour to the west, beyond which is the much-photographed Lycian sarcophagus which seems to float above the water, the level of which has risen since it was carved. To the south, across the sound, is the long ridge of the island of Kekova; and in the bay are a number of small islands that were quarried down to the waterline in antiquity. East of the Kale is a necropolis with scattered tombs among veteran olive trees, one of which

well merits its inclusion in Thomas Pakenham's *Remarkable Trees of the World*. A longer, and rougher, walk from Üçağiz to the west along the shore leads to Aperlae. Here too there was a harbour. The quays are under water but can be easily made out. The anchorage was protected by a short promontory opposite, while the town was defended by a spectacular circuit of ashlar walls, much of which is relatively well preserved.

The road to Üçağiz descends to a wide valley which is visibly prosperous and evidently supported the two Lycian towns that lay on its southern side, Apollonia and Tyberissus: Apollonia, off a side road near the village of Kilinçli, is

Sarcophagi at Tyberissus.

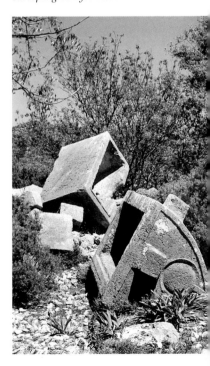

memorable not least for the wonderfully haphazard distribution of the tombs; while Tyberissus spreads from the hills to the east of the road that leads downwards, across a stony terrain that is not kind to hoofs or walking boots, to Üçağiz. Below the 'city', rising from the valley floor, is a substantial outcrop, appropriated for a number of commensurate tombs. But the larger necropolis is higher up, reached by a path that strikes upwards to double-back up the western flank of the hill. The buildings on the acropolis are not large, but no one will be disappointed of the contrasting views over the enclosed valley to the north and southwards towards Kekova.

Less easily found is the smaller settlement of Istlada to the east. The easiest way to reach this is to motor on, passing the outcrop with the tombs and crossing a low pass. After 1.4 kilometres/0.9 miles, the ridge to the right falls away and is little above the level of the road. A rough road between plastic tomato houses leads to an ancient track, partly rock-cut, and still used by herdsmen. This crosses the ridge, and passes an ancient cistern. The way descends steeply, to turn between a number of terraced houses of early date, some of which survive to full height. Here one has a rare sense of the domestic building of the Lycians. The masonry is for the most part irregular. A sharp cry from a shepherdess on the hill above apart, there is no human sound. Time has passed by. Istlada was never a town in our sense. Her territory cannot have been large. But her modest existence was no doubt aided by cultivation of the shelf of level and cleared ground below the ruins, around which richer inhabitants chose to place their sarcophagi, all virtually identical in detail. The place has particular charm in spring, with carpeting daisies, white and yellow, a pale wild gladiolus, a lurid purple vetch and other flowers.

Istlada is the most intimate of Lycian sites, and there are few more enchanted places in which to spend a quiet afternoon. Equally atmospheric in a very different way is Hoyran. This is hardly 3 kilometres/1.9 miles away as the crow flies and could doubtless be reached by rough tracks through the hills. But for those who do not yearn for a stiff climb of over 305 metres/1,000 feet, the easier course is to return to the main road and turn eastwards, passing Cyaneae and proceeding for a couple of miles beyond Yavu to a side road on the right. The road winds upwards to a village high on the escarpment. Near the first group of modern houses, facing east, is one of the more remarkable tombs of Lycia. Above the fictive beams there is a frieze with a man reclining between a dozen figures, whose grouping is remarkable not least for its rhythm. The road ends after a further 1 kilometre/0.6 miles. The acropolis is 0.5 kilometres/0.3 mile away on the crest of the ridge. Either make through the houses and then turn south on an ancient path, still in regular use, that curls round to further ruins or take a track on the left which leads directly to the spectacular cluster of sarcophagi east of the acropolis. The finest is of house tomb type, with a worn relief in two tiers of men, some of whom are seated, on one side; nearby is a pillar tomb with a relief of a man.

Thorny scrub now protects the acropolis. On my first visit, I scrambled up a spine of rock, not at all expecting what I was to see: the full panorama of Kekova and the sound, with Istlada and Teimiussa at my feet. The acropolis is cleverly

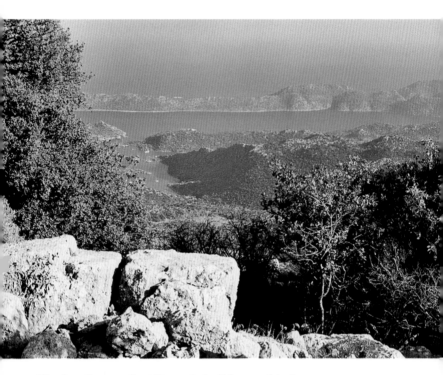

View from the acropolis at Hoyran to the Kekova roadstead.

constructed, partly hewn from the rock, with some fine early masonry and much inferior later patching and additions. A door survives at the south-east of the original fort. The space enclosed is relatively small. No serious attacker could have been repelled for long and the fortress must surely have had a subsidiary function as a signalling post. On the south side several tiers of rock-cut buildings survive, with holes for floor timbers and numerous recesses. The most ambitious, apparently part of a monastery, is a little to the east. This has a handsome door: the monolithic left jamb and lintel are decorated respectively with three and with two bosses; the rock-cut right jamb is not bossed. Behind is one of the many rock-cut flights of steps. The path through the necropolis is also ancient, with carefully cut steps where necessary. There is a strong scent of bay leaves, which an old man has been harvesting.

95

XANTHUS

❖

XANTHUS was always the most considerable city of ancient Lycia. And despite the – fully authorized – removal of so much sculpture from the site to the British Museum in 1842, the modern visitor quickly senses this. The position is commanding, dominating the eastern bank of the Xanthus River, now the Eşen Çay, which cuts southwards towards the sandy coast. The low ground of the valley must always have been intensely cultivated, and remains so, as large areas of protective plastic sheeting attest. To the east are the rugged ridges of the Ak Dağ, to the west a chain of hills, the Cragus and the Anticragus, which fall away on their further side to the coast. Access to the Xanthus valley from the sea was controlled to the west by the well-preserved fort of Pydnae. The Turkish name of this, meaning 'steading of the infidels', is readily understandable and even now the place is usually deserted, although few finer or more complete examples of Greek polygonal masonry can be found. Opposite Pydnae, 5 kilometres/3 miles east of the river, was the major port of Roman Lycia, Patara, with a fine triumphal arch, an elegant temple, an impressive Hadrianic granary and the celebrated theatre, until recently filled by the encroaching golden sand: recent archaeological campaigns have clarified the development of the town but the Temple of Apollo, celebrated from early times, has left no visible trace.

Nothing is known of the foundation of Xanthus, but the city was already of importance in 540 BC, when its citizens set fire to the acropolis and their families

to avoid submitting to the Persian Harpagus. The fifth century BC was a period of prosperity under light Persian control. Xanthus submitted to Alexander and was then fought over by his successors. As the dominant city in the Lycian League, Xanthus played a major part in local resistance to Brutus in 42 BC. This culminated in a closely fought siege, in which, once again, the men of Xanthus chose to destroy their families rather than surrender. None the less the city would recover her position, retaining her pre-eminence under the Roman Empire and into the Byzantine era.

Approaching from the modern village of Kinik, the road crosses the lower part of the town, the first significant relics of which are a Hellenistic gateway and the Arch of Vespasian hard by on the left, and opposite what remains of the Nereid monument, the sculpture from which is now in London. Ahead on rising ground is the Lycian acropolis. The visible polygonal masonry, of the fifth century BC, is easily distinguished from the Byzantine work to the north. Immediately beyond is the fine Roman theatre of the mid-second century AD, to the construction of which the Lycian plutocrat Opramoas of Rhodiapolis contributed no less than 30,000 denarii. To the west of this are two of the more spectacular monuments of the city: a pillar tomb surmounted by a sarcophagus apparently of Hellenistic date and the celebrated, although probably misnamed, Harpy Tomb. This massive pillar tomb is some 8 metres/26 feet high. The reliefs of the tomb chamber on top were taken to London and sensibly replaced by casts in 1957. To the north of the stage building of the theatre is the agora; and at the north-east corner of this is what is perhaps the most significant monument of Xanthus, an obelisk with

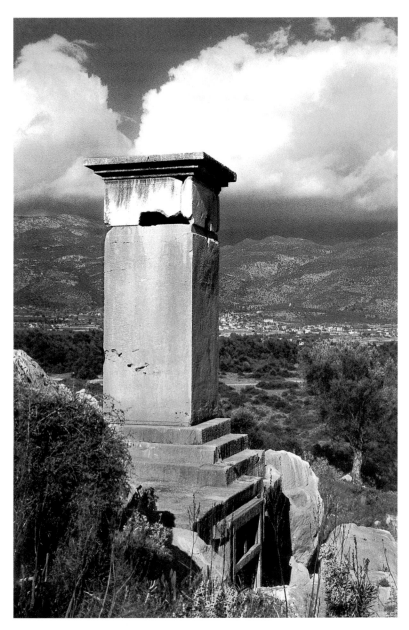

Xanthus: the Pillar Tomb.

inscriptions in Lycian – of two types – and in Greek.

To the east a substantial area of the Roman and early Byzantine town has been partly excavated. There are the footprints of two substantial churches. Beyond, nearer the eastern wall of the city, is a scattering of early tombs, including two Lycian sarcophagi with sculpted lids, one showing a boar hunt. The city walls look over lower ground and should be followed northwards, to the site of the Lion Tomb (the original is now in London) and a further group of funerary monuments with a particularly appealing tower tomb. Beyond these, amidst scrub, are the remains of the Byzantine monastery that took the place of what had been the Roman acropolis.

The pagan inhabitants of Xanthus could boast a shrine that came to rival the Temple of Apollo at Patara. Some 3.5 kilometres/2.2 miles downstream is the Letoum, the sanctuary of Leto. The future mother of Apollo and Artemis, Leto sought water to assuage her thirst, but was denied it by Lycian peasants. She returned and transformed them into frogs, as anyone who has heard the determined croakings at the Letoum in the spring can almost believe.

Although waterlogged, the site is strangely appealing. The sacred spring fed a considerable nymphaeum and there were three small temples. More substantial is the Hellenistic theatre to the north. The flanks are of beautifully disciplined masonry and the north-eastern passage to the cavea is decorated with masks of Silenus, Dionysus and other deities. The cows that graze in the orchestra are too used to stray tourists to interrupt their chewing. Nearby is an unusually refined tomb, the doors decorated with leaves at the corners.

96

PINARA

❖

NORTH of Xanthus the eponymous valley rises, at times almost imperceptibly. The most accessible ancient city is Tlos. This was visited by Sir Charles Fellows in 1838 and drawn in 1842 by William James Müller, who went on to exhibit pictures of the acropolis hill. Of the many tombs the most remarkable, with a relief of Bellerophon, is on the north face of the rock. Elsewhere much survives of the Roman bath complex and the theatre is impressive. Yet despite these advantages, Tlos lingers less in the memory than its western neighbour, Pinara.

From afar the great eastern cliff of the upper acropolis of Pinara is readily made out, high in the writhing mass of the Cragus massif. The defensive possibilities of the position must have been recognized from the earliest of times, and it may be that Pandarus, a Lycian archer who according to Homer fought for the Trojans, was from Pinara. The historical record is virtually a blank and yet the ruins establish that for many centuries the city flourished.

A recent road brings the visitor to a point below the lower acropolis. This is a spine of rock, which at its southern end falls away in a cliff to the bed of what after the rains is a surging stream. Not far above the streambed, near a cluster of tombs at an angle of the cliff, is the so-called Royal Tomb. This is exceptional in scale and remarkable for its reliefs, particularly four showing cities in the entrance. These cannot be specific views, but offer valuable evidence of the appearance of Lycian towns, with battle-

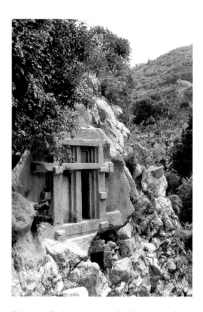

Pinara: the lower acropolis house tomb.

mented walls – Pinara itself was not walled – grand public buildings and, of course, the great tombs, so carefully silhouetted against the skyline. Higher up, near the tip of the ridge, is another unusual tomb. Of the so-called house type, it is surmounted by a pointed arch, at the top of which is a pair of ox horns.

The centre of ancient Pinara lies strewn across the sloping ground on the further side of the lower acropolis and stretches to the foot of the upper acropolis. To the north, a relatively level area may represent the agora. The small odeum backs on to the lower acropolis. Nearby is a stretch of defensive wall. Little has changed since the time of Fellows and Müller, whose watercolours of Pinara are particularly beautiful. And it is a pleasure to wander in the town,

chancing on the ruin of a Byzantine church, or making for the unusually big sarcophagus that stands proud well down the slope. But it is the setting that most stirs the imagination: the massif across the streambed to the south and, above all, the vertiginous cliff face of the upper acropolis, that rises to a height some 457 metres/1,500 feet above the town. The pigeonhole tombs carved in two groups into this are oddly mesmerizing; and even today excavating these would be no easy operation.

To get to the upper acropolis it is necessary to climb up a low ridge to the south of the cliff and then to struggle up a steep path, regularly eroded by the winter rain. The going is quite rough. But there is a reward for perseverance. For although, a medieval fort apart, there is little to see on the scrub-covered sloping surface of the hill, the whole site is at one's feet. Returning to the city demands less effort but more care, as there is a good deal of loose scree. But even so it was surprising to be told on my last visit by the newly appointed guardian when he learnt where I had been that I must be a descendant of a mountain goat.

Most tourists may not have time to visit the upper acropolis. But no one should miss the most substantial building of ancient Pinara, the Greek theatre, north-east of the lower acropolis. This was built against an isolated hill, which accounts for its excellent state of preservation. The cavea is largely intact: there are twenty-seven rows of benches, accessed by ten stairs. The lower courses of the stage building also survive. But even when complete this would not have blocked the spectator's view to the great cliff that must always have been the most conspicuous feature of ancient Pinara.

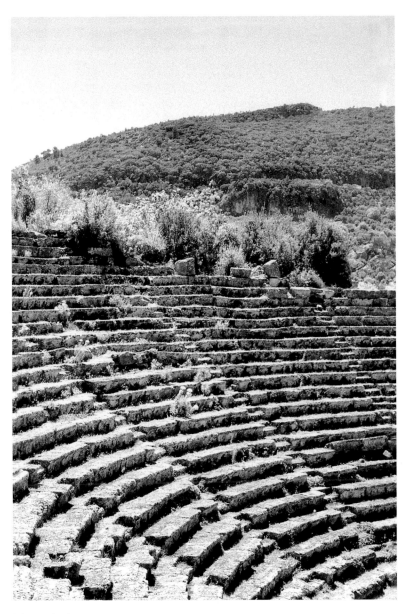

Pinara: the theatre.

97

SIDYMA

❖

HIGH to the west of the Xanthus valley, spread across a level shelf on the flank of Mount Cragus, some 1,750 feet/533 metres above sea level, round the modest village of Dodurga, are the appealing ruins of Sidyma. The city was probably an ancient foundation and may be mentioned on a Lycian coin of the second century BC, but is not certainly recorded until the following century. As the ruins attest, it enjoyed a long, if modest, prosperity under Roman rule. This continued in the early Byzantine era. The place makes a single appearance in the historical record: a sick soldier called Marcian was left there during a campaign against the Sassanians; he was tended by two brothers who took him hunting; as he slept, one of the brothers saw an eagle alight on him, and later asked what the soldier would do for them were he to become emperor; he did in 450 and appointed them to public offices.

Part of the charm of visiting Sidyma is the steep road that climbs inexorably

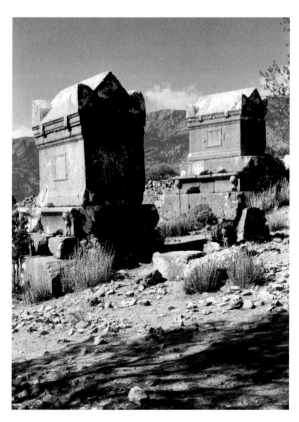

Two tombs.

upwards. Even in summer, when Zanthus and the other sites in the valley below can be uncomfortably warm, it is relatively cool. The village occupies part of the centre of the ancient city, and inevitably much has been lost as a result. The rear wall of a stoa dedicated in the reign of the Emperor Claudius (41–54) can be made out. The acropolis was on the hill to the north, round the south-east of which runs a long section of the partly polygonal defensive wall. Above this was a theatre of which Bean saw six rows of benches.

What make Sidyma so appealing a site are the tombs, many of which are spread over the ground to the east of the village. These are of varying types. There is a simple pillar tomb. There are numerous sarcophagi, differing from those of other Lycian towns by having triangular pedimented ends to the lids. Some of these are clustered to visual effect, while two are placed on a single base: these were made for two men called Aristodemus, perhaps father and son, one of whom was a doctor in the imperial service. Another has eroded reliefs of putti on the corners of the lid. The most remarkable tomb is of temple form. This evidently had a portico in antis, now fallen. A substantial slab of the roof is in place, and happily the carved decoration of the ceiling, with square compartments framing heads in full-face and rosettes that have happily been spared from the elements.

Sidyma is a site to savour. There is no obvious circuit to follow, as you pick your way between the tombs. The position must always have seemed striking. And it is not difficult to understand why a court doctor who must have prospered elsewhere chose to be buried in what was evidently his ancestral city.

98
CADYANDA

FETHIYE, the ancient Telmessus, is alas no longer as rewarding a site as it must have been before urban sprawl crept towards the great tombs carved into its cliffs. But the heat and dust of the modern town are quickly left behind on the road inland to the north-east, through a still untrammelled valley, to Üzümlü. Despite a sign invoking Robin Hood, Üzümlü is a quiet sleepy market town. The ruins of Cadyanda are on the pine-clad hill to the south. A road cuts to the east. Shortly after a pansiyon (whose name, 'Far from the Madding Crowd', may irritate those like me who are unable to admire Hardy), an unmetalled lane curls up through woods.

Cadyanda was a city by the fifth century BC. Yet of its history we know very little. A footpath from the ticket office (not always manned) circles the site. After the heat of Fethiye, it is a relief to be in the shade and – at nearly 914 metres / 3,000 feet – to catch the wind. For those who do not want to wander at will, it may make sense to make the initially steeper anticlockwise circuit.

After a few minutes, this climbs to a fine stretch of the city wall, of excellent polygonal masonry. Immediately within this is the jumbled stage building of the still only partly excavated theatre, with its elegant tiers of seats and a continuous bench with a high back above, set into the hillside below a high retaining wall. One can only hope the remaining rubble will be left in place and the handful of shading pines spared.

Above is a fortified enclosure, roughly square, from which a splendid section of

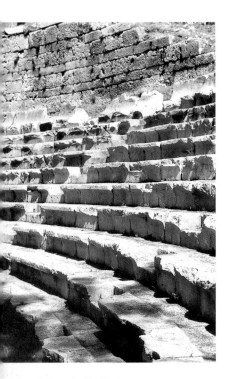

Cadyanda: the theatre.

the city wall crosses a wide gully. Here, rather unusually, there are windows, two small, two rather larger, with cuttings for solid grilles and bars. Further on, the hill falls away to the east and the wall is less well preserved. The path cuts through the trees for the eastern end of the stadium. The footprint of this is clearly visible, and a section of slumped benches remains on the north side. To the northeast of the stadium was a substantial reservoir – Cadyanda was in far too elevated a position for an aqueduct to have been feasible. Above the steps, and appropriately at the very summit of the hill, is what remains of an elegant temple, with a few fluted column drums.

The urban area spread across the slope to the north. But little of substance survives. Altogether more impressive is the large Roman bath complex, of beautifully cut ashlar, to the south of the stadium: this was built under Vespasian.

To the west of the stadium further sections of the city wall follow the crest of the hillside, with plunging views to Fethiye – which is some 18 kilometres / 11 miles away – and to the coast. Lower down are the happily unkempt remains of a stoa and associated buildings. From here the path winds past the elegant steps of a heroon to meander through a very substantial necropolis, in which the activity of treasure-hunters is only too evident. The views downwards do not pall.

The finest of the tombs of Cadyanda, of about 400 BC, are far down the hill on the old footpath from Üzümlü. Roughly 2 kilometres / 1.2 miles from the ticket office, the road turns sharply downwards to the right. A reasonably obvious path leads downhill, criss-crossing the bed of a narrow stream. After a walk of some ten minutes, the Turkish flag can be seen through the trees. Above – and to the right – of the streambed, there is a clearing, with house tombs carved into outcrops of rock. Opposite these is a further tomb, cut into a boulder that has slipped at an angle of 45 degrees. The rather simple façade does not prepare one for the vigorous reliefs of the sides of the tomb. On the left a man lies, rather confidently, on a couch. Death may not have frightened him. Opposite, on the north side, a horseman rides down a soldier and is about to despatch another, who is already forced to one knee and unable to use his spear or defend himself with his shield. The Lycian warrior could not afford to falter.

99
KAYA KÖYÜ

FEW places in Turkey are more eerie than Kaya Köyü, which spreads across the southern flank of a valley 14.5 kilometres/9 miles south of Fethiye. The road climbs through pinewoods and on the descent from a pass one looks across to a whole town of square stone houses, almost all in ruin. While one small chapel is perhaps of early date, what is visible of the former Greek town of Livizzi is largely of the nineteenth century. So too are the main churches. The upper church is off a forecourt with a pebble mosaic, vaulted and with traces of late baroque plaster decoration. The lower church, further west, is similar but in rather better condition, with the carcass of its iconostasis. A shallow dome is inserted rather uncomfortably into the vaulted ceiling. Nearby is the charnel house.

Livizzi and her inhabitants paid a heavy price for the nationalist ambitions of the Greek leader, Eleftherios Venizelos, and those who supported him, not least Lloyd George, who had not forgiven Turkey for its victory at Gallipoli. That Greece so overplayed her hand contributed to the rebirth of Turkey and to the tragedy of Smyrna, of which the repercussions were experienced throughout Asia Minor.

The visitor to Kaya Köyü, wandering up the curving lanes between the roofless houses, has a palpable sense of the brutality that can arise when the tectonic plates that govern peoples are irresponsibly set in motion. The people of Livizzi had lived on easy terms with their Ottoman neighbours – which were par-

alleled in such architectural details as the window frames of the lower church – but they inevitably lost their homes in the population exchange that followed the Greek defeat in 1922. It is to the credit of the owners of the few inhabitable houses that one senses a spirit of reconciliation. As the evening sunlight catches the narthex of the upper church, with its mouldings of simulated rope, and glances upon the broken walls of a thousand houses, one wishes that those in the West who seek to intervene in countries they don't understand would take careful note.

The abandoned town, late afternoon.

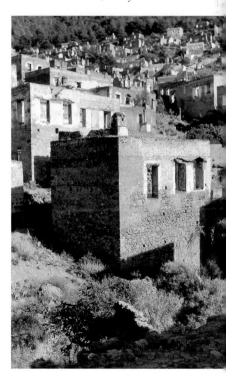

100

CAUNUS

CAUNUS was a Carian city and not a Greek colony. Its Carian name was Kbid and inscriptions show that the Carian language survived for a considerable period. From the sixth century BC there are references to the city, whose political fate reflected that of its neighbours, whether in the heroic struggles between the Greeks and the Persian kings – whose satrap of Caria, Mausolus, did much to Hellenize Caunus during his rule (377–53 BC) – or under Alexander and his successors. Caunus was captured for Ptolemais Sotor in 309 BC, and retained by the Ptolemies until the second century BC, when it was sold to the Rhodians. They in turn were supplanted by Rome in 167 BC. Mithridates seized Caria in 88 BC, and subsequently Caunus remained in dispute between Rhodes and Rome, until the latter secured the whole of Asia Minor. Comments by the ancient geographer Strabo indicate that, despite Caunus's importance as a port, her climate was believed to be unhealthy – because of the heat, and the local fruit, to which was attributed sickness (mosquitoes were more probably responsible). An inscription on the site makes it clear that the trades in both slaves and salt were of particular importance to the city's economy.

The best way to visit Caunus is to cross by rowing boat from Dalyan across the eponymous river, the ancient Calbis, and see, looming above the reed beds that fringe the channel, the great tombs carved into the cliff. The easternmost group, directly above the modern cemetery, is the most striking. There are seven tombs with temple façades. Five replicate Ionic porticoes in antis, with pairs of columns. Dominating these is the more ambitious unfinished façade with a portico in antis of four columns: the rock has been cut away from the top to just below the level of the capitals. A rough path – which the authorities have tried to block – leads up the hill and crosses to the adjacent cluster, in which it is possible to walk through the passage behind the finer of the two temple tombs. Further west at the bottom of the cliff, a third group of tombs, with numerous pigeon-holes, is reached by a farm track. Datable to the fourth century BC, the tombs are of a specifically Carian type, the distribution of which centres on Caunus.

A kilometre/0.6 miles west of the modern landing stage is the acropolis hill, some 150 metres/492 feet high. With its steep flanks, this lent itself naturally to defence and was evidently the stronghold known as the Herakleion, conquered in 309 BC by Ptolemy. Later fortifications girdle the rock at lower levels. To the west, built against the hill, is the outstanding monument of Caunus, the theatre. North of the theatre on a low ridge are a fascinating circular structure identified as a measurement platform, the recently excavated remains of a church and a substantial bath complex. This is exceptionally well preserved and there are plans to create a museum within it. Through a grille can be seen what survives of the Exedra of Protagenes, a monument that originally supported five bronzes by the artist who is known to have worked at Rhodes in 306 BC and was both a friend and rival of the painter Apelles.

Below the ridge a series of descending terraces have been identified and partly

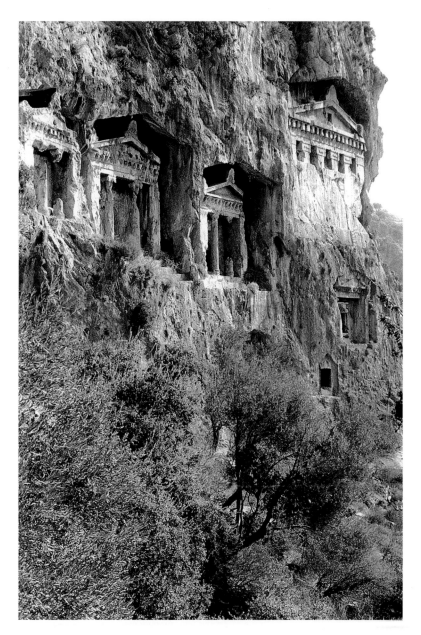

The pedimented tombs, with the unfinished tomb on the right.

excavated, including the large terrace of a temple and the precinct of Apollo. Under this is the well-restored north stoa of the agora. At the further end is a monument to Quintus Vedius Capito, with an unusually elegant inscription. To the east are the bases of other monuments and beyond these the now reconstructed fountain building. On the south-west side of this is a text setting out details of customs and harbour dues. Below is the sizeable pool of the main harbour, now cut off from the sea by two millennia of silt. To the left, protecting the anchorage on its more exposed southern side, is the lower acropolis, with the remains of some large structures. The ridge linking this to the upper acropolis, and controlling a second harbour to the south, was defended by the city wall, and the western end of the lower acropolis was strongly fortified.

The Hellenistic city wall continued from the opposite side of the harbour, climbing to run above the northern flank of the Baliklar hill that dominates the site, and thus to overlook the southern end of Lake Köyceğiz to the north. The furthest stretch was probably originally built under Mausolus, while the western section, the masonry of which is of fine quality, is Hellenistic. It was ambitious to construct a wall enclosing so considerable an area that could never have been inhabited. But as a result the city walls of Caunus rival those of Iasus and Cnidus, and are outshone only at Heracleia.

Today, particularly in the summer, Caunus is very much on the tourist trail. But the magical way the site rises up from the silted ground to be reflected in the water, and the unforgettable views from the acropolis over the river as this twists towards the sea, distinguish it from the rival cities and towns of ancient Asia Minor.

101
LORYMA

❖

MARMARIS may once have had charm. It now boasts all the amenities that I would rather live without. But the jagged Loryma peninsula which stretches south-westwards is for the most part unscathed. From early times this wild territory was controlled by Rhodes, itself settled before Homer's day by Dorians. The three original cities of the island coalesced as a new state with a new capital, Rhodes, in 408 BC, and in the ensuing period the mainland territory of this, the Rhodian Peraea, was steadily expanded. Caunus and Stratoniceia were subsequently lost, but Rhodes held the peninsula at least until the second century AD.

South of Marmaris, on a small headland just beyond the suburban sprawl, is a small wooded promontory. Much of the wall of the town of Amos can be followed round the crest of the hill. There are vestiges of a temple and, further west, built against the hill, a better-preserved theatre, appropriate in scale for what can never have been a large community.

The Loryma peninsula is still ill served by roads. The best, on the western flank, turns inwards from the village of Bozburun, rising up through another, Teslica, before descending in stages to the coast at Serçe Liman. Two kilometres / 1.2 miles beyond Teslica there is evidence of a large settlement on the right, and to the east, among trees by a stream, a substantial Hellenistic building of excellent masonry. Further on, to the right, are the ruins of a late village built with pillaged material. To the left of the road, at a low pass, is the polygonal wall of a temple with a number of scattered pyramidal blocks, of between two and four steps, that have been regarded as bases for offerings. The road now descends, passing a section of polygonal wall, olive presses and another four steps, to the protected roadstead of Serçe Liman. Here there are a few houses and in the morning, if luck holds, a fisherman will be prepared to take a passenger. For the ancient tracks to Loryma are no longer easily passable and, as her Rhodian masters must have felt, the natural approach is from the sea.

I was fortunate. A middle-aged couple were on the point of setting out to check their nets. We passed a single fisherman in an even smaller boat – which on the return we would tow back to Serçe Liman – and followed the inhospitable coastline to the west. After half an hour of gentle chugging, the boat headed into a deep bay, Bozukkale, with one of the safest anchorages on the peninsula. This was used by the Athenians in the Peloponnesian War and before the Battle of Cnidus in 395 BC, and was the *raison d'être* of the Rhodian town of Loryma, which survived into the Byzantine era. The town itself has left little trace. But above, on the narrow crest that runs to the headland south-west of the bay, is the magnificent Rhodian fortress that defended it. This is some 320 metres/1,049 feet long and roughly 30 metres/98.4 feet wide; the walls are of more or less regular courses of lightly-bossed ashlar blocks; and there are five square towers overlooking the harbour and four on the landward, south, side. At either end were round towers, of which that above the headland has gone. In the walls there are five narrow gates and two

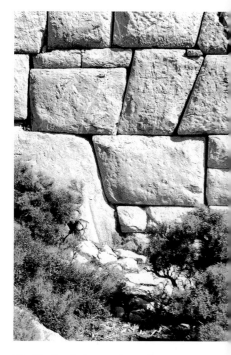

The Rhodian fortress: polygonal masonry of the south wall.

channels to drain water, but within the enceinte, excavated cisterns apart, nothing but the untamed bedrock. Inscriptions near the south-eastern gate, as Bean records, refer to the cult of Zeus Atabyrius.

While I wandered about, the fisherman's wife sold their catch to an enterprising restaurateur who clearly caters for passing yachtsmen. Loryma is a place to linger in, but I was happy to leave before other strays arrived to break in on the magic of an unclouded morning. A further fortress is on the hill two hours' scramble to the north; with the thought of returning some day to see this, I let the rhythm of the engine reconcile me to half an hour of indolence.

102

CNIDUS

❖

THE Torinese architect Giovanni Battista Borra, travelling in 1751 with the English tourists Robert Wood and James Dawkins, prepared the first detailed map of the ruins at Capo Crio at the extreme western tip of the Datça peninsula. And the port of Cnidus with its double harbour was understandably to attract archaeologists of later generations: Sir Charles Newton working for the British Museum in 1857–8, and more recently – and scientifically – the Americans and teams from the British Museum and Konya University.

At Cnidus the hand of man directly complements that of nature. The original city had – as Professor Bean established – been built roughly at the central point of the peninsula, north of the modern town of Datça, where a low-walled acropolis can still be made out near the mole of an ancient harbour. This city, conveniently placed for the best agricultural land on the peninsula, was settled at an early date by Dorians from the Peloponnese. By the sixth century the Cnidians were in a position to plant a colony of their own in Sicily. This was later transferred to the Lipari Islands. Inevitably the Persian destruction of Lydia in 546 BC changed the regional balance of power and Cnidus was not exempt, passing from Persian to Athenian and subsequently Spartan control, before reverting to Persian rule in 387 BC. Some two decades later the city was transferred to its present site. The reason for so dramatic a decision was clearly to take advantage of the place's potential as a port. Deveboynu, Capo Crio, was then an island, but it was realized that this could be linked to the mainland by an artificial isthmus, which would create harbours at each side. The east-facing ground of the former island became a prime residential area, while the more level area on the mainland, laid out on a south-facing grid plan, was used for the major public buildings. To the north the site was protected by a ridge that rises steeply to the east.

In antiquity, as now, many visitors arrived by sea. On land the approach is from the east. The road crosses the line of the city walls and passes a fragmentary odeum. Much more impressive is the

The lower theatre, seats.

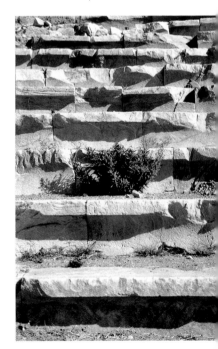

lower theatre, to the right of the road, with thirty-five rows of seats in a gleaming pale stone. From this one looks out across the larger, southern harbour, protected by two moles, and at the terraces on the former island. The inevitable restaurant has sprung up on the isthmus. To the west of this is the smaller military harbour, referred to by Strabo as the 'trireme harbour', where there was room for twenty such vessels and which could be protected by a chain across the narrow fortified entrance. Excavations have revealed a series of buildings to the north of the isthmus. The commercial heart of Cnidus was the agora, with a substantial stoa backed by a particularly striking retaining terrace wall. To the west of this a stepped paved road leads upwards to the religious centre of the city, with the foundations of temples and of one of the Byzantine churches that succeeded these. Some of the masonry that has been unearthed repays close attention, for the ancient quarrymen and masons could achieve a remarkable precision. Further north, against the cliff, is the elegant circular temple identified by some as that of Aphrodite Euploia, of which only the podium survives. Following the lower line of the hills to the east, one comes to the large, but ruinous, upper theatre, and to the Sanctuary of Demeter, where Newton excavated the celebrated statue of that deity now in the British Museum.

The walls of Cnidus are by any standard impressive. Particularly fine is the great rounded tower at the foot of the former island controlling the narrow entrance to the trireme harbour. The line continues to the north-east above the shore and then strikes up the spine of the ridge to the north of the city, rising to the splendid acropolis, where the hill falls away at the eastern end. Here there is a

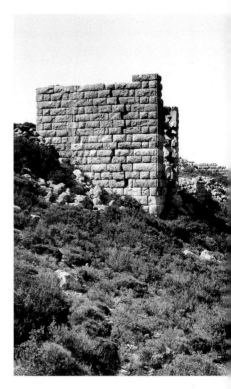

The acropolis.

spectacular sequence of towers, all rectangular and many standing to full height, as the inaccessibility of the acropolis hill has discouraged pillage. The masonry is of regular ashlar blocks.

From the northern wall and the acropolis the defenders of Cnidus could monitor any hostile movements, by sea or land. Cnidus and its harbours are at one's feet, and one presides, as it were, over the meeting of the Mediterranean and Aegean seas. Part of the fascination of Cnidus is that one can make so sweeping a survey of the whole city, yet also, chancing for example on a game board cut into a pavement, feel so close to those who lived there over two millennia ago.

The ancients respected the balance of life and death. The great necropolis of Cnidus stretches to the east of the city walls, and some of the mausolea abut on the modern road, which adheres to the line of the original route. The most celebrated of the tombs of Cnidus was, however, high on a cliff above the sea a good kilometre / 0.6 miles to the south of this. The lion that crowned this is now in the Great Court of the British Museum, but part of the base and much fallen masonry are in place above the ramp constructed when the lion was removed in 1858.

The old road to the east can still in part be traced, and some 10 kilometres / 6.2 miles from Cnidus, on a section of this leading from the village of Çeşme towards the site of the city of Tropium, famous in antiquity for its games, is the still substantial carcass of a bridge of about 300 BC. Built of ashlar blocks of varying height, this crossed a ravine. In summer the river is dry; but the force of the water after rain is shown by the distance travelled by some huge stones which have been dislodged from the bridge. There was a single triangular or trapezoidal arch, best preserved on the east side. Massive abutments survive and the road was brought down to the level of these by cuttings. No one who seeks out the bridge will regret the brief walk from Çeşme.

103

STRATONICEIA AND LAGINA

❖

STRATONICEIA was one of the more difficult sacrifices from the predecessor of this book. I first went when the site was still occupied by a village and well remember the bemused look of a man who had gone out of his way to help when I gave him a, to me, precious packet of Bath Oliver biscuits. A decade later the village had been abandoned and the pretty mosque was disintegrating. This has now been put in order; and much more of the ancient city has been revealed.

Stratoniceia was the successor of a Carian settlement, but owed its name to Stratonice, wife successively of Seleucus I Nicator and of his son and co-ruler, Antiochus, after both of whom numerous cities were named at the turn of the third century BC. The subsequent history of the place was turbulent until the long centuries of Roman peace. Thereafter it sank into obscurity.

The road from the south-west leads past a necropolis, to near the little mosque, which faced the cobbled street that runs towards the centre of the site. The first lane on the right heads south for the theatre, which is cut into the northern flank of the acropolis hill. Originally of the Hellenistic period, this was altered to accord with Roman requirements in the period of Augustus. Much of the cavea is intact, although on the west side part of the seating has slumped as the result of an earthquake. Above the theatre is a small and poorly preserved but splendidly sited Ionic temple. From the top of the theatre it is possible to sense the scale of the ancient city. To the north is the out-line of the temenos of a temple. Passing this, turn right by the as yet unexcavated remains of a bath complex. Ahead, on the left, is the handsome bouleuterion, once thought to be a Temple of Serapis, of the early first century AD. The masonry is of excellent quality: there are numerous graffiti on the pavement.

From the east side of the bouleuterion take a path northwards, passing a number of scattered houses, now deserted, to reach the recently excavated stretch of the colonnaded street which ran to the remarkable North Gate. The western arch of this has long been known, but it was not until the recent excavation that it was established that this was the left-hand of a pair of gates on either side of a semi-circular nypmhaeum, each flanked by columns, of which one on the west survives intact. This lavish structure of the mid second century AD marked the start of the processional way to Stratoniceia's sanctuary at Lagina.

Much of the city wall can be traced. The section to the east of the North Gate is particularly satisfying. At a weak salient there is a Hellenistic fortress that was re-commissioned by the Byzantines, who used the spoil of earlier buildings, including many column drums and decorated friezes. Further on in the wall of a ruined modern house there is a particularly crisp relief of an axe. Making back to the centre of the former village, north of the mosque is the gymnasium. This must be the most beautiful of the structures of Stratoniceia; the detail of the central exedra and of the flanking rooms, in gleaming white marble, is of the finest quality.

Stratoniceia boasted two sanctuaries, Lagina and Panamara. I have not been to

Stratoniceia: the gymnasium.

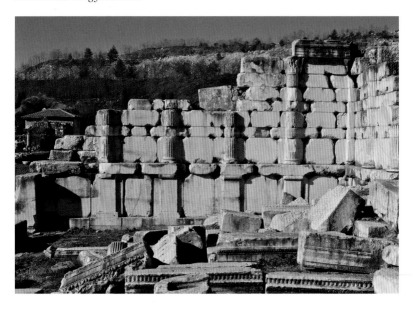

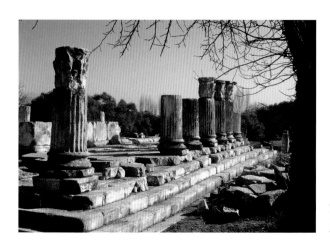

Lagina: the Temple of Hecate.

the shrine of Zeus Panamarus. Less excusably, I had not been to the Temple of Hecate at Lagina until recently, and am grateful to Patricia Daunt who urged me to go.

Like so many places that it was once difficult to get to, Lagina is now readily accessible, although not by the original processional route. The road passes a pool and then descends towards the terrace on which the ruins lie. An ancient olive of prodigious girth that offers shade in the car park sets the scene. A path leads gently down to the enormous precinct, measuring 149 × 134 metres/ 490 × 440 feet, originally reached through the propylon on the left. This was entered by a curved portico – with beautifully laid curved paving – and a flight of steps descended to the precinct. This was lined by stoas. That to the left of the propylon, on the south, was lined with rows of benches: the others, of which that to the west is the best preserved, had Doric colonnades. In the centre of the precinct is the Temple of Hecate, a goddess of Carian origin, whose arcane cult was related to those of Artemis and Demeter, and who was believed to control the key to the gate of the Underworld. The temple has been dated to about 50 BC. The order is Corinthian; and enough survives, or has been put back in place, to give some impression of the elegance of the whole. There are graffiti on some of the steps of the podium. While the reliefs discovered in 1891–2 are in the Archaeological Museum at Istanbul, much finely carved material cleared from the temple is laid out to the north. The sections of ceilings are of particular interest. Aligned on the temple to the east is an altar, also on a stepped podium: the patterned frieze on the base is unusually refined. The numerous monuments in front of the west stoa testify to the conviction of the cult of Hecate.

Unlike Stratoniceia, from which the billowing smoke of a factory can be seen and which will soon be affected by noise from a new highway, Lagina is a place of quiet harmony – as it cannot have been during the annual festivals when the key of Hecate was processed to Stratoniceia and back.

104
BEÇIN

THE ancient city of Mylasa was the power base of the Hecatomnids, until Mausolos selected Halikarnassos as his capital. It sprawled across two low hills. The modern Milas is not at first sight a place of promise for the sightseer. Yet, with a little patience, something of the pattern of the past emerges. The second century AD Baltali Kapi ('Gate of the Axe') is an arch of considerable refinement. A little way to the west, on the Hisarbaşi Hill, is a temple of which a single column stands: the site has now been excavated to reveal the substantial stepped podium. Much of the area within the partly-extant temenos walls has also been cleared and a number of good Ottoman houses within these have been restored. But inevitably the monument of ancient Mylasa has to be the Gümüşkesen, an elegant Hellenistic mausoleum a mile or so west of the centre, almost screened by trees from modern buildings.

Mylasa dwindled in importance with the Roman decline, but in the fourteenth century its strategic position led the Turkic Menteşe to select it as their seat. In Milas itself, their advent can be sensed in a trio of mosques, of which the Ulu Cami of 1398 is the most conspicuous. But it is at Beçin, less than four kilometres to the south, that their presence is more powerfully felt.

Beçin, a sloping flat-topped outcrop surrounded by steep cliffs, must always have lent itself to defence. It may indeed have been the original acropolis of the Carian founders of Mylasa. From below, the turreted walls seem to grow from the rock. At the most accessible, south-western, point a substantial tower, adorned by two pillaged lions, projects to protect the path upwards, cut in places through the bedrock. This must originally also have served as the processional way to the Hellenistic temple, part of the stepped podium of which hangs to the right above the path just before the inner gate. The interior of the fortress was inhabited until relatively recently: modern houses, many partly constructed with ancient blocks, fall into decay, and there are the eroded walls of earlier structures.

Not content with constructing the fortress, the Menteşe built energetically

Steps of the Greek temple and medieval tower.

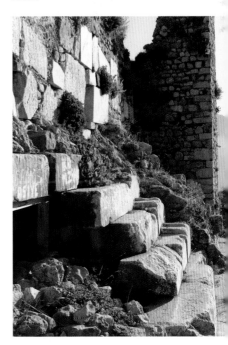

on the ground that rises to the west from below the fortress. First comes the substantial Büyük Hamam, the central room (iliklik) of which had a dome supported on pendentives with leaf motifs. The road upwards passes a türbe and the Orhan Camii, with a handsome door and a floor of reused marble blocks, to reach the recently-restored Ahmet Gazi Medrese founded in 1375 by the self-styled 'Great Ruler, the Sultan of the Coasts'. The detail of the recessed portal has been thought to echo Gothic buildings, and as his claim implies Ahmet was at least interested in controlling maritime trade.

Higher up are a small fountain and, to the left of the road, the substantial block of the Kizil Han. Most travellers and their animals were accommodated in the long hall on the ground floor, but more distinguished visitors would have been housed in the two rooms of which there is evidence on the upper floor. Interesting as the Islamic buildings of Beçin are, it is their setting that most appeals. This cannot really be said of their counterparts in Milas, although areas of old housing do, just, survive near the souk and the Hisarbaşi Hill.

105
LABRAYNDA

LABRAYNDA entered the historical record shortly after 499 BC when Carians fleeing from the victorious Persians retreated to the sanctuary there. Approaching now, it is not difficult to understand why it was thought a sacred place. The modern road does not follow the ancient paved sacred way from Mylasa but winds up a long ridge: at length, beyond the pines there is a glimpse of distant poplars – in the time of Herodotus there were planes – and of a substantial rock below the crest.

The cult of Zeus Statius was favoured by the Hecatomnids, satraps of the Persians who became the *de facto* rulers of Caria. The founder of the line, Hyssaldomus, came from Mylasa: his son Hecatomnos followed him and was succeeded by his own son, Mausolus (ruler in 377–51 BC), who transferred his capital to Halikarnassos. Mausolus projected a comprehensive redevelopment of the sanctuary, employing the architect Pytheos who was to design his own monument, the Mausoleum of Halikarnassos, the sorry vestiges of which can be seen at Bodrum. The project was continued under his brother Idrieus, who succeeded his older sister Artemisia, widow of their brother Mausolus, and was married to his, and their, younger sister Ada: and it is Idrieus's name that is found in the dedication of several buildings at Labraynda.

The steeply sloping position lent itself perfectly to the creation of a processional route. The official entry does not follow this, so after buying a ticket it makes sense to cut to the right, and to start with the steps of the south and east propylons, both built for Idrieus, just above the splendid stretch of the south wall of the precinct beside the modern road. By the south propylon is the 'Doric House', also of Idrieus's time: the church between the propylons is of course a later insertion. From the terrace between the propylons a wide flight of steps leads upwards. Beyond this a smaller flight mounts to the right to a terrace across which, at an angle, is a stoa also dedicated by Idrieus, against which a pretty fountain house was placed. At the west end of the terrace is the so-called Second Andron, dedicated by Mausolus: the smaller, Third Andron is immediately to the south of this.

The Temple of Zeus, now much reduced, was accessed from a high terrace on the east, with a stoa on its north side which was dedicated by Mausolus. The Ionic temple, built for Idrieus, was built on the site of an earlier shrine. What survives is so insignificant in relation to the buildings behind this that it is evident that destruction was deliberate. Across the west terrace is the First Andron, again dedicated by Idrieus. This is the most complete major building at Labraynda. The large chamber must have functioned well for assemblies, with its ten large windows, originally fitted with shutters the cuttings for the fixtures of which can be seen. To the north of the andron, behind a portico in antis are two rooms of unequal size, again built for Idrieus: piers were subsequently added to the larger of these to support a dome.

Some way above the stoa of Mausolus is a particularly distinguished tomb. The path behind this leads up the acropolis hill. This was defended by a circuit of

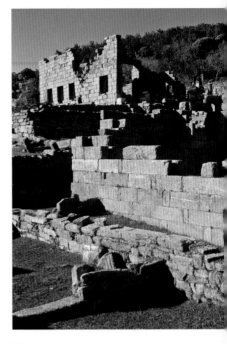

The approach to the sanctuary.

walls that have been attributed to Idrieus's widow – and sister – Ada, whose stronghold of Alinda is only 26 kilometres/15 miles away though the hills. The most interesting stretch exploits the rocky outcrop on the west side which is visible on the approach.

Mausolus's great monument has largely gone. But at Labraynda one can still sense that he was a ruler of taste with an atavistic devotion to the cult of Zeus Statius which his brother respected. It is not surprising that centuries later Christians sought to supplant the cult by building relatively modest churches of their own.

106

HERACLEIA AD LATMUS

THE most dramatically sited of the coastal cities of Caria was Heracleia, below the rock-strewn mass of Mount Latmus. The strange magic of the place was recognized in antiquity, for it was in a cavern on the mountain that the moon goddess Selene saw the sleeping Endymion, whom Zeus permitted to dream for eternity. Heracleia was a significant port, but gradually the Gulf of Latmus was cut off from the Aegean by deposit from the River Meander, to become the brackish Lake of Bafa.

The approach is from the southern tip of the lake. The mountain rises to the east. Strange protuberances of rounded rock erupt. There are necropolises by the shore and the towers of the town walls catch the eye. Of the Hellenistic and Roman city much survives among the houses of the modest village of Kapikiri: the Hellenistic agora with a well-preserved warehouse below; the small Temple of Athena, perched on an outcrop to the north; an eroded Roman theatre among olive trees; fluted marble column drums here; Hellenistic walls there; numerous tombs; and, not least, the modest curved shrine of Endymion near the lower walls.

It is for the walls that one is drawn irresistibly back to Heracleia. There is perhaps no comparably complete enceinte of the third century BC on such a scale. The construction of this has recently been plausibly attributed to the Macedonian general, Pleistarch, who controlled much of Caria early in the third century, after whom the city was briefly called Pleistarcheia. For the stren-uous it is best to start the circuit north of the village – where it was originally linked with an island, itself later built on by the Byzantines. For the steep climb up the jagged ridges one is rewarded as each tower comes into view, the mortarless masonry of the highest quality, the line taking every possible advantage of the terrain. On some exposed sections, all that is left are the footings for the bigger outer blocks and the smaller inner ones carved into successive outcrops. The views over the lake, with its several islands, and upwards to Mount Latmus are breathtaking; so too are the carpeted anemones of spring and the tall white flowers of the autumn. The walls mount inexorably. At times the ascent is vertiginous. But at length the ridge falls away to a narrow valley, and the line of the walls turns to the south. It is here that some of the most spectacular – and best-preserved – towers are found. The wall descends no less majestically than it has climbed. One looks up at the mountain and down across lower, but hardly less contorted, ground to the wild rocks on which are the two modest acropolises of Heracleia's predecessor, the Carian town of Latmus, which Pleistarch suppressed when he founded his new city.

The ruins of Latmus are most easily approached from a valley 1.5 kilometres/0.9 mile south of Heracleia. A path along the northern margin of this skirts fields and scattered tombs and then turns up a narrow defile. There are more tombs – most only dug after the town was abandoned; there are terrace walls and flights of steps. The site spreads over four subsidiary valleys. And because this was abandoned when Heracleia was built and hardly used in the Byzantine period, Latmus is the most complete extant early Carian town. Rocks were

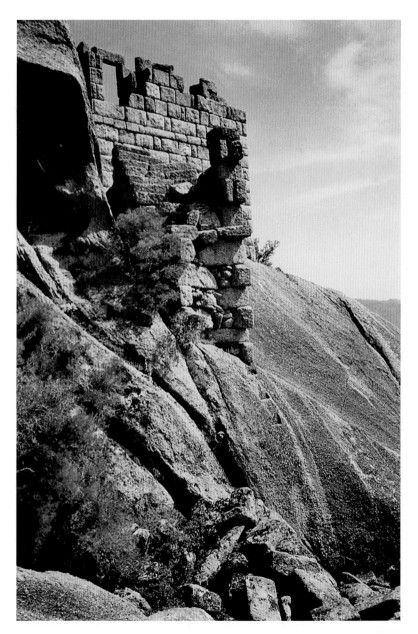

A stretch of the walls, showing cuttings for blocks below the broken section.

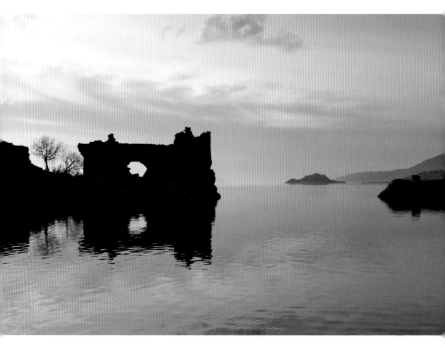

Heracleia: Byzantine monasteries in Lake Bafa, towards dusk.

commandeered; numerous post holes and excavated cupboards can be seen; and many walls survive. There are two substantial square blocks, both in prominent positions, which were evidently in domestic use. And high up are the two small fortresses or acropolises, one on the line of the walls near where it is crossed by the rough track that leads north to Heracleia. Although the scattered olive trees are still pruned, the place is abandoned; birds of prey swoop, and an echoing pattern of knocking tells of the persistence of lust-struck tortoises.

The slopes of Mount Latmus have held other secrets. Only relatively recently, Annelise Peschlow-Bindokat and her colleagues have discovered numerous Neolithic drawings on rock faces which are spared flood water or drips from above. Most of these are clustered near the ancient routes that cross the massif. There are representations of men and women, of herds and animals. The symbolism of these is the domain of the ethnographer, their message only partly comprehensible after the passage of 10,000 years: for certainly Neolithic man did not intend a group of leaping figures to evoke the 'disco' of which an elderly guide spoke. The German archaeologists have also charted a network of narrow paved roads across the mountain: these also are probably due to Pleistarch, who presumably understood that trade through the rough terrain justified the expense of creating roads of a type for which there was no regional precedent.

In the seventh century AD Latmus became a major centre of Christianity. A Byzantine fort was constructed at Heracleia itself in the angle between the southern wall and the shore. Others were built on the promontory 3 kilometres / 1.9 miles to the north and at the next city up the coast, Myus, where cotton fields have now taken the place of the sea. There were monasteries on the islands in the lake – the most spectacular on that north of the fortified promontory. There were hermitages on the slopes above Heracleia, and, far below the summit of Latmus, the fortified Yediler monastery. The monks may have learnt from the survival of the drawings by their Neolithic predecessors. For, just above the monastery, an overhanging rock was muralled with vigorous scenes from the life of Christ, including the *Baptism*, the *Transfiguration*, the *Crucifixion* and the *Lamentation*. Richard Chandler was taken in 1765 to the Pantocrator cave high within the walls of ancient Latmus where other murals survive. As he wrote: 'It is in one of the most wild and retired recesses imaginable.'

No tourist can hope to find his or her way on the slopes of Latmus without help. And Kapikiri with its pansiyons (my preference is for the Agora) is the perfect place from which to explore these. It is also an excellent base for visitors to such nearby Carian sites as Euromus and Labraynda or Heracleia's more successful rival, the former port of Miletus and its dependent sanctuary at Didyma.

Heracleia: neolithic drawing below Mount Latmos.

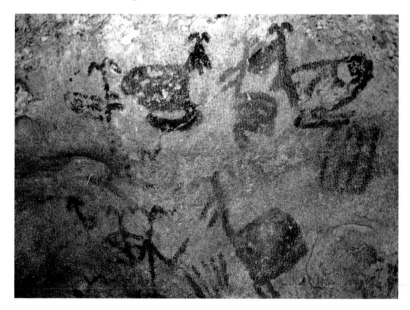

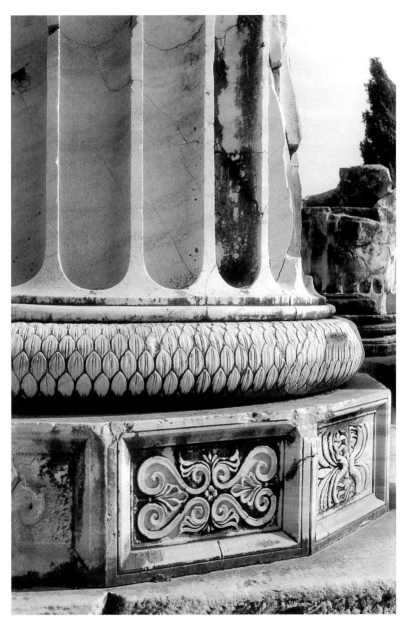

The Temple of Apollo, base of fluted column of the east portico.

107

DIDYMA

❖

MILETUS was one of the great cities of Greek Asia Minor in the seventh and sixth centuries BC, her fortune owed to the excellence of her port. Renowned for her early philosophers and her role in the abortive revolt of 500–494 BC against the Persians, Miletus remained the most important coastal town between Ephesus and Halikarnassus, and it was not until the Byzantine era that she was cut off from the sea by the silt of the Meander. From afar, the vast and wonderfully preserved theatre, a Roman reconstruction, dominates the site. To the east was the harbour, with both Hellenistic and Roman monuments, including the Delphinium and two agoras, which lead back in an arc to the impressive bath complex of the Empress Faustina, Marcus Aurelius's rather grasping wife. There is an informative site museum, with a striking early inscribed kouros as well as other sculpture and smaller finds from both Miletus and Didyma.

From the Delphinium a sacred way led some 15 kilometres/9.3 miles to the Sanctuary of Apollo at Didyma, which was controlled in antiquity by Miletus. The place, just above the coast, was a shrine before the advent of the Greeks. The archaic temple, of the early sixth century BC, which overlay an eighth-century predecessor, was destroyed by the Persians. Alexander determined to replace it, and on an even larger scale. Seleucus Nicator employed Paionios and Daphnis as architects: work proceeded for centuries and was still unfinished when the oracle's cult was overtaken by the rise of Christianity.

The approach to the temple is not promising. The nearby town is swollen with houses built for sun-loving expatriates, and the enclosure is almost surrounded by roads and modern buildings. Yet despite this, the temple must be the single most beautiful classical monument in Asia Minor. And enough of this survives for one to be dazzled by the ambition of its double peristasis of Ionic columns, by the variety of the decoration of the paired bases of the outer columns at the east front and by the splendid scale of the central open cella round the inner sanctuary of which only the lower courses survive. Masons' marks abound, whether on the walls of the cella or, on a smaller scale, in the two narrow passages through which this is approached: had the temple been completed these would have been erased. Magnificent as the east elevation is, the long lateral flanks of the temple are equally impressive; and on the west the excavators took care to leave the sprawled drums of a column in the positions where these were found. The columns were brought from a quarry near Lake Bafa. Many of the intended 120 columns were never erected, and of those that were some, including one of the three that still stands, were never fluted, while many bases were left uncarved.

The southern face of the podium of the temple doubled as the flank of the stadium, which clearly had an important part in the religious life of Didyma. Many of the benches bear the names of those who used them – links with individuals of whom otherwise we know nothing. Equally personal are the game boards scored into the pavement of the temple itself, doubtless when the authority of both Apollo and his priests had waned.

108

PRIENE

❖

THE original city of Priene on the northern side of the estuary of the Meander is said to have been founded by a grandson of the last king of Athens. The coast was already in retreat as a result of the constant action of the river, and a new site was being developed on the southern flank of Mount Mycale, when Alexander the Great came in 334 BC. The new Priene continued to flourish, under the rule successively of Lysimachus, of the Attalids of Pergamum and of Rome, but gradually declined, so that the visitor sees what is in effect a Hellenistic city. The ruins, explored in turn by Chandler for the Society of Dilettanti and by German archaeologists, are remarkably complete.

The modern approach is from the east. The Hellenistic walls follow the contour of the slope and run up to the cliff face of the mountain. Much of the grid of streets can still be followed: paving stones are carefully grooved to discourage slipping on the steeper inclines, and many of the cross-streets are partly stepped. Near the centre are the three best-known monuments of Priene: the elegant bouleuterion or council house; the remarkable Hellenistic theatre, the original stage building of which was moved backwards by the Romans, yet preserved whether for economy or in a spirit of piety; and, set on a magnificent terrace, the Temple of Athena, for which Alexander paid, with five beautiful re-erected columns. Northwest of the temple, below the cliff, is the Sanctuary of Demeter and her daughter, Core, with the lower courses of a small temple, surrounded on three sides by narrow passages, and the adjacent sacrificial pit, into which the blood of the animal offerings drained. The most interesting Byzantine church is by the theatre, the stepped pulpit still in place. To the left of the main street, as this descends towards the west gate, is what remains of a synagogue, built in the Byzantine period. The site is shaded by a canopy of pines, but cyclamen and thyme abound.

At the southern extremity of Priene, just within the walls, is the monument in the city where one perhaps feels closest to the ancient world, despite the proximity of the modern road. The gymnasium was paid for, in about 130 BC, by a benefactor called Moschion. The central palestra was flanked by stoas. The best preserved is on the north. The central room of this, the ephebeum, bears the elegantly carved names of hundreds of

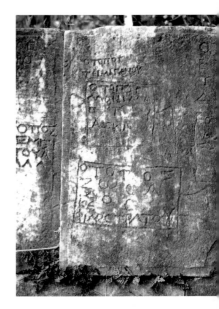

Athletes' names in the gymnasium.

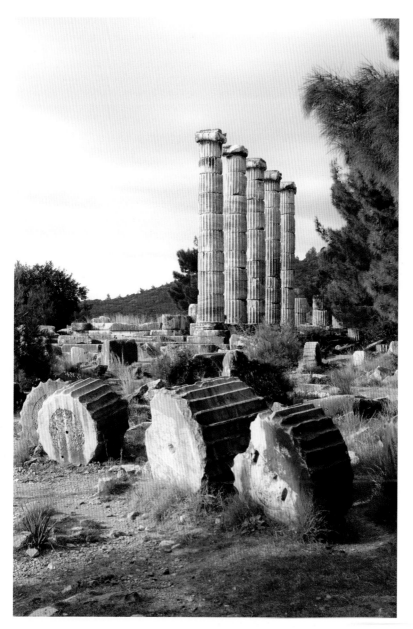

The Temple of Athena.

the boys – ephebes – who studied there. To the west is the room where the athletes washed, the water flowing from spouts with lion masks. East of the gymnasium was the stadium, in which both the Hellenistic and the Roman starting lines can be traced.

The visitor to Priene is ever conscious of the looming presence of Mount Mycale to the north. The ascent is not for the unsteady. Strike up the scree-strewn slope from above the theatre to the eastern corner of the cliff. From this an obvious scramble leads upwards. After 6 metres / 20 feet or so, you reach the steps cut in the rock when the new Priene was founded. These follow natural fissures in the cliff, turning as these dictated; two thousand years of exposure have eroded the vertiginous stairway, which eventually reaches a grassy slope just below the crest. The acropolis, the ancient Teloneia, where soldiers served three-month periods on guard, covers an unexpectedly large area. No fortification was necessary above the cliffs, but to the north there was no such natural barrier and walls

were built. Much survives of the Hellenistic line, including some splendid towers: the walls were restored, and reinforced, by the Byzantines. The characteristic Hellenistic masonry, with disciplined courses of finely prepared ashlar, is readily distinguished from that of the Byzantines, with smaller blocks and a cement core.

Within the walls little can be made out: a building here, a cutting there. But shards, ancient or Byzantine, are ubiquitous. Noises rise from the valley and one may hear the call of shepherds on the hillside beyond the walls. The valley of the Meander is at one's feet. The descent is as dramatic as the climb. A third of the way down, I saw a tortoise on one of the steps. There it could hardly survive. Should I take it up or down? Alas, I did not need to decide, for the creature was dead, its shell cracked when it crashed down from the cliff top in the brief hour since I had passed. Only now, when writing this, does it register how lucky I was not to have been in the way.

109

ALINDA

❧

FOR those who prefer classical sites that have not been excavated, the ruins of Alinda, perched upon a steep hill that overhangs the busy agricultural town of Karpuzlu, has a special magic. Carian in origin, the city enters the historical record in a dramatic way. Queen Ada, sister of Mausolus and widow of his brother, Idrieus, was driven from Halikarnassos by a younger brother, Pixodarus, and withdrew to Alinda. From there she emerged to meet Alexander in 334 BC, offering to help him gain her former territories. He agreed to be adopted by Ada and, after Caria had been conquered with her help, left her to reign as queen. It has been suggested that Alinda was the Alexandria ad Latmos which later could boast of a sculpture of Aphrodite by Praxiteles, and Alinda certainly became a strongly hellenized city.

From a distance the main monuments are clearly visible: the extraordinary, and extraordinarily well-preserved, market building 99 metres/325 feet in length, cut into the flank of the slope above the modern town; and much higher up the theatre. The visitor will not find it difficult to reach the former. The lower storey, with a series of doorways that also served to admit light, two arched and ten not, opening to small rooms used for shops with small storerooms behind, is reached from a terrace, itself with a handsome retaining wall. The middle storey, lit from small windows on the west, had rooms of more regular size. The top floor, the configuration of which cannot be fully established, was level with the agora on the east side. The masonry of the west front is remorseless in precision and the building as a whole is perhaps the masterpiece of Hellenistic commercial architecture.

The stoas of the agora do not survive, but the fine east wall of this, set against the hillside, does. Further on to the right is the more accessible of the two main gates in the city wall. An obvious path climbs upwards to the theatre, picturesquely shaded by olive trees. The stage building, which has collapsed, was enlarged in conformity with Roman requirements, but otherwise the Hellenistic building survived unaltered. The masonry is excellent, with carefully graded blocks. Higher up, near the top of the hill, there is a fine Hellenistic tower, placed to watch over the valley to the

The market.

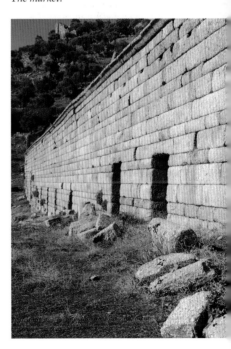

north-east and associated with the characteristically Carian city wall, that took full advantage of the terrain. Within the walls are the remains of numerous houses which establish that the area was densely inhabited in antiquity.

The acropolis is separated by a saddle from a higher hill on the west. This too called for fortification. A wall south of the saddle linked the city wall to those of this second acropolis. It too was inhabited: there are hints of houses and, on the right just back from the cliff edge, a row of six cisterns. There are two towers at the further, west, end, where the ground falls steeply away to a second saddle, crossed by an aqueduct of which four elegant arches survive.

We can see Alinda very much as Richard Chandler did in 1765. And despite the sounds that rise up from the town, the place has an immemorial air. A horse grazes in the agora. Tourists are few; a dog watches patiently as an elderly couple gather in their olives.

110

GERGA

GERGA can boast no major monument to rival those of the cities of inland Caria. But for those who savour the unusual, it is a fascinating place. Of Gerga's history nothing certain is known. Remote in a sequestered valley it must have succombed in turn to successive rulers of the area. Gerga's inhabitants were presumably of Carian stock and unquestionably were resistant to Hellenistic tastes. Their monuments are of Roman date, but bear very little resemblance to those of other sites in the area. Their eccentricity reminds us of the tolerance of Rome for those of their subjects who posed no threat.

In the past those who followed Professor Bean's directions and set out across the elegant bridge over the River Çine, the ancient Marsyas, near Incekemer, and then walked uphill to the north came across the first of a number of large Greek inscriptions naming Gerga. The track is not demanding and part of the charm of the expedition, a walk of several miles, is that one sees vignettes of a rural life still remarkably untouched by what we term progress. But the realignment of the main road from Yatagan to Aydin mean that this approach is now more complicated. Just north of Eski Cine, a road on the right is now signposted to Gerga. This climbs up through the villages of Ovacik and Kirsakkaler. The rest must be done on foot, but finding adequate directions may not be easy.

Gerga is a most eccentric site. Nothing there would have satisfied Vitruvius. There are some houses built of rather

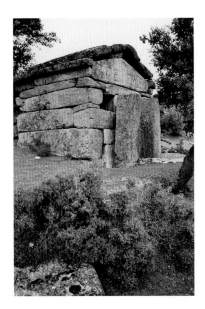

Gerga: the temple.

crude masonry. There is a small temple, still roofed, of solid, indeed ostensibly indestructible, form, with the word 'Gergas' firmly inscribed, in Greek rather than Latin letters, on the large block above the doorway. There are some puzzling open-fronted buildings, which Bean suggests may have been fountain houses. There are a few sculptures with no pretension to refinement. And there are two pyramidal stelae. These also are both inscribed 'Gergas'. Bean was understandably fascinated by the place and something perhaps of Gerga's appeal will be lost when the archaeologists have been able to explain the oddities of its buildings. Certainly a morning at Gerga raises more unanswered, and perhaps unanswerable, questions than a day in many more celebrated ancient sites.

111

NYSA

❖

THE Meander was the principal river of Caria, rising in the undulating ranges of central Anatolia and writhing westwards in the manner that gives it its name, before taking a most southerly course to the sea. The valley was one of the great trade routes of Asia Minor, and must always have been agriculturally rich. East of Priene the first major site is Magnesia ad Meandrum, with the evocative ruins of the Temple of Artemis designed by Hermogenes of Alabanda – the enclosure of which Strabo deemed superior to that of the Artemisium at Ephesus – a theatre and an extensive bath complex. Further on, swallowed by the sprawling town of Aydin, is the site of Tralles, source of one of the most beautiful sculptures in the Istanbul Archaeological Museum.

Altogether more memorable, north of the village of Sultanhisar, astride a stream that rises high on Mount Messogis, are the ruins of Nysa. A few days before I set out on my first visit to Turkey, Victoria Macdonagh told me that this was the one place I should not miss. I would not have done so, but I have thought gratefully of her since.

Nysa seems to have succeeded an earlier settlement, or settlements, founded by Spartans, and may have been named after 200 BC for a woman of the Seleucid family. The wealth of the place is indicated by the generosity of a citizen, Chaeremon, to Rome during the Mithridatic War. One of his relations married a daughter of Mark Anthony, his daughter by whom became Queen of Pontus and Cappadocia.

The approach road climbs to the north, passing an arch of what must have been a large gymnasium. Park when the theatre comes into sight, just beyond the ticket office. At your feet is the unexpected footprint of the western half of the stadium falling away to a deep ravine, carved by a stream that was channelled through a tunnel in antiquity: the opposite side of the stadium can be seen on the further bank. To the northwest is the recently excavated library, which stands to two storeys and is after that at Ephesus the most remarkable building of the kind in Asia Minor. As at Ephesus the books, or rather scrolls, were shelved in receesses in internal walls, which were divided from the outer ones by galleries to minimize the risk of damp. The recessess were ranged round a central reading room on two levels that ran the full height of the building: small rooms on the upper floor were used for archives. That Nysa boasted so splendid a library comes as no surprise, for there was a proper tradition of learning in the city. Here Aristodemus taught rhetoric and grammar respectively in the mornings and evenings: his pupil, the geographer Strabo, is the source of much of the information we have about the place.

The theatre is the most impressive monument of Nysa. There is one diazoma, with twenty-three rows of seats below and twenty-six above, reached respectively by nine and seventeen flights of steps. The Roman stage building was enriched with reliefs, which are now in the museum at Aydin. The

Nysa: the Roman tunnel.

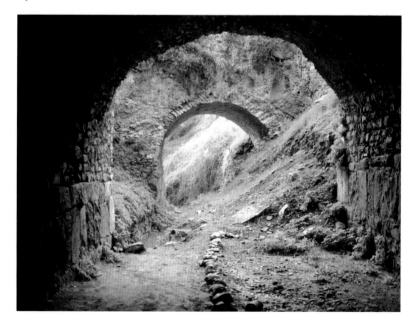

112

APHRODISIAS

APHRODISIAS was one of the great cult centres of ancient Asia Minor, and now is among the most impressive of the classical sites of Turkey. Inhabited at least from the early Bronze Age, Aphrodisias was stated by Stephanus of Byzantium to have originally been named after Ninos, King of Assyria. The worship of Ishtar, the Assyrian and Babylonian goddess of love, was with time subsumed by that of Aphrodite. Around the sanctuary of the goddess a settlement grew up. But it was not until the second century BC that Aphrodisias became a significant city. Mark Antony may have helped to secure freedom from tax for Aphrodisias from Rome. The city's glory days were, however, in the imperial period, her wealth implied by that of a priest, Attalus Adrastus, who contributed 122,000 denarii for public buildings and left over twice as much for gymnastic causes. In addition to the Temple of Aphrodite, major public buildings were erected. But Aphrodisias was not walled until the fourth century AD, the Antioch Gate bearing a dedication to the Emperor Constantius II (323–61). Aphrodite was not, of course, a deity who could readily be assimilated within the Christian religion. Yet none the less Aphrodisias survived into the Byzantine period: a great church took the place of the temple and the theatre was adapted as a fortress. But gradually decline set in. By the nineteenth century the village of Geyre sprawled among the ruins.

Most visitors come to Aphrodisias from the north west, where the tributary valley of the Dandalas meets the

streambed lies below the south-eastern angle of the cavea. For some 90 metres/ 295 feet it runs through a tunnel, lit by a single shaft in the vault, which turns to the right. Walking through the tunnel, one realizes what an impressive feat its even longer counterpart under the amphitheatre must have been. On the eastern bank among the olive trees are further buildings, including the fine council house or odeum, with a semicircle of twelve rows of benches. This has now been more fully restored and the row of columns behind it has been re-erected, while the street on which these stand has been cleared. Further east is the agora, many of the columns of the north and east stoas of which have been re-erected. Excavation continues.

Meander, below the site of the former city of Antiochia ad Meandrum. Flanked by hills, the valley is a couple of miles wide. The country is particularly beautiful in the spring when the fresh verdure is answered by the blossom of the orchards that cluster about the small villages with their pencil-sharp minarets. Philip Glazebrook in his *Journey to Kars* (1984) describes the place, using a pseudonym, soon after the last of the villagers of Geyre had been cleared from the site. The pansiyon of Mr Mestan where he stayed is still visible but no longer in business.

The tourist should begin in the exemplary museum, recently enlarged. Partly because of the ready availability of the local white marble, a notable school of sculptors developed at Aphrodisias and a foretaste of their achievement is offered by some dozens of blocks with well-carved masks outside the entrance. In the museum itself, exhibits explain the development of the town, and give some idea of the sophistication of civilized life there. But it is the sculpture that holds the attention. The statues of deities are outshone by a remarkable group of portraits, many of which are compellingly individualized. That of Flavius Palmatus is an arresting late example. No other provincial city of the ancient world produced such assured images in comparable number. A major new gallery has been built for the reliefs from the Sebasteion and the statue in a bluish marble of a horse from the Basilica.

Excellent as the museum is, it is exhilarating to escape the modern buildings and to wander among the monuments of the ancient city. Here, archaeology and nature seem in rare harmony. Poplars echo columns. And beyond the city walls

Aphrodisias: a mask by the museum.

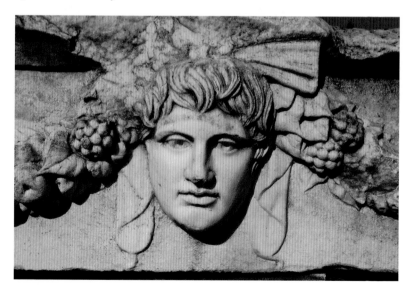

the hills are never out of sight. Because so many tourists arrive by bus there is a more or less 'official' circuit. But those who can should take time and wander at will. At Aphrodisias retracing one's steps and criss-crossing the city is always satisfyinging.

To the south of the museum is the Sebasteion of the first century AD with its two porticoes, one of the most beautiful structures at Aphrodisias, overhung by trees. The eastern end of the south portico has now been partly reconstructed. Beyond, a track between fields leads towards the southern walls, of which a substantial section survives. Returning towards the centre of the city, there is a wonderful sequence of ruins: the Theatre Baths, the piazza beyond and, at an angle to the left of it, the stage buildings of the admirably preserved theatre, which was built against the tell of the Bronze Age settlement. The acanthus-carved pilasters of the baths are of the admirably crisp quality one comes to expect of Aphrodisian sculpture. Partly because it was encased in a Byzantine fortification, the theatre is one of the best-preserved buildings of the city. It originally seated some 1,700 spectators. The proscenium with its reliefs was paid for by Gaius Julius Zoilus, who had been freed by Julius Caesar, and dates from 40–30 BC. But the theatre was adapted under Antonius Pius and Marcus Aurelius to meet the Roman taste for animal and gladiatorial displays. The stage building is notable for the numerous inscriptions recording imperial missives.

The tell behind the theatre is the best point from which to survey the city. To the north-west, formerly identified as an agora, was a park surrounding a long pool with semi circular ends: west of this is the Portico of Tiberius behind which

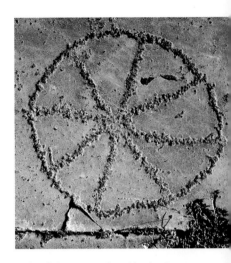

Aphrodisias: a game board in the theatre.

are the Baths of Hadrian (AD 117–38), one of the more substantial extant complexes of Aphrodisias: this has recently been restored.

To the north of the pool is one of the most appealing buildings of its type, the elegant odeum, with its tiers of white marble seats and a carefully restored opus sectilium floor. Beside the odeum is what remains of the episcopal palace built in Byzantine times. This was well placed, for immediately to the north was the fifth-century Byzantine church, in fact of cathedral scale, of which part of the apse survives, as do many of the columns. The church replaced the great Temple of Aphrodite, which in earlier centuries had been the very *raison d'être* of Aphrodisias. And it is clear that the Byzantine builders endeavoured to incorporate as much as possible of the previous Hadrianic structure in their scheme. The fluted white marble columns are particularly elegant, and I now realize how vulnerable these are. For by

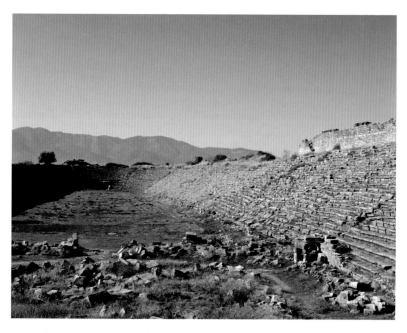

Aphrodisias: the stadium, looking west.

chance, on my second visit in the spring of 1991, I saw desperate workmen, who had been burning scrub nearby, putting damp mud on columns which had been caught by the flames and were literally crumbling before my eyes. Kenan Erim's expression of despair when thanking me for my snapshots made me realize how wholly remarkable his achievement was in both excavating and caring for the ruins of Aphrodisias. His enthusiasm was crucial in securing the funding that was necessary and, most suitably, he is buried by the reconstructed Tetrapylon, to the east of the great temple.

Perhaps the best-preserved building of Aphrodisias is the stadium at the northern side of the city. Aligned approximately from east to west, it is 262 metres / 859 feet long and up to 59 metres / 193 feet wide, with slightly elliptical sides. The thirty-odd rows of benches could have accommodated up to 30,000 spectators. In Byzantine times, perhaps after the theatre was damaged by an earthquake in the seventh century, the eastern end of the stadium was remodelled as a small arena, but little evidence of this alteration is now visible. With its waving wild flowers the stadium is a wonderfully atmospheric place, not least in the evening, when the shadows lengthen and shroud the hills to the west. But once I was there soon after dawn, guided to a gap in the site fence by Mr Mestan's dog, when it seemed ridiculous to wait three hours for the official opening time.

As a casual glance at the plan of Aphrodisias shows, the city walls follow a line that incorporates the stadium. Few tourists pay much attention to the walls, but these too are most impressive. Marble that might elsewhere have been carefully husbanded was ruthlessly recycled by the fourth-century masons. This can be seen, for example, in the stretch of the wall to the east of the stadium, which includes the north-east gate, tucked into an angle. This was never as significant as the West or Antioch Gate, the point of arrival for those who had come by way of Antiochia ad Meandrum.

Outside the walls lay the necropolises of Aphrodisias. These were extensive but contain no tombs of especial note. Altogether more remarkable are the marble quarries 2 kilometres / 1.2 miles away to the north. Their proximity made possible the extraordinarily lavish decoration of the great monuments of Aphrodisias. Those who do not have time to visit them can gain an impression of their eerie fascination from John Julius Norwich's introduction to Kenan T. Erim's *Aphrodisias: City of Venus Aphrodite*. Published in 1986, this is a compelling account of the place by the archaeologist whose name will always be associated with it.

113
LAODICEA

FEW families gave their names to as many cities in antiquity as the Seleucids. Laodicea is probably named after Laodice, wife of Antiochus II who reigned from 261 BC and divorced her in 253. The site may already have been sacred to Zeus. This occupies a low but level hill set back from the River Lycus (now the Cürüksu), the valley of which formed a natural route from that of the Meander, of which the river is a tributary, to Pisidia and the Pamphylian coast. Laodicea shared this advantage with Hierapolis, across the valley to the east, and Colossae. In 188 BC the area passed to Pergamon, and thus in 133 to Rome, the Attolids' chosen heir. Cicero, then Governor of Cilicia, worked at Laodicea in 50 BC. Like Colossae, Laodicea had a Jewish colony – permitted to worship but not, in 62 BC, to send subventions to Jerusalem. The existence of Jewish communities in both towns may explain the early advent of Christianity: Laodicea is mentioned in Saint Paul's Epistle to the Colossians and as one of the seven cities of Asia in the Book of Revelation.

The approach off the road between Denizli and Pamukkale is from the south-east. The car park is near the centre of the hill, just before the gate built in the Byzantine era when the defended area was reduced. Ahead is the so-called Syria Street, much of the colonnades of which have been re-erected, although one travertine pier has been left slumped across the paving stones. The columns are of different widths and a few are of coloured, rather than the usual white, marble. Excavation has revealed, on the

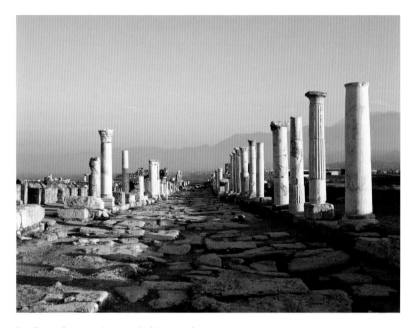

Laodicea: the central street, looking south.

right of the street, a substantial mansion and, set back off a cross-street, a massive church. Beyond this, set in a colonnaded court, is a partly re-erected Corinthian temple: the large room visible through the glass floor was used to store documents in the Christian period. Further on is the lower level of a large nymphaeum, recorded in 1961–63 before any other work had been done in the area, beyond which parts of a fine row of columns on a side street have been put back in place.

Rather remarkably Laodicea had two substantial theatres, both cut into the flank of the hill, the larger facing northeast more or less behind the temple, the other facing north-west near the northern tip. Both remain very much in the condition that they were seen by the Torinese architect, Giovanni Battista

Borra, who recorded them in his capacity as draftsman to Wood and Dawkins in 1751. Much of the stage building of the smaller theatre would appear to be intact, but it is the undisturbed state of both theatres that makes these, with their partly displaced seating, seem so moving.

On returning to the excavated area, cross Syria Street to find a charming small building, the Club House of the Greens, built in the late third century for charioteers, as an inscription above the entrance states. The entrance hall has four modest columns and there are two other rooms. Behind this is an agora with a monument at the centre. On the line of the cross-street on which the large church stands as this crosses to the south-west at a high point is a modest-looking but crucial structure from which water was distributed. The area beyond this has not been excavated. There are scattered blocks and here and there evidence of buildings. Where the ground falls gently away, there is clear evidence of a small odeum, most of the seating of which has fallen away. This was set above the large level area of the south agora, the wall of the stoa on the opposite side of which partly survives. Beyond this is the picturesque carcass of a substantial bath complex, built under Hadrian, that hangs above the large stadium. This was dedicated to the ruling emperor, Vespasian, and consecrated by the father of the future Emperor Trajan in AD 79. That it was paid for by a Laodicean donor indicates the prosperity of his city. Famed in antiquity for its wool, this was also – as indeed the existence of its Jewish colony implied – a significant trading post. Long neglected, Laodicea can now take its place as one of the more impressive classical sites of Asia Minor.

114
HIERAPOLIS

BY ANY measure Hierapolis is an extraordinary place. The fiercely white terraces, which from Laodicea across the valley of the Lycus might be mistaken for the waste of a gargantuan industrial complex, were formed by calcium bicarbonate in the water of the warm springs that emerge from the limestone and created petrified pools and cascades. The ancient city is on the broad terrace above these. It may have been a Seleucid foundation, but may derive its name from Hiera, wife of the putative atavar or founder of the Attolid dynasty. Under Eumenes II of Pergamon it was a key frontier fortress of his expanded realm, passing to Rome on the death of the last of his line in 133 BC. It is to the long Roman occupation and its Byzantine sequel that the key monuments of Hierapolis are due. Like Laodicea, the city was a major centre of the wool trade: its hot springs ensured that it became a place of cult and thus of pilgrimage. What the Plutonium was to the ancients, the antechamber as it were to the Underworld, the Martyry of Saint Philip would become to the Byzantines. Like their Roman predecessors, Turks have an understandable taste for hot springs: and when I first visited Hierapolis in 1987 the city was blighted by inappropriate buildings round the central pool. This has happily been corrected: the city is now approached on foot from the mother of all visitor centres just outside the south gate of the Byzantine wall.

Tempting as it is to pass through the gate, there is a case for following the stretch of wall to the left as far as a

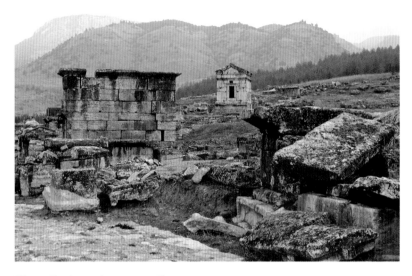

Hierapolis: the northern necropolis.

postern: be careful not to damage minor phenomena of the place: raised water channels, the sides of which have petrified. Within the walls there are shaded terraces from which to view the cascades. Ahead is a major Roman bath complex which is surprisingly well preserved. The northern section houses the museum in barrel-vaulted halls of appropriate scale. In addition to the smaller finds, there is a substantial collection of sculpture: a sulky image of Attis, and a number of sarcophagi, including one of Sidemara type from Laodicea. The late second-century reliefs from the stage building of the theatre are placed in a separate room. There are vigorous representations of the gods with scenes from their lives – Adonis sits on the lap of Venus – and wild Dionysian festivals: intended to be seen from a distance, these are not of very refined quality. Outside in the garden there are some notable

architectural fragments, among the more unusual capitals with paired sphinxes from the agora.

East of the museum is the modern enclosure round the pool, which is still in use. On the other side of this is the massive carcass of the nympheum, behind which is the Plutonium, visually unimpressive but a remarkable phenomenon. Recorded by Strabo, this was a gas-filled passage that was regarded as the entrance to the Underworld. Beside it was the Temple of Apollo of which relatively little survives. Ahead, set against the hillside is the very substantial theatre, now entered from above. The reconstruction of the stage building is undeniably impressive, but here restoration has somewhat diminished the appeal of the place.

North-east of the theatre is the Martyry of Saint Philip. The apostle was thought to have been buried in a tomb

round which a small shrine was constructed. From the terrace by this a grand
flight of steps, turning sharply to the
right, climbed to the martyry, a large
fifth-century structure radiating from a
central octagon in a commanding position overlooking the city. This is a relatively recent discovery and has been
tactfully restored.

Descend towards the centre of the city,
either going as far as the central axial
street, now known as the Via Frontinus,
or turning off on one of the narrower
parallel paved roads to pass the not very
substantial remains of the Byzantine
cathedral, before taking a side street to
the Via Frontinus just south of the large
Byzantine Gate. This was built when
troubled times meant that Hierapolis
had to be defended, as had not been
necessary during the long centuries of
the Pax Romana. North of the gate is a
fine stretch of the Roman street. Many
columns have been re-erected, but on the
left a sequence of Byzantine shops are
built out in front of the colonnade. Further on, to the right, was the large agora,
beside which is the handsome latrine
building with a central row of columns.
Beyond this is the Arch of Domitian (AD
84–5), with later round towers at either
side. The road continues northwards,
passing a second massive baths, to reach
one of the most impressive of Roman
necropolises, unequalled in Asia Minor.
The road climbs slightly and then curves
leftwards as this descends, flanked by
numerous mausolea, many of which are
of considerable size. Clustered along the
road, these seem to jostle for position, as
no doubt those whom they commemorated had done in life. There was no
doubt a frisson in the notion of being
entombed in a city with so direct a link
to the Underworld.

<h1>115</h1>

<h1>EPHESUS</h1>

❖

THE splendid ruins of Ephesus represent not the original Greek city of that
name but its successor, founded by Lysimachus, who laid out its extensive walls.
On Lysimachus's death in 281 BC, the
city passed to the Seleucids. In 190 BC it
was secured by Eumenes II of Pergamum, whose nephew Attalus III bequeathed his state to Rome. Ephesus
became the greatest entrepôt on the
Aegean, with a population of 250,000.
Her importance made her a natural focus
for the missionary zeal of Saint Paul. In
imperial times silting, caused in part by
agricultural exploitation inland, began to
affect the harbour. In the fifth century
two major Christian councils were held
at Ephesus, but the city was already in
decline and within a century the site was
apparently abandoned in favour of that
of the modern Selçuk.

Early visitors were drawn to Ephesus
not least by the search for one of the
wonders of the ancient world, the Temple of Artemis, which was finally found
in the Victorian era by J. T. Wood: the
remains, outside Selçuk, although much
eroded, are oddly moving, not least
before dusk.

For the active, and adequately clothed,
visitor, the most memorable way of
approaching Ephesus is to park south of
the Magnesia Gate and climb the flank of
Mount Coressus, which dominates the
site and is considerably higher than
Mount Pion, which lies within the walls.
Lysimachus's splendid wall with its
towers, four-square, crowns the crest.
The thorny bushes are vicious, but in

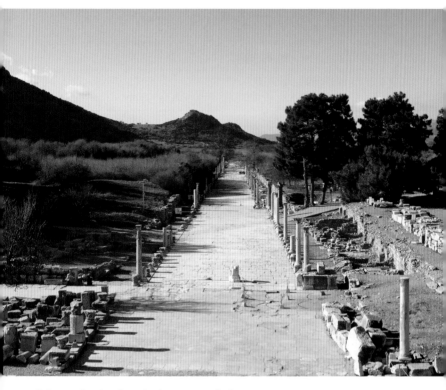

Ephesus: the view from the theatre towards the port.

spring cyclamen and various types of orchid more than compensate. The ridge descends gradually and the line of the walls ends beyond the so-called Tower of Saint Paul at the side of the former harbour. Turn inland, making for the marble-paved road, restored by the Emperor Arcadius (AD 395–408), which led from the harbour to the theatre. The saner visitor will make for the main entrance to the north of the site and reach the road not far from the theatre

The enormous theatre, in which Saint Paul denounced the worship of Artemis, was built againt the flank of Mount Pion and is substantially of Roman date. Alas, this has been vigorously restored. Turn right on the street (the 'Marble Street'), with raised pavements on both sides, that passes the lower agora and a supposed brothel. Below the bend of the street, where this turns sharply to the east, is one of the most celebrated buildings of Ephesus, the library built by Consul Gaius Julius Aquila (110–15) in memory of his father, who is buried there. The façade, of two storeys enriched with niches and columns, has been brilliantly reconstructed by the Austrians, who have excavated at Ephesus since 1896: look closely at the columns, some of which are veined with purple, while others are yellow. Parts of the building are double-skinned to protect the precious books from damp. No comparable Roman library exists in Asia Minor, for that at Nysa is considerably smaller in scale, and few buildings are more eloquent of the lavish taste of the early imperial era. The architect was evidently aware that the façade would be seen obliquely by those who descended towards it on the 'Street of Curates'. To the right of the library is the imposing triple archway to the lower agora dedicated to Augustus and his son-in-law Agrippa by two former slaves. This was one of the largest structures of the kind in Asia Minor: many columns of the stoas have been re-erected.

Above the library the 'Street of Curates', which leads upwards towards the Magnesia Gate, is lined with buildings of interest: a public lavatory, with some of the original marble seats, followed by a small temple dedicated to the Emperor Hadrian on the left. Behind this is a large bath complex, the main room in which is presided over by a statue of Scholastica, a Christian, who paid for its restoration in the fourth century. The side street that leads to the baths is, like so many others at Ephesus, well preserved. Many of the paving stones were scored though after these were laid down to afford greater grip: there are numerous other examples of this necessary practice at Ephesus.

Opposite these, and behind a Byzantine fountain, are the recently excavated

Ephesus: the Library of Celsus.

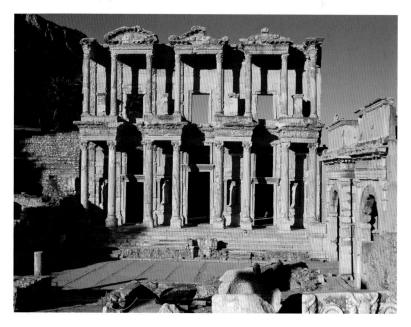

terraced houses, many with rooms that survive to full height and retain not only marble and mosaic pavements but also marble wall facings and almost complete painted mural schemes. Pompeii and Herculaneum apart, there are few places in which one is so close to the *douceur de vivre* of Roman provincial life, with a rectangular marble bath, the personal lavatory of C. Vibius Salutaris and graffiti recording payments for figs and barley. The remarkable ivory relief in the site museum at Selçuk (Room 18) was found in a room with murals of putti. The presentation of the houses cannot be faulted, but the protective structure has not proved to be dustproof. Higher up the road, the series of monuments continues, more impressive in conjunction than individually.

The Nymphaeum of Trajan, of which there is a token reconstruction, was the source of the statue of Dionysius in the museum. Ahead is what survives of the Hercules Gate, beyond which on the left are the Hydreion, a fountain with imperial statues, and the monument of Caius Memmius, grandson of Sulla. Elements of this are arranged in what has been termed 'a Cubist modern architectural collage'. Diagonally opposite, where the street turns to the right, is the Monument of Caius Sextilius Pollio, flanked to the right by the Fountain of Domitian. Further on, to the right, are the substantial storerooms below the terrace of the destroyed Temple of Domitian: it then turns at a right angle to run to the Magnesia Gate, passing between the south wall of the south or State Agora and the relatively unimposing semi-circular water distributor that was so vital to the city. Smaller than the lower agora, and less well preserved, the south agora had an important place in civic life. Behind

the north-eastern stoa is the bouleuterion, the lower section of the benches of which are in place, and beside this, the Temple of Divus Julius and Dea Roma, honouring Caesar and Rome. To the left of this is the Prytaneium, dedicated to Vesta and the source of the two statues of the Ephesian Diana in the museum. To the east of the agora are the Baths of Varius.

West of the main entrance a track leads to the great monument of Byzantine Ephesus, the church of Mary, itself a reconstruction of a Roman building of uncertain function. It was here that councils of the church were held in 431 and 449, but by the seventh century the cathedral had been transferred to the church of Saint John at Selçuk. Thick scrub discourages interest in other structures nearby.

One of the great monuments of Ephesus, not officially accessible, is beyond the main car park. The stadium, built like the theatre into the flank of Mount Pion, dates substantially from the third century. Although it was robbed when the Byzantines constructed the vast castle above Selçuk, much survives. At the far end is a round space for gladiatorial fights; and Bean suggested that some of the rooms were used to house the wild animals whose despatch gave such delight to a Roman audience. Below, and a little to the north, is the large gymnasium given to Ephesus by Publius Vedius Antoninus in the second century.

Ephesus was a populous city. Now it is a magnet for tourists. At holiday times numbers can be oppressive, so there is a case for going in the winter. It is most conveniently visited from its successor, Selçuk. The castle there is not open to the public and the basilica of Saint John is the victim of a too enthusiastic restoration. But the surviving arches of the Byzantine aqueduct still stride through the commercial heart of the modern town and the large Seljuk İsa Bey Camii with a dedicatory inscription of 1375 is both distinguished in detail and impressive in design: like both castle and basilica it was built of stone appropriated from the ruins of Ephesus. No visitor, however, should miss the splendid new site museum. The sculpture is particularly impressive, ranging from early kouroi to statues from the Fountain of Trajan, the frieze of the Temple of Hadrian and a notable group of Roman portrait busts.

116

TEOS

❖

NO area of Asia Minor is more favoured by nature than Ionia. But much of the Ionian coastline has been brutally developed and inevitably the context of some of the Greek settlements has suffered, not least to the north of Ephesus. One exception is Notium on a high ridge above the shore. Little survives: but what remain of the western walls and the podium of the modest Temple of Athena above these retain their magic.

Notium controlled the nearby sanctuary at Claros, where recent excavation has greatly enhanced understanding of the shrine of the Clarian Apollo. A ruined propylon leads to the much-robbed temple, where the oracle pronounced in a now flooded chamber. Happily those who quarried the site had no use for the massive fragments of colossal statues of Apollo, of Artemis and Leto. One lies by the temple and the others have been re-erected above this. Notium's near neighbour to the west, Ledebus, has been desecrated by building, and few will wish to search out its time-abused walls.

Further west was the much more important city of Teos, with its two harbours. This, Freya Stark wrote in 1954 (in *Ionia: a Quest*), was the Ionian city where she would have chosen to live. Possibly colonized initially from Orchomenos in the Peloponnese, Teos became one of the major cities of Ionia. The Ionian inhabitants left rather than submit to Persian rule, but many returned and in 494 BC their city made a significant contribution to the Carian fleet that was destroyed by the Persians at Lade. Teos flourished as a commercial seaport and its wealth can be judged from its contribution of 5,000 containers of wine to support Antiochus III in his unsuccessful struggle with a Roman navy. It was the city of Anacreon, pioneer of poets of love.

The city itself has been spared recent building. But the northern harbour at Siğacik is now a concrete fringed marina, while the southern harbour is partly overlooked by a massive holiday development. From the site entrance follow signs for the acropolis, a low oval hill that was close to the centre of the city. There are the footings of early walls, and, at the east end, a substantial platform. To the south, built into the slope, is the theatre, a building of particular moment in a city that was the first base in Asia Minor of the Artists of Dionysius, professional actors and musicians. The lower section of the cavea is tolerably well preserved and elements of the stage building are also in place, built, like much of Teos, in a bluish limestone from the much-quarried hill beyond Siğacik.

South-east of the theatre is the elegant bouleuterion, the least robbed of the monuments of Teos: eleven rows of benches are in place. As was usual, the building was beside the agora, the stoas of which are reduced to stacks of heaped stones. Between the agora and the southern harbour are a few farmsteads: a dog flushes out game for its master; and geese cackle unseen. The harbour itself is much silted up. The ancient mole on the southern spit continues the alignment of the Hellenistic city wall. Vessels were

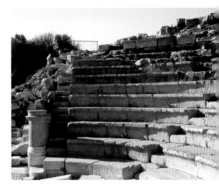

Teos: the bouleuterion.

tied up to the pierced projecting blocks, several of which are still in place. Although the water level has risen since antiquity, small boats of fibreglass are now moored to the mole.

Heading back, follow the sign to the Temple of Dionysius, looking out on the way for a long cistern with a series of arches on its northern side. The temple was the celebrated monument of Teos. It was designed by Hermogenes of Priene and built during the reign of Antiochus III, who with his sister Laodice was also worshipped there. The temple was first surveyed in 1764 by the indefatigable Dr Chandler for the Society of Dilettanti. His pioneering publication of 1769 is invaluable because the site was energetically robbed in the nineteenth century. Mercifully, enough survives of the temple and its temenos to give one at least a sense of what has been lost.

117
TIRE AND BIRGI
❖

THE Islamic monuments of western Anatolia deserve to be better known. And a sightseer who needs time to digest his impressions of the great classical sites should consider a day's excursion, perhaps from Selçuk, to Tire and Birgi. Selçuk, until 1914 known as Ayasuluğ, became in 1345 the capital of the emirate founded by Mahmed Bey who named it after his father, Aydin. Mahmed's son, Isa Bey, selected an architect, Ali, of Damascene extraction to build the huge mosque that bears his name at Selçuk, and many smaller monuments in the town date from his reign. In 1390, when Sultan Beyazit I took the emirate, Isa Bey, who had married a daughter of the Sultan, was constrained to transfer his base to Tire, some 39 kilometres/24 miles inland, on the south flank of the productive valley of the Kücükmenderes, the ancient Cayster. The family regained a brief independence after Timur's defeat of Beyazit in 1402, as their former property was returned. Timur himself was entertained at Tire in the winter of 1402–3.

Inevitably, Ottoman rule was reimposed. Most of the monuments of Tire reflect the prosperity of the ensuing period. On the western outskirts of the town, still happily rural in context, is the beautiful fifteenth-century Yavukluoğlu Mosque and the associated medrese. Many of the most interesting buildings are clustered near the souk. The small Şegh Hüsumattin mosque of 1384 has a stumpy spiralling minaret. Nearby are the Tahtakale mosque with a brick minaret and the large fifteenth-century

Kutu Han, now under restoration. A little to the south is the Yeni Cami of 1597, with a good portico and a large prayer hall with a contemporary marble mimber, a clone as it were of the architecture of Sinan. Just to the west is the ambitious bedesten, founded by Ibn al Melek, with a massive central hall.

The most appealing mosque in the town is a few streets to the west: the Yahşi Bey Camii, founded by an official of Sultan Murat II who endowed it in 1441, with a polychrome brick minaret and a central domed court opening to a pentagonal prayer hall under a memorable fluted semi-dome. This was the building in Tire that most impressed the indefatigable traveller Evliya Çelebi in 1671: he stated that there were 144 mosques, 30 medreses, 13 baths and 26 hans in the town. What remains is thus but a fraction of what there was; and although much old domestic building survives, recent prosperity has inevitably affected the character of Tire.

Birgi, 32 kilometres/20 miles eastwards, was Mehmed Bey's original capital. For him in 1312–3 was built the Ulu Cami high on a terrace above the river bed that divides the town. Much classical spoil was used. The mosque was planned like a basilica with five aisles. The walnut mimber of 1322, signed by Muzuffereddin Ibn Abdülvahid, is of exceptional quality and the carved window shutters are also remarkable. The soaring minaret is decorated with chevrons of glazed brick, the blue of which echoes that of the sky. Beside the mosque is the türbe of Mehmed Bey (1334), where he and three of his sons including Isa Bey are buried under a mesmerizing dome with a delicate centerpiece set in a field of concentric chevrons in turquoise and red brick, that

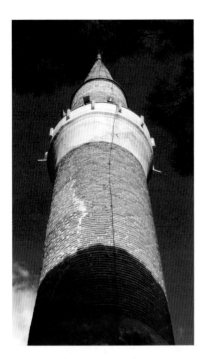

Birgi: the tiled minaret of the Ulu Cami.

are in turn framed by an elaborate frieze. Nothing, alas, survives of the palace where Mehmed entertained the great Moroccan traveller, Ibn Battuta, in 1333.

The charm of Birgi is owed both to its position and to the survival of a surprising number of good houses, the tractors parked beside which indicate the occupation of their inhabitants. One house stands out, the Çakirağa Konaği on the right bank of the river. Completed for a successful merchant, Şerif Ali Ağa, who died in 1837, this must be one of the most appealing private house of its date in Turkey. The centre is recessed and many of the rooms on the first and second floors are decorated with floral designs, the charm of which is owed to their lightness of touch.

118

SARDIS

SARDIS was the capital of the kings of Lydia. Their kingdom was won by Gyges from the uxorious Candaules and subsequently became a considerable power. Gold from the Pactolus, the small river that crosses the site, was used for the celebrated coins of the last king, Croesus, who was defeated and captured by the Persian King Cyrus in 546 BC. Sardis survived the fall of the Lydian kingdom: it flourished under Rome and became the seat of a bishopric ranking sixth after Byzantium. The Sassanids in the seventh century and Timur in 1401 sacked the place: and mud from the friable mass of the acropolis hill completed its destruction. Early travellers found the site of the city, still abandoned. When in 1879 the Antiquarian Society of Boston planned to work in Asia Minor, the influential Harvard professor Charles Eliot Norton asked Ruskin: 'What do you think of Sardis as a point of attack – with all the wealth of Croesus to tempt us?' Assos was chosen; but Sardis's turn would come.

The acropolis is on an isolated hill to the west of the river: of the surviving fortifications most are Byzantine. On the northern slope can be made out the outline of the Roman theatre, with a stadium below. The line of the ancient road from the east continues to the modern village of Sart. To the right is a section of the Roman town excavated by the Americans. Behind an unusually fully documented street of shops, one with its own lavatory, is the large synagogue, energetically restored. North of this is the palestra, dominated on the west by the prodigious gymnasium dedicated to the sons and wife of Septimius Severus. The vast court of this, originally roofed, has been largely rebuilt. The west wall must always have seemed theatrical, and restoration has not enhanced its charm.

Half a mile south, beyond an area of excavations that are of limited appeal, is the monument for which Sardis is justly celebrated, the Temple of Artemis. Try to go early, when the sun still falls from the intended angle on the eight extant columns of the east façade, two preserved to full height, although with their beautiful Ionic capitals somewhat out of line. The temple was begun in about 334 BC, but left unfinished. The eastern portico was erected in a second campaign, of c. 175 BC, but once again work lapsed. In about AD 150, the scheme was modified and the eastern half of the cella was re-dedicated to the reigning emperor, Antonius Pius. The main structure was built. But resources evidently ran out before the revised project was fully realized. The columns were to have been fluted, but in the event this was achieved only with the internal ones of the east portico; elsewhere a substantial skin of stone that was intended to be cut away is still in place. Similarly, while some of the bases were carved with acanthus and other floral patterns, with wreaths or guilloche, many more remain undecorated.

The rise of Christianity meant that the temple became obsolete. A small church, itself subsequently contracted, was set against the south-east corner. The edifice later became a quarry, but happily not before erosion had ensured a measure of protection. Mud washed from the acropolis hill to the east engulfed the site. And when the temple was seen by Dr Jacob Spon, co-author of *A Journey to Greece* (1682), and by Chandler, only the upper

parts of the extant columns were visible, saved doubtless by the fact that these were not easily re-usable. The sloping line of the surviving section of the cella wall corresponds with that of the protective mud.

Truncated as it is, the temple is intensely beautiful. The impeccable construction of the walls is matched by the refined detail of the completed bases. Moreover, the building is wonderfully sited, with views up to the acropolis and to the equally striking ridge on the west. When there is cloud, sunlight plays on the hills. And in a sudden storm the stone blackens. In summer, the hillside

The Temple of Artemis.

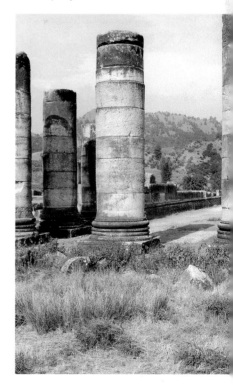

above the temple cascades with purple thistles of varying types and other plants.

There are other antiquities to see at Sardis, individual tombs and necropolises, as well as sections of the Byzantine fortifications, built when retrenchment was evidently the order of the day. But none perhaps is more evocative than the four piers of a substantial church north of the modern road and more or less below the theatre. Now half-lost among trees and tillage, these were built of the recycled spoil of classical Sardis. Marble column drums and delicate cornices were put to service amidst the rubble.

119

MANISA

❧

THE visitor to Manisa, unless he goes to the Archaeological Museum, has little reason to sense that the city had a pre-Islamic existence. The Lydians and the Seleucids left nothing. No building of Roman Magnesia ad Sipylum or its Byzantine successor survives. Magnesia was captured in 1313 by Saruhan Bey (d. 1345), Turkish founder of an emirate that fell to Mehmet Çelebi, a son of Beyazit I, in 1405.

The town stretches up the slope of a steep hill, the Sandik Tepesi. On a terrace high above the modern centre is the earliest significant monument, the Ulu Cami, begun under Isak Bey, Saruhan's grandson, in 1367. Spoil from earlier buildings is almost ostentatiously paraded in the outer walls. The courtyard, with a single arcade on the north and double ones at either side, leads to the domed prayer hall. The associated hamam has recently been restored.

Pioneering as this is in some ways, the Ulu Cami is inevitably overshadowed by the remarkable Ottoman mosques below. The earliest of these is the Hatuniye Camii, which with its subsidiary buildings was built for Hüsnüşah Hatun, wife of Beyazit II, by her son Şehinşah, who like other Ottoman heirs apparent was sent to Manisa to learn the art of ruling. The mosque is on Bursa Caddesi, in the heart of the market area. One can only regret that the beautiful portico has been glazed in.

The two most impressive, and indeed ambitious, Ottoman mosques are close together, directly under the Ulu Cami, and no doubt deliberately dwarf the nearby türbe erected by Isak in memory of Suruhan Bey. The earlier, the Sultan Camii, was built in 1522 by Süleyman the Magnificent in the name of his mother, Ayse Hafize Hatun. It faces the medrese, behind which is the solid hamam of 1540, still in use. To the west of this is the former hospital of 1535, now a museum of the history of medicine. Extensive as this is, the Sultan complex is outshone by that of the Muradiye mosque, built in 1582–5 for the future Sultan Murat III, who was to choose Manisa as his capital. This is a sophisticated design by Sinan, executed by his accomplished successor, Mehmet Aga. The mosque is placed on rising ground, of which full visual advantage was taken. The interior is particularly successful, a wholly effective unitary space. Fine Iznik tiles adorn the mihrab and are used for the calligraphic panels above the windows. The marble mimber, partly pigmented, is also original. On the left is the imperial loge.

The mosque is adjoined by the large medrese, also to a design by Sinan. This serves as the Ethnographical Museum. In the arcades round the central court are shown sculptures that belong to the adjacent imaret (soup kitchen). The collection ranges from the fossilized footprint of a neanderthal, dated about 25,000 BC, to a small statue of Marsyas, illicitly excavated near Serigol and returned from the USA in 1994 (a smuggled metal bed has as yet to be disgorged by the J. P. Getty Museum). Some of the sculptures shown outside are also of interest: a broken Roman relief of Orion; four tombstones to gladiators; an eloquent fragment with a soldier crouching before a mounted conqueror; a Roman gentlewoman whose son is presented by a maid; a Byzantine relief of a deer.

The major monuments of Manisa deserve to be better known. But the very success of the thriving modern city and the waves of construction this has brought make it harder for the sightseer to concentrate on what he has come for.

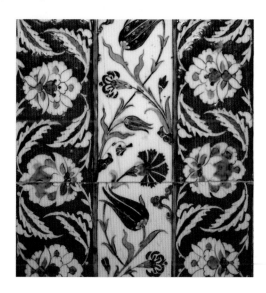

Muradiye mosque, Iznik tiles.

120

PERGAMUM

❖

PERGAMUM was a relatively obscure town until its status was transformed as a result of the decision of King Lysimachus, successor to Alexander the Great in most of Asia Minor, to place part of his treasure there in the charge of an able associate, Philetaerus. On the king's death, the latter took control. In 263 BC he was succeeded by his adopted son, Eumenes. His heir, also adopted, Attalus I (241–197 BC), was an outstanding warrior, whose achievements enabled his successor, Eumenes II, to embark on a major programme of building at Pergamum. Both Eumenes II and his brother Attalus II (150–38 BC) were fanatical book collectors. Attalus II was not only a patron of the arts but also a pioneering collector of sculptures. The line ended with his eponymous nephew, who bequeathed the kingdom to Rome in 133 BC. Thereafter Pergamum lost its political importance, but not its prosperity, under Roman control.

The ideal approach to Pergamum is from the north-west: the old road from Ayvalik winds for miles through the umbrella pines of the valleys watered by the Madra Daği. After a gradual descent, the acropolis hill of Pergamum looms. On the left, across the valley, is the most spectacular section of the Roman aqueduct, which brought water from the mountain to the city. The obvious route to this leads past a farm with five loose and very vociferous guard dogs.

Modern Pergamum spreads out from the site of the early town west of the acropolis. Allow a good four hours to see the acropolis satisfactorily. The modern road snakes up to reach the much-reduced south-east section of the walls built under Eumenes II. Above the site entrance the contiguous palaces of the Attalids are on the high ground to the right, built up against the city wall. Opposite, and a little below the King's Palace, are what remains of the Altar of Zeus – the sculptures from which, now in Berlin, represent the high point of Pergamene art. Beyond this is the Precinct of Athena in which Attalus II's sculpture collection was displayed: on the north side is the library; in the westernmost room are holes for the wooden bookcases in which the scrolls were kept. Higher up is the partly reconstructed

The aqueduct.

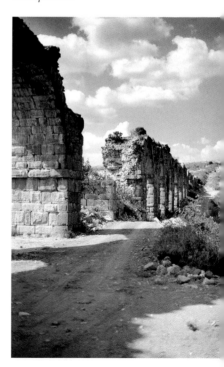

Temple of Trajan with its stoas; the columns ordered for the south stoa proved to be too small and had to be raised on high bases, with slightly uneasy visual results. To achieve the space needed for the Trajaneum, a great terrace was constructed. The passages and storerooms within this are most impressive. If time permits, go on to the northern towers of the city wall. Outside these are the footings of the Roman arsenal, and there is a good view of the aqueduct and the hills beyond.

Return to the Precinct of Athena and look down over the beautiful Hellenistic theatre, built perhaps under Eumenes II. A tunnelled staircase descends to it. The fall of the hill explains the almost precipitous slope of the theatre. The best place to inspect the prodigious masonry of the terrace of the Temple of Trajan is from the north-east corner of the upper diazoma. At the foot of the theatre there is a terrace, with holes for the upright posts of the Attalid stage building, which was replaced in Roman times. The terrace continues on the right to the beautiful small Temple of Dionysus, built against the cliff. Letters on some of the blocks of the podium show that the positioning of these was worked out in advance of construction; the marble blocks that covered the evidence have gone.

The main entrance to the theatre was at the southern end of the terrace. Follow the line of the hill – and of Eumenes' walls – to the Temenos of Demeter, where goats outnumber tourists. The two re-erected columns of the propylon, built for the wife of Attalus I, are rare examples of the Aeolic order, with capitals of palm leaves. From the propylon one reaches the upper and most remarkable of the three terraces of the prodigious gymnasium complex, which

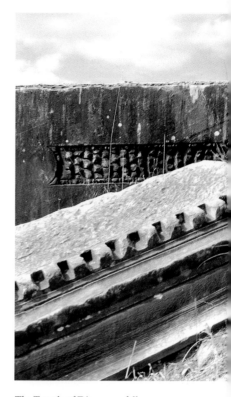

The Temple of Dionysus, fallen masonry.

incorporated two sets of baths. The Attalid phase of the construction is in the local ansedite stone, the Roman additions introducing mortar and marble. The splendid stair from the middle to the lower gymnasium, used for boys, was built under Eumenes II.

Below this is the main road down to the ancient city. Much of the paving is original. Beyond is the house of a rich Roman consul tactfully named Attalus. Below, near a turn, is the lower agora. Above the gymnasium the road turns sharply, passing the covered ruins of a substantial house with fine Roman mosaics. Other buildings off the street include a small council chamber. Higher up, the road crosses the upper agora and then forms – and indeed determines – the eastern line of the precinct of the Altar of Zeus.

Descending to the modern town, one cannot fail to be struck by the vast brick hulk of the second-century Temple of Serapis, subsequently the basilica, known now as the Kizil Avlu, or 'Red Hall'. Shorn except at its topmost level of marble enrichment, this vies in size with the great thermal buildings of Rome itself. It is flanked by two equally remarkable domed rotundas, that to the north now being used as a mosque. The vast precinct is now partly built over: to achieve the required space it was necessary to build two parallel tunnels to cover the River Selinus. The restoration of the complex is the most recent achievement of the long-standing association of German archaeologists with the excavations at Pergamum.

On the north of the modern town is the little-visited Roman amphitheatre, which straddles a narrow valley with a stream that could be controlled for the water displays the Romans relished. Three arches of the upper level are visible, but much of the rest is smothered by a millennium and a half's accumulation of soil. None the less what remains is strangely moving, despite the detritus in the streambed.

At the western end of the centre of the modern town is the excellent museum, another German contribution. Beyond, more or less opposite the larger of two vast tumuli now hemmed in by housing, is the road to the Asclepieum, which drew so many visitors to Pergamum in classical times. The cult of Asclepius was brought to the city from Epidaurus in the Peleponnese in the fourth century BC. Galen, who was born at Pergamum, practised here, and, as Professor Bean commented, the sanctuary was a cross between the spa at Droitwich and Lourdes, retaining its popularity throughout the Roman era. A colonnaded street leads up to a rectangular enclosure, flanked to left and right by stoas, of which that on the north is the better preserved. To the left of the propylon is what remains of the Temple of Asclepius, built to the highest standard in about 150 AD. Beyond is what may have been the Roman treatment centre, a circular building with an impressive ground floor. From this a Roman tunnel crosses diagonally to near the centre of the enclosure, emerging by one of the sacred pools. Opposite, at the west end of the northern stoa, is the much-reconstructed theatre. The visitor may be startled to hear tanks firing in the military range nearby; after a surfeit of ill-comprehended antiquities, nerves can be frayed. As I pottered, an Englishwoman sought to drag her man away:

'Come on, we spent too long with the tortoise.'

'No, we didn't. It was nice.'

121

ASSOS

❖

ASSOS has many claims on the tourist. Her history is remarkable, her ruins and her position are equally spectacular; and recent development in her successor village of Behramkale has been carefully controlled.

Assos was founded early in the first millennium BC by settlers from Lesbos, whose former island is in sight, across the Bay of Edremit. The advantages of a readily defensible position above a natural harbour on a relatively inhospitable coast must have quickly been recognized. Dominated in turn by Lydia, Phrygia and the Persians, Assos came into its own in the fourth century BC under Hermeias, a eunuch who had studied under Plato and patronized Aristotle, who was to marry his niece. The sophistication of Hermeias's court is also demonstrated in the walls of the city, which imply a knowledge of the virtually contemporary defences of Messine in the Peloponnese. Cleanthes, the Stoic, was born at Assos about 331 BC and over four centuries later Saint Paul walked to the town. With the Byzantines, an inexorable process of decline began. Excavation commenced in 1881, supported by the Antiquarian Society of Boston.

The approach to Assos from inland passes a substantial fourteenth-century bridge over the River Satnioeis before reaching a fine stretch of the Hellenistic walls below the modern village. This climbs up the northern side of the acropolis hill. Many of the old houses now serve as pansiyons. At the highest point of the village is the simple fourteenth-century mosque, built inevitably of spoil from the ancient town. Above, higher up, is the entrance to the archaeological site by the line of the Byzantine walls, built when the town was contracting in size. On a shelf at the summit is the sixth-century Temple of Athena, some of the Doric columns of which have been re-erected, although the sculpture excavated there is now at Ankara. Many visitors will be more moved by the sight of Lesbos in the haze of evening light than by the scattered capitals of the temple itself.

From the acropolis can be seen the lower town, part of which has been excavated. It is possible to scramble down to the east, and wander through what remains of the bouleuterion, the agora with the north and south stoas and the area of the Hellenistic shops. Yet further down is the large, but substantially reconstructed, third-century theatre, which is also accessible from the metalled road to the harbour. West of the agora is the very damaged gymnasium, not far below the formidable southern cliff of the acropolis hill. The setting has a particular appeal, with fig trees that tempt both the indigenous squirrels and the importunate tourist.

The Temple of Athena.

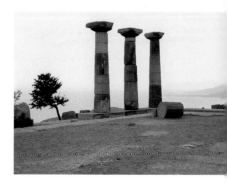

The wonder of Assos is, indubitably, the splendid section of the fourth-century BC wall which plunges from the rock of the acropolis and runs downhill towards the enclosed harbour. This can of course be reached from the gymnasium nearby, but is most impressive when seen from the outward approach. The modern route to the harbour, already mentioned, crosses the original road to the main gate, which is flanked by numerous Hellenistic and Roman tombs that have recently been unearthed. The gate is defended by two towers, and parts of the adjacent wall stand to a height of 14 metres/46 feet. Higher up, just beneath the acropolis, there is a smaller postern. The masonry is of exceptional quality and can hold its own with that of any fortification of the period, whether in Asia Minor or mainland Greece.

122

NEANDRIA

THE Troad has inevitably held a special interest for generations of visitors to Asia Minor. Homer's epic account of the fall of Troy – however and by whomever composed – had a central place in the evolution of classical civilization. And the coach tours that descend on the site that the German archaeologist Heinrich Schliemann established as that of the city pay homage to a long tradition. The successive layers of occupation began early in the third millennium BC. The city walls are not insubstantial and the archaeologists have made dramatic contributions to our understanding of what has been revealed. But the visual impact of the place is limited.

Eighteenth-century travellers in pursuit of Homer's heroes, Hector and Achilles, did not have the disadvantage of knowing where the historical city of Troy lay. Some were impressed by the ruins of Alexandria Troas, which are strewn across a surprisingly long stretch of the coast. The baths, paid for by Herodes Atticus in about 135 AD, are noble in scale, as befitted a major public building in a city visited by Saint Paul on two occasions. This had been founded – under the name of Antigonia – by Antigonus I Monophthalmos, one of Alexander the Great's generals, and was subsequently, in 301 BC, renamed after Alexander himself by Lysimachus. The city, like others near the coast, was robbed for its masonry by the Ottomans, and much that was described by Chandler in 1765 has long since disappeared.

High on the escarpment overlooking Alexandria Troas is the more ancient city of Neandria, whose people were moved to Antigonia at its foundation. Neandria itself had been founded in the seventh century BC, on a promontory that descends from Çigri Daği, the ancient Mount Ida. A modern road climbs up the southern flank of the mountain. North of the summit a track leads off to the west, crossing a low rise. The mountainside is rocky; and the marvellously complete enceinte of the Greek city seems to grow almost naturally out of the landscape. The walls defend an area roughly oblong, some 0.5 kilometres/0.3 mile wide and three times as deep, enclosing ground shelving gently westwards on the south side, but which falls away to the north. The walls were constructed of stone from the hillside. From the east gate – to which the track leads – the circuit can be walked, with successive towers and posterns, all calculated to take full advantage of the position. Little survives within the walls: scatterings of shards and the scant ruins of a small temple, the rare Aeolic capitals from which are in the Archaeological Museum at Istanbul. It is for the walls that one has come; and above all for the commanding prospects across the coastal plain of the Troad. Even in summer the place is abandoned. Birds call; and at length lightning from sable clouds hovering above the hills to the east makes it clear that it is time to leave.

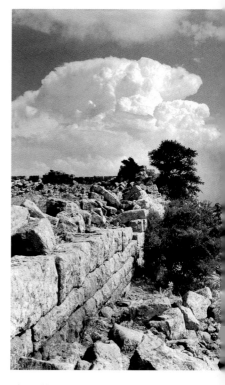

The walls, a storm coming on.

123

EDIRNE

❖

NOW close to the frontiers with both Bulgaria and Greece, Edirne is the successor of Adrianople, named after the Emperor Hadrian in 125 AD. The main entrepôt of Thrace and a major garrison town on the Via Egnatia which linked Rome with Constantinople, Adrianople came to be seen as a key to the defence of the latter. Its fall to the Ottomans in 1362 marked a decisive stage in the decline of the Byzantine Empire. Renamed Edirne, the city was to be the Ottoman capital until the conquest of Constantinople in 1453.

Most of the major monuments of Edirne are concentrated in the centre of the town, round the Eski Cami of 1402–14. This was designed by Haci Alaettin from Konya. The plan is similar to that of the Ulu Cami at Bursa, which Edirne had replaced as the capital, and the interior is notable for the vast calligraphic inscriptions. To the right of the mosque is the Rüstem Paşa Keravansaray of about 1560, now a hotel, the earliest of a number of major buildings in the city by Sinan. Nearby is Mehmet I's bedesten, still in use as a market. To the west is Sinan's Semiz Ali Paşa Çarşisi, which although damaged in 1992 still does service as a bazaar. By the north entrance of this complex is the Kule Kapisi, a gate to which is the only significant survivor of the pre-Ottoman walls of Adrianople.

Diagonally north-west of the Eski Cami, across the central Hürriyet Meydani, is Murat II's Üç Şerefeli Camii, which took its place as Edirne's Friday mosque in 1447. There are four minarets, all differing in detail. The innovative courtyard was enriched with columns and marbles taken from Roman and Byzantine structures. The domed prayer hall was bigger than any previously built by the Ottomans and is supported on only two free-standing piers to achieve maximum visibility for the faithful; but the result is spatially awkward.

The most remarkable building of Edirne is unquestionably the Selimiye Camii, planned for a suitably commanding site east of the Eski Cami in 1569 for Sultan Selim II. The architect was the octogenarian Sinan. The mosque is preceded by a majestic colonnaded courtyard with an elegant central sadirvan. There are four soaring minarets, all with three balconies. The domed prayer hall, resting on eight dodecagonal piers, is marginally larger than that of Haghia Sophia. The calligraphy of the dome, the refined carving of the mihrab and mimber and the beautiful Iznik tiles – blue, turquoise, red and green – all contribute to a mesmerizingly satisfying unity. The Selimiye Camii demonstrates how rigorously the aged Sinan analysed the occasional awkwardness of his earlier imperial mosques and is unquestionably his surpassing achievement.

Of the other Ottoman monuments of Edirne, one should not be missed. North of the centre of the city, across one of the three extant early bridges across the River Tunça, is the Beyazit Külliyesi, which makes an unforgettable impression when its many domes are reflected in the water, particularly during the winter floods. Beyazit II instructed his court architect, Hayrettin, to create the vast religious and medical complex, which was built between 1484 and 1488. At the centre is a substantial mosque, the plan of which recalls the Yeşil Camii at Bursa. More interesting are the medical school

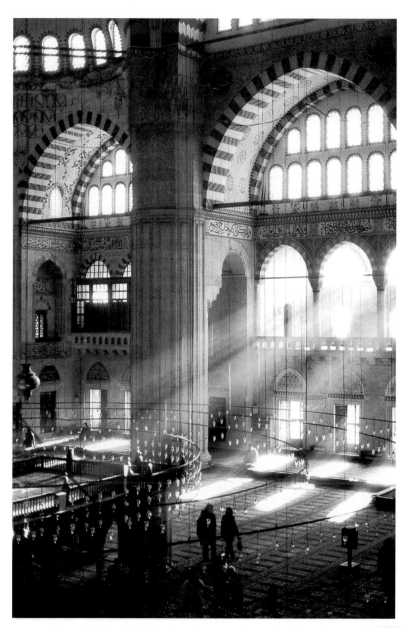

The Selimiye Camii, interior.

and the lunatic asylum, conceived on lines that would have put such establishments of early modern times in the West to shame. The inmates of the asylum were treated in a domed hexagonal building in which six iwans open off a central rotunda. Yet ultimately it is less the ingenuity in the plan of the complex that impresses than the remarkable sense of social responsibility which this implies. No later Ottoman building of the type was conceived on so heroic a scale.

GLOSSARY

Acropolis Fortress of a city or town
Agora Square or marketplace
Asclepieum Shrine of Asclepeius
Ashlar Squared blocks of stone, laid in courses

Basilica Roman hall with lower side halls, which served as the model for many Byzantine churches
Bedesten Domed building in a market for the storage and sale of valuables
Blazon Coat of arms
Bossed masonry Blocks of stone, with roughly cut projecting outer surfaces
Bouleuterion Meeting place of a council

Caddesi Street
Cami, camii Mosque
Cardo (cardo maximus) Main street of a Roman town
Cavea Semi-circular auditorium of a theatre
Cella Central hall of a temple
Çeşme Fountain
Cuneiform Pictogrammatic script evolved in Mesopotamia

Deësis Representation of Christ flanked by the Virgin and Saint John the Evangelist
Delphinium Shrine to Apollo
Denarii Coins
Diazoma Horizontal passage in a cavea

Exedra Semi-circular recess
Ephebeum Place for training youths

Garderobe Lavatory
Gavit Narthex of an Armenian church
Glacis Smooth sloping area, rock-cut or built, at an angle below a defensive wall
Gymnasium Palestra for the training of youths

Hamam, hamami Bath
Han Caravanserai
Harem Women's quarters
Heroon Shrine to demi-god or hero
Hippodrome Place for horse and chariot races
Hüyük Tell, tumulus

Iwan, eyyan Vaulted or domed recess, open at one side

Kale, kalesi Castle
Kanak House
Kapi, kapisi Gate
Kilise Church
Kouros Archaic Greek statue of a male nude
Kufic Stylized script used in early Islamic period
Külliye Mosque complex, or religious foundation
Kümbet Tomb

Latin cross Plan of church with transepts
Loge Loggia, i.e. for the sultan, in a mosque
Macellum Food market
Mausoleum Tomb

Medrese or medresesi Koran school
Megaron Palatial hall
Mescit Small mosque
Mihrab Niche in a mosque, set in the direction of Mecca
Mimber Pulpit in a mosque
Minaret Tower of a mosque from which a muezzin delivers the call to prayer

Narthex Vestibule at the west end of a church
Necropolis, necropoleis Cemetery
Nymphaeum Ornamented fountain

Oculus Circular opening in a roof
Odeum (or odeum) Small theatre-like building used for councils, meetings, etc.
Opisthodomos Porch at the rear of a temple
Opus Alexandrinum Mosaic inlay in marble or stone paving
Orchestra Circular space in the pit of theatre, used for the chorus or actors

Palestra Training place for athletes
Parecclesion Side chapel in a church
Paşa Pasha
Plutonium Shrine of Pluto
Portico in antis Portico set back between walls ending in pilasters
Proconnesian marble Marble from island of Proconnese in the Sea of Marmara

Propylon Entrance gate

Saray, sarayi Palace
Sadirvan Ablution fountain in a mosque courtyard
Sebasteion Shrine of Sebaste (i.e. Augustus)
Selamlik Male quarters of a palace
Semahane Hall in a tekke used for ritual dancing
Şifahane Hospital
Souk Market
Spina Central barrier in an amphitheatre
Stadium Building for races by runners and other athletic activites
Stela, stelae Narrow upright slab with inscription
Stoa Porticoed building with a wall at the back

Tekke Dervish monastery
Tell Mound formed by the debris of long-term occupation
Temenos Sacred enclosure
Tersane Dockyard, arsenal
Tetrapylon Four-sided arch at the intersection of major roads in a Roman city
Tumulus Mound
Türbe Tomb

Vizier Ottoman official

PEOPLES AND DYNASTIES

Abbasids Dynasty founded by Abu al-Abbas which conquered Syria in AD 750 and transferred the caliphate to Baghdad in 762.

Ak Koyunlu White sheep Turkomen.

Armenians Indo-Europeans who settled in former Urartian territory in the second millennium BC and subsequently held fluctuating kingdoms, with capitals at Ani, Van and elsewhere, refugees from which settled in the eleventh century in Cilicia, where their kingdom endured until 1375.

Artukids Descendants of Sukman, son of Artuk, who seized Hasankeyf in 1102 and ruled it until 1232.

Assyrians People of the Mesopotamian state of Assyria, which maintained trading colonies in Anatolia from early in the second millennium BC.

Attalids Kings of Pergamum who succeeded Attalus I (241–197 BC).

Ayyubids Rulers of much of western Mesopotamia, including Urfa, who took Ahlat in 1207 and Hasankeyf and Diyarbakir in 1231/2.

Bagratids Georgian dynasty.

Byzantines Successors to the empire transferred from Rome to Byzantium, or Constantinople, in AD 330.

Carians Tribe that inhabited Caria, the territory stretching south from the River Meander, before the arrival of the Greek colonists.

Cavdar Tatars Tribe from central Asia that settled in western Anatolia.

Comneni Imperial house of Trebizond (1204–1461), founded by descendants of the Comnenos family, emperors of Byzantium in 1081–1185.

Danishmenids Seljuk dynasty with a substantial principality in northern Anatolia, including Sivas, Amasya, and Kayseri, who were defeated by the Seljuks of Rum in 1178.

Georgians People based to the east of the Black Sea and subject in turn to Persia and Rome, who adopted Christianity in AD 330. The fluctuating Georgian kingdoms were under pressure from more powerful neighbours, and their state was effectively destroyed by the Mongols in 1386.

Hatti People occupying much territory subsequently held by the Hittites from c. 2500 BC.

Hittites People who reached central Anatolia c. 2000 BC. Their empire based at Hattusas was founded in the seventeenth century BC, and at its zenith controlled Babylon. The Hittite language was Indo-Germanic.

Hurrians The Hurri or Hurrians emerged in eastern Anatolia in about 2300 BC and from c. 1530 until c. 1350 BC controlled an empire in Syria.

Il-Khans Mongol dynasty descended from Hulagu which dominated central Anatolia after the defeat of the Seljuks in 1243.

Kara Koyunlu Black sheep Turkomen.

Karamanids Ruling dynasty of Karaman who succeeded to the control of a significant area of the Seljuk Sultanate from c. 1300, and were ousted by the Ottomans under Mehmet II.

Kurds People who have inhabited much of south-eastern Anatolia, as well as parts of Iraq and Iran, from early times.

Lydians The Lydian kingdom controlled a stretch of north-western Anatolia from the eighth century until 550 BC from their capital at Sardis.

Mameluke Military oligarchy of Turks and Circassian converts to Islam and their descendants, who effectively controlled Egypt for a millennium and were defeated in Asia Minor by the Ottomans in 1485–91.

Mangujakids Rulers of the upper Euphrates valley, including Divriği.

Mongols Grouping of tribes from central Asia, united by Genghis Khan (b. 1155), whose armies proved irresistible. The Mongol empire was divided in 1227, but its components continued to flourish, encouraging trade. The Mongols defeated the Seljuks in 1243 and a massive immigration from the east followed under Il-Khanid rule.

Omayyads Rulers of an empire founded by the fifth Caliph, Muawiya, at Damascus in 661, who were succeeded in 750 by the Abbasids.

Ottomans Turkish nomads from east of the Aral Sea who reached Iran in the eleventh century. The Osman tribe under Ertogrol received land from the Seljuks. His son Osman extended his territory, and in 1326 his son Orhan won Bursa, which became the Ottoman capital, subsequently to be succeeded by Edirne and, in 1453, by Istanbul. The empire, controlling an arc of territory from the Balkans to North Africa, was at its zenith under Süleyman the Magnificent (1529–66) and the dynasty endured until 1922.

Phrygians People from Macedonia or Thrace who arrived in Anatolia late in the second millennium BC and by c. 750 controlled the area between the Greek colonies in Ionia and Urartu in the east. The dissolution of the kingdom followed King Midas's defeat by the Cimmerians.

Saltukids Rulers of Erzurum, until 1232.

Sassanians Rulers of Iran.

Seleucids Seleucus Nicator secured the largest of the successor states of the empire won by Alexander the Great (356–23 BC). Based at Antioch, his heirs controlled an empire that was to be challenged from the east by the Parthians and from the west by Rome.

Seljuks Seljuk was a Turkish prince who became a Muslim in about 1000. His successors built up a major empire, Alp Arslan, defeating the Emperor Romanus decisively at Manzikert in 1171. The Seljuks of Rum were founded by a dissident relation of the Great Seljuks. His grandson Masud made Konya his capital in 1135; the sultanate was at its zenith under Alaeddin Kaykubad I (1219–36), and its power was broken by the Mongols in 1243.

Turkomen Nomads of Turkic origin from central Asia who from the eleventh to the fourteenth centuries occupied much of Anatolia: see Ak Koyunlu and Kara Koyunlu.

Urartians In the ninth century BC the Urartians built up an empire centring on Lake Van; after they were defeated at the end of the seventh century by the Assyrians and Cimmerians, Urartu dwindled in importance.

CHRONOLOGY

BC

c. **8000–5000** Neolithic period.

c. **3200–1800** Early Bronze Age.

c. **2500–2000** Hatti culture.

c. **2000** Arrival of Hittites in Anatolia.

c. **1700–1200** Hittite kingdom and empire.

c. **1200–700** Late Hittite period.

c. **1100–1000** Greek settlements on the Aegean littoral.

855–585 Urartian empire.

c. **800–500** Rise of Phrygian, Lydian, Carian and Lycian powers; development of Greek coastal cities.

546–40 Emperor Cyrus of Persia's conquest of Lydia and the Greek cities.

522–486 Reign of Emperor Darius I of Persia.

494 Ionian revolt against Persian rule.

336–23 Reign of King Alexander the Great.

334–33 Alexander the Great's conquest of Asia Minor.

325–133 Kingdom of Pergamum.

321–95 Seleucid kingdom.

295 King Seleucus I occupies Cilicia.

190 Roman victory over King Philip V of Macedonia at Magnesia.

133 Pergamum bequeathed to the Roman Republic.

83 Roman victory over King Mithradates VI of Pontus.

27 BC–14 AD Reign of the Emperor Augustus.

AD

17 Roman annexation of Commagene.

43 Lycia incorporated in the Roman Empire.

117–38 Reign of the Emperor Hadrian.

330 Nomination of Byzantium as capital of the Roman Empire by the Emperor Constantine.

391 The Emperor Theodosius I selects Christianity as the official religion of the Empire.

527–65 Reign of the Emperor Justinian.

636 Arab victory over the Byzantines at the Battle of the Yarmuk.

1071 Seljuk victory over the Byzantines at Manzikert.

1071–1287 Seljuk sultanate of Rum.

1096 First Crusade.

1134 Konya selected as the Seljuk capital.

1204 Fourth Crusade; Latin conquest of Constantinople.

1246 Mongol defeat of the Seljuks.

1261 Byzantine reconquest of Constantinople.

1299 Osman recognized as Sultan.

1365 Edirne selected as the Ottoman capital.

1413 Sultan Mehmet I restores the Ottoman Empire.

1453 Sultan Mehmet II's conquest of Constantinople, which became the Ottoman capital.

1520–66 Reign of Sultan Süleyman I the Magnificent, marked by significant territorial advances in Europe and elsewhere.

1683 Failure of the Ottoman siege of Vienna.

1853–56 Crimean War, in which Turkey was allied with England and France.

1878 Congress of Berlin, resulting in territorial losses by the Ottoman Empire.

1909 Deposition of Sultan Hamid II.

1913 Peace of London, entailing further territorial losses in Europe.

1914–18 Turkey supports Germany in the First World War.

1921–22 Turkish forces under Mustafa Kemal reverse the Greek occupation of western Anatolia.

1923 Treaty of Lausanne, which led to the exchange of population with Greece; selection of Ankara as capital.

1924 Abolition of the caliphate.

1938 Death of Atatürk.

INDEX